D0927804

"The book is a pleasure to read, but no less learned for that. There is great depth of learning on show here, but Koller manages somehow to wear that learning relatively lightly—an impressive feat."

—DANIEL RYNHOLD, professor of modern Jewish philosophy, Yeshiva University

"One would have thought that centuries of dissecting twenty-odd verses of Genesis from every perspective imaginable have exhausted their meaning. Yet Koller, with his erudite grasp of both biblical literature and the longue durée of the Jewish interpretive tradition, unbinds the Akedah to reveal its philosophical and theological grandeur. As he unravels it, he wrests it from the grip of the dominant and dangerous interpretation that faith justifies violence and redirects our attention to the message that resounds in God's warning to Abraham: 'Do not lay a hand on the boy!'"

—JAMES A. DIAMOND, Joseph and Wolf Lebovic Chair of Jewish Studies, University of Waterloo

"Aaron Koller leads his readers on a journey through a stunningly wide range of material—ancient, medieval, and modern; Jewish and Christian; Hasidic, Misnagdic, and secular; some scholarly, some poetic, some dug up by archaeologists—without ever losing focus or clarity. Wearing his massive learning lightly, he helps readers learn from these sources even as he shows them how to critique them on ethical and intellectual levels. His own interpretation of this deeply (and troublingly) influential narrative is at once respectful of the biblical text and religiously sensitive."

—BENJAMIN D. SOMMER, professor of Bible and ancient Semitic languages, Jewish Theological Seminary, and winner of the Goldstein-Goren Prize for Best Jewish Thought

"Koller's bold claim that 'one person's religious fulfillment cannot come through harm to another' stands alone as a textually rooted, morally compelling vision for sincere faith in a modern world that too often finds form in false fundamentalisms. *Unbinding Isaac* should be required reading for all of us seeking the voice of the ethical imperative in religious community."

—YEHUDA KURTZER, president, Shalom Hartman Institute of North America

"Amid countless commentaries on the Akedah, Aaron Koller's powerful, gracefully written work is brilliant, refreshing, and new. Harvesting generations of scholarship in Bible, rabbinics, and Jewish thought, medieval and modern, he deftly inlays their voices in their own times and places as they speak to us. His reading of the Akedah is timeless and urgently timely. Respectfully critiquing prevailing interpretations, he daringly proposes that the Akedah teaches ethics not as a submission to the holy but as the deepest teaching of theology."

—YEHUDAH MIRSKY, professor of Near Eastern and Judaic studies at Brandeis University and author of *Rav Kook: Mystic in a Time of Revolution*

"The story of the Akedah in Genesis 22 raised doubts and confusion in ancient times. How and why did God command Abraham to slaughter his son? What is the relationship between this story and the practice of child sacrifice that was common in the biblical period, in Israel and in some of the neighboring people? . . .

Most of the time, scholars who have dealt with this text did so from one perspective, depending on their area of expertise: biblical scholarship, the study of antiquity, the study of medieval Jewish thought, or scholarship on modern philosophy.

The impressive book by Aaron Koller is unique in that it combines all of the perspectives mentioned above in a single package. In this way, the story of the Akedah is newly illuminated in a particularly exciting and convincing way."

—ISRAEL KNOHL, Yehezkel Kaufmann Professor of Bible, Hebrew University of Jerusalem

UNBINDING ISAAC

University of Nebraska Press
Lincoln

UNBINDING ISAAC

*The Significance of the Akedah for
Modern Jewish Thought*

Aaron Koller

The Jewish Publication Society
Philadelphia

Acknowledgments for the use of copyrighted material appear on page 155, which constitutes an extension of the copyright page.

Library of Congress Cataloging-in-Publication Data
Names: Koller, Aaron J., 1978– author.
Title: Unbinding Isaac: the significance of the Akedah for modern Jewish thought / Aaron Koller.
Description: Lincoln: University of Nebraska Press, [2020] | Includes bibliographical references and index.
Identifiers: LCCN 2019041688
ISBN 9780827614734 (hardback)
ISBN 9780827618435 (epub)
ISBN 9780827618442 (mobi)
ISBN 9780827618459 (pdf)
Subjects: LCSH: Isaac (Biblical patriarch)—Sacrifice. | Bible. Genesis, XXII, 1–19—Criticism, interpretation, etc.
Classification: LCC BS1238.S24 K65 2020 | DDC 222/.1106—dc23
LC record available at https://lccn.loc.gov/2019041688

Set in Merope by Mikala R. Kolander.

To my parents,

Elayne and Jerry Koller

שותא דינוקא בשוקא או דאבוה או דאימיה

"The child's speech outside
comes either from his father
or from his mother."

(Bavli *Sukkah* 56b)

CONTENTS

ILLUSTRATIONS

ACKNOWLEDGMENTS

The work on the material in this book began back in 2008–9, when I taught a class on Jewish biblical interpretation at Drisha in New York City. For part of the year, we studied the 'aqeda as a test case, investigating the ways the text had been understood by classical and modern interpreters. Kierkegaard was not on the reading list, but he was on my mind, and over the course of the year, some of the core ideas now in this book—most centrally, Maimonides' interpretation of the text—began to take shape.

Over the decade since then, this work has taken various shapes and forms. I am most profoundly indebted to my good friend Elie Jesner, who has been a true ḥavruta for nearly twenty-five years, distilling his erudition and humanism in ways that have constantly enriched me. On the pragmatic level, he read drafts of a number of chapters and suggested numerous improvements and corrections, sharing his knowledge of both classical Jewish texts and modern philosophy. My colleague Dr. Daniel Rynhold improved this work with many suggestions and critiques, and also provided some important references; for other references, I am indebted as well to Dr. Joshua Feigelson. Dr. Eliyahu Stern and Dr. Jess Olson responded to some of my questions on modern intellectual history and Jewish thought, and helped me think through some of the issues in the intellectual history of the time. A Kierkegaard reading group in 2016, in which Dr. Sam Fleischacker and Dr. Viren Murthy participated, was instrumental in broadening my perspective on Kierkegaard and his thought.

This work began in the classroom and continued to a large extent in various classrooms. My students in Drisha were an ever-eager group of learners and critics, from whom I learned at least as much as they learned from me. I have, more recently, taught an undergraduate course on the 'aqeda (a spelling henceforth abandoned) at Yeshiva University. The rigorous environment of a YU classroom ensured that every analysis had to be worked out in great detail, distilled to its essence, and then analyzed from every angle. The students in each class were scintillating conversation partners, and also produced remarkably high-quality work of their own, which in turn informed my own thinking. It is a pleasant obligation to single out papers by Tzvi Cantor on Rav Shagar's essay discussed in chapter 1, and Noah Marlowe on Rabbi Norman Lamm's sermon, discussed in chapter 7.

Some of the early writing of this material happened in the incomparable atmosphere of the Shalom Hartman Institute in Jerusalem. I am grateful to Dr. Donniel Hartman for providing a vibrant and comfortable place to work during a sabbatical. Among the extraordinary fellows of the institute, my thanks go to two in particular. Professor Israel Knohl encouraged me to draft a proposal for this book and then served as a constantly fascinating interlocutor and next-door neighbor once I arrived. Professor Avi Sagi, from whose many publications I had learned much before arriving in Jerusalem, further enriched my understanding through numerous conversations once I was there.

In the last stages of the writing process, The Jewish Publication Society director Rabbi Barry Schwartz provided important guidance, and the JPS managing editor Joy Weinberg went through the manuscript line by line, ensuring that the book will be far more easily readable and understandable than it would have otherwise been. To the staff at the University of Nebraska Press, too, I am grateful for their fine work in producing this book.

I am endlessly thankful to, and more thankful for, my partner Shira Hecht-Koller. Her empathy, humanity, and generosity of spirit is reflected in some of the thinking in these pages. On the practical level, Shira's insights and sharp comments on parts of the book consistently led to better analysis and clearer writing, and a suggestion of hers led to an important reorganization of the chapters. Shira's parents, my amazing parents-in-law, Sara and Rabbi Michael Hecht, have been warm and supportive regular presences in all of our lives. Dalya and Shachar have been with us longer than the work on this book; Amitai and Aiden came along later and joined the party. They have all contributed in ways large and small to this project. More importantly, they have contributed to our studying and struggling with the Jewish texts and tradition that are so central to our lives. You are all children of the twenty-first century, and understand better than we do what this young century has already wrought. Imma and I hope that you continue to study and continue to struggle, and that you leave the world and the Jewish tradition richer for your efforts.

Finally, to my parents, Elayne and Jerry Koller. One hardly needs a special reason to express gratitude to one's parents. This is especially so in my case, as I am fortunate to have loving, supportive parents who provided me with strong role models and an excellent education, and yet always encouraged me to follow my own path. As the epigraph says, a child's speech often reflects the discourse in the childhood home. In my case, and the case of my brother and sister, this is easy to see: learning and values, cosmopolitan and Jewish, permeate my parents' home.

Still, in the context of this particular book, it seems appropriate to thank them for the very basics: thanks, Mom and Dad, for not sacrificing me. When I was a teenager, they told me a joke:

> How old was Isaac at the Akedah?
> No idea, but he couldn't have been a teenager, since then it wouldn't have been a sacrifice.

I'm not sure exactly what they meant by telling me that, but I'm sure it was an expression of love. And I hope they accept this book as a small token of my love in return.

HOW TO USE THIS BOOK

To best utilize the resources in this book, access its complementary study and discussion guide at https://jps.org/books/unbinding-isaac. The guide will help readers think critically about the sources discussed throughout the book; provides the full text of some of the primary sources that rabbis and educators will find useful in teaching the material; contains guiding questions that can be used in classes and discussion groups; and includes certain scholarly sources that educators and scholars may find helpful in their further study and research.

INTRODUCTION

The Challenge and the Power of the Story

וַיְהִי אַחַר הַדְּבָרִים הָאֵלֶּה וְהָאֱלֹהִים נִסָּה אֶת אַבְרָהָם.

וַיֹּאמֶר אֵלָיו "אַבְרָהָם!"

וַיֹּאמֶר "הִנֵּנִי."

וַיֹּאמֶר "קַח נָא אֶת בִּנְךָ אֶת יְחִידְךָ אֲשֶׁר אָהַבְתָּ אֶת יִצְחָק וְלֶךְ לְךָ אֶל אֶרֶץ הַמֹּרִיָּה וְהַעֲלֵהוּ שָׁם לְעֹלָה עַל אַחַד הֶהָרִים אֲשֶׁר אֹמַר אֵלֶיךָ."

וַיַּשְׁכֵּם אַבְרָהָם בַּבֹּקֶר וַיַּחֲבֹשׁ אֶת חֲמֹרוֹ. וַיִּקַּח אֶת שְׁנֵי נְעָרָיו אִתּוֹ וְאֵת יִצְחָק בְּנוֹ. וַיְבַקַּע עֲצֵי עֹלָה. וַיָּקָם וַיֵּלֶךְ אֶל הַמָּקוֹם אֲשֶׁר אָמַר לוֹ הָאֱלֹהִים.

בַּיּוֹם הַשְּׁלִישִׁי וַיִּשָּׂא אַבְרָהָם אֶת עֵינָיו וַיַּרְא אֶת הַמָּקוֹם מֵרָחֹק.

וַיֹּאמֶר אַבְרָהָם אֶל נְעָרָיו "שְׁבוּ לָכֶם פֹּה עִם הַחֲמוֹר וַאֲנִי וְהַנַּעַר נֵלְכָה עַד כֹּה וְנִשְׁתַּחֲוֶה וְנָשׁוּבָה אֲלֵיכֶם."

וַיִּקַּח אַבְרָהָם אֶת עֲצֵי הָעֹלָה וַיָּשֶׂם עַל יִצְחָק בְּנוֹ. וַיִּקַּח בְּיָדוֹ אֶת הָאֵשׁ וְאֶת הַמַּאֲכֶלֶת וַיֵּלְכוּ שְׁנֵיהֶם יַחְדָּו.

וַיֹּאמֶר יִצְחָק אֶל אַבְרָהָם אָבִיו וַיֹּאמֶר "אָבִי."

וַיֹּאמֶר "הִנֶּנִּי בְנִי."

וַיֹּאמֶר "הִנֵּה הָאֵשׁ וְהָעֵצִים וְאַיֵּה הַשֶּׂה לְעֹלָה?"

וַיֹּאמֶר אַבְרָהָם "אֱלֹהִים יִרְאֶה לּוֹ הַשֶּׂה לְעֹלָה בְּנִי."

וַיֵּלְכוּ שְׁנֵיהֶם יַחְדָּו.

וַיָּבֹאוּ אֶל הַמָּקוֹם אֲשֶׁר אָמַר לוֹ הָאֱלֹהִים.

וַיִּבֶן שָׁם אַבְרָהָם אֶת הַמִּזְבֵּחַ וַיַּעֲרֹךְ אֶת הָעֵצִים וַיַּעֲקֹד אֶת יִצְחָק בְּנוֹ
וַיָּשֶׂם אֹתוֹ עַל הַמִּזְבֵּחַ מִמַּעַל לָעֵצִים.

וַיִּשְׁלַח אַבְרָהָם אֶת יָדוֹ וַיִּקַּח אֶת הַמַּאֲכֶלֶת לִשְׁחֹט אֶת בְּנוֹ.

וַיִּקְרָא אֵלָיו מַלְאַךְ ה' מִן הַשָּׁמַיִם.

וַיֹּאמֶר "אַבְרָהָם אַבְרָהָם!"

וַיֹּאמֶר "הִנֵּנִי."

וַיֹּאמֶר "אַל תִּשְׁלַח יָדְךָ אֶל הַנַּעַר וְאַל תַּעַשׂ לוֹ מְאוּמָה כִּי עַתָּה יָדַעְתִּי
כִּי יְרֵא אֱלֹהִים אַתָּה וְלֹא חָשַׂכְתָּ אֶת בִּנְךָ אֶת יְחִידְךָ מִמֶּנִּי."

וַיִּשָּׂא אַבְרָהָם אֶת עֵינָיו וַיַּרְא וְהִנֵּה אַיִל אַחַר נֶאֱחַז בַּסְּבַךְ בְּקַרְנָיו.

וַיֵּלֶךְ אַבְרָהָם וַיִּקַּח אֶת הָאַיִל וַיַּעֲלֵהוּ לְעֹלָה תַּחַת בְּנוֹ.

וַיִּקְרָא אַבְרָהָם שֵׁם הַמָּקוֹם הַהוּא ה' יִרְאֶה אֲשֶׁר יֵאָמֵר הַיּוֹם בְּהַר ה'
יֵרָאֶה.

וַיִּקְרָא מַלְאַךְ ה' אֶל אַבְרָהָם שֵׁנִית מִן הַשָּׁמַיִם.

וַיֹּאמֶר "בִּי נִשְׁבַּעְתִּי נְאֻם ה' כִּי יַעַן אֲשֶׁר עָשִׂיתָ אֶת הַדָּבָר הַזֶּה וְלֹא
חָשַׂכְתָּ אֶת בִּנְךָ אֶת יְחִידֶךָ, כִּי בָרֵךְ אֲבָרֶכְךָ וְהַרְבָּה אַרְבֶּה אֶת זַרְעֲךָ
כְּכוֹכְבֵי הַשָּׁמַיִם וְכַחוֹל אֲשֶׁר עַל שְׂפַת הַיָּם וְיִרַשׁ זַרְעֲךָ אֵת שַׁעַר
אֹיְבָיו. וְהִתְבָּרְכוּ בְזַרְעֲךָ כֹּל גּוֹיֵי הָאָרֶץ עֵקֶב אֲשֶׁר שָׁמַעְתָּ בְּקֹלִי."

וַיָּשָׁב אַבְרָהָם אֶל נְעָרָיו.

וַיָּקֻמוּ וַיֵּלְכוּ יַחְדָּו אֶל בְּאֵר שָׁבַע.

וַיֵּשֶׁב אַבְרָהָם בִּבְאֵר שָׁבַע.

Afterwards, God tested Abraham, and said to him, "Abraham."

He said, "I am here."

He said, "Now take your son, your only one, whom you love, Isaac, and go to the land of Moriah, and offer him there as a burnt offering on one of the hills, which I will tell you there."

Abraham woke up in the morning and saddled his donkey; he took his two servants and his son Isaac. He split the wood for the sacrifice, and got up and went to the place of which God told him.

On the third day, Abraham lifted his eyes and saw the place from afar.

Abraham said to his servants, "Stay here with the donkey, and the boy and I will go up to there; let us bow down, and then return to you."

Abraham took the wood for the burnt offering and placed it on his son Isaac. He took the fire and the knife, and the two of them walked together.

Isaac said to his father Abraham, saying, "Father!"

He said, "I am here, my son."

He said, "Here is the fire and the wood, but where is the sheep for the burnt offering?"

Abraham said, "God will see for himself the sheep for the burnt offering, my son."

The two of them walked together.

They came to the place of which God told him. Abraham built there the altar. He arranged the wood, he bound his son Isaac, and he placed him on the altar, above the wood.

Abraham stretched out his hand and took the knife to slaughter his son.

The angel of the Lord called from heaven and said, "Abraham, Abraham!"

He said, "I am here."

He said, "Don't stretch your hand against the boy, and do not do anything to him, for now I know that you are a fearer of God, as you have not spared your son, your only one, from me."

Abraham lifted his eyes, and saw—behold!—a ram having been caught in the thicket by his horns. Abraham went and took the ram, and offered it as a burnt offering in place of his son.

Abraham called the place "The Lord will see," which is why it is said today, "On the mountain of the Lord He shall be seen."

The angel of the Lord called Abraham a second time from heaven.

He said, "I swear by myself," says the Lord, "that because you have done this and not withheld your son, your only one, I will indeed bless you and greatly increase your descendants like the stars of the sky and the sand on the shore of the sea, and your descendants will inherit the gates of their enemies, and all the nations of the world shall bless themselves by you, since you have obeyed me."

Abraham returned to his servants.

They got up and walked together to Beer-sheba.

Abraham dwelled in Beer-sheba.

These three hundred words have haunted readers for thousands of years. The story is compact, taut, almost telegraphic in its style, pausing for no details, no drama; there is only one brief dialogue, and no introspection at all. The paucity of literary details contrasts sharply with the power of the story told: one imagines a horrifying revelation, tortured deliberation, and alternately innocence, dismay, terror, and steely determination on the part of the characters, but none of this is reported. This clash of style and substance has made the Akedah, the "binding," one of the most enduringly terrifying stories in the Bible.

Unlike some of the "texts of terror" elsewhere in the Hebrew Bible, the Akedah can be read to all audiences. In fact, in the Jewish tradition it is singled out as the reading for Rosh Hashanah, when all men, women, and children can be expected to be present, and it is mentioned repeatedly in the prayers of that day. If it does not immediately provoke revulsion, the terror of the story increases the more one dwells on it. The text can, and has, provoked diametrically opposed responses, to God, to Abraham, and to Isaac.

How overwhelming is the might of God! How mysterious God's will! How profound is the call to abandon past and future for the sake of a present with God. How awe-inspiring is the religion that promises a glorious future to one prepared to sacrifice everything. How *other* is God, who expects God's followers to follow to any place that God shows them.

What kind of monstrous god commands the sacrifice of a child? What kind of cruel deity promises his devoted follower a family, takes decades to deliver on the promise, then demands the child back — only to step away from that demand at the last minute and claim it was all a test? Can such a God be worshiped? Can such a god even be tolerated?

How sublime is Abraham's faith! One stands in awe at the devotion of a man willing to give up, to sacrifice, his most precious possession, for which he prayed and waited many decades, for no particular reward, alone on a mountaintop. How magnificent is the soul of such a man, how perfect, how worthy of reverence and awe.

What kind of a monstrous parent *obeys* such a command? Is God's will really so clear that Abraham should murder someone because of what he thinks God wants? Is God's favor really so valuable that Abraham would turn on his son to stay in God's good graces? Can a person who is capable of murder for God really be a patriarch, a hero, a role model for an entire nation?

And Isaac—what a perfect lamb, prepared to go to his death without even the benefit of having heard God's voice. An unblemished sacrifice, stretching out his neck for the easy passage of the sharp blade, never having yet lived but ready to die for the sake of his father's faith. What an exemplary model of filial obedience!	What sort of lamb was Isaac, allowing himself to be brought meekly to the slaughter for his father's sake? If Abraham wanted to please God, did Isaac have to play along? Should he not have protested—or at least demanded his share of the reward?

Such conflicting responses—all of which will be discussed further over the course of this book—have not just engaged, but tortured readers for many years. Over the course of centuries, the story has sat at the intersection of text and life. In every generation, readers have turned to it for help in thinking about the most difficult and traumatic aspects of their own religious lives and in turn have bequeathed to the text a profound, intense, multivalent set of meanings upon which other people can draw.

Contemporary readers are often left with the sense that "anyone who has studied the Akedah, and then gone back and studied it again, knows that all the questions that the Akedah raises are far better than any of the answers that have been suggested" and that "it is most likely that until the end of days, many Jews will read the Akedah twice a year and tremble, and anyone who has any sort of ethical sensibility will continue to protest and not to understand."[1] But texts that are read, and re-read, cannot mean nothing. And in fact, this particular text has always *meant* something, although that meaning has often changed. It has inspired, instilled fear, provided a pious model, and driven people away. It remains among the best-known biblical texts, and yet among the most challenging.

Challenges of an Unadorned Text

The narrative itself is unadorned. We hear nothing of what the characters wear, what they look like, or what they say to each other—all common features of biblical narratives. We also lack details that seem central to the story: how old, for instance, is Isaac? Is he a boy of five, an adolescent, an adult? The midrash, associating this story with the following one of Sarah's death, puts Isaac at age thirty-seven; one *Targum* from Byzantine Palestine makes him thirty-six; the commentator Abraham ibn Ezra surmises that he was around thirteen; the Jewish artistic depictions of the scene from antiquity and the Middle Ages consistently portray him as a young boy, no more than seven or eight. This matters profoundly for the dynamics of the story, but the text itself is mute.

The story is also unadorned by any background. Many great stories draw their pathos and their power from the narrative of a mesmerizing individual making his or her way through the world against the backdrop of grand events. In Homer's *Iliad* we are captivated by the anger of Achilles and the passion of Paris, whom we follow through a momentous clash between the Greeks and the Trojans. *War and Peace* tells of five families on the background of the French invasion of Russia. The personal drama of Shakespeare's *Julius Caesar* plays out against the political drama of the late Roman Republic. The story of *Hamilton* is a powerful narrative of an individual in the context of an epoch-altering revolution, a "world turned upside down."

The Bible, too, knows how to combine the personal with the national in stories. The literary portraits of the central characters of the biblical narrative are compelling in part because of the times through which they live and which they shape. The life of Moses is the birth of the nation. The biography of David is also the rise of the monarchy in Israel. The personal animosity between Mordecai and Haman is tied in with the genocidal plot hatched against the Jews throughout the

Persian Empire. Much of the power of these stories comes from this background. The individuals are not just individuals. They are living through history and sometimes creating that history.

Not so Abraham. Here there is no background. When did this story take place? Nothing is said. What towns did he pass by on his way to the land of Moriah? We are not told. What did those townspeople think of him? Were they at peace, or was a war raging? Who controlled the territory? Was there cultural change in the air? All of these are topics not broached. The great twentieth-century literary scholar Erich Auerbach famously argued that the story of the Akedah is "fraught with background,"[2] but there simply is no background. We can look nowhere but at Abraham and Isaac, climbing a mountain alone, with a knife in a hand and a voice in an ear. Abraham confronts us at every turn. He is present throughout—and three times says "I am here." He says "I am here" to God when first commanded; he says "I am here" to Isaac when the son turns to the father in confusion; he says "I am here" when the angel calls from heaven. Abraham is *here*, directly in front of us, and there is nothing behind him. Looking so intensely at characters so austerely sketched is difficult. We wish for more background.

The Average Jew and the Akedah

The average Jew, from antiquity and on, could not escape the Akedah. It is worth observing just how many encounters a Jew would have had with the story if she or he entered a synagogue in the Land of Israel fifteen hundred years ago.[3] The worshiper might, first of all, have literally stepped on a depiction of the story, as for instance in the Beit Alpha or Sepphoris synagogues: the presence of these mosaic floors meant that any time there were people in the synagogue, they would be confronted with the image of the Akedah.

After the visual encounter would come the liturgical encounters. The Akedah was invoked on fast days, with the cry "May He that answered

Fig. 1. Mosaic floor from the Beit Alpha synagogue, Beit She'an, sixth century CE. From Elazar Sukenik, *The Ancient Synagogue of Beit Alpha*, plate 19, by permission of the Hebrew University Magnes Press.

Abraham our father on Mount Moriah answer you and hearken to the voice of your crying this day" (*Mishnah Ta'anit* 2:4), and had a prominent place in the prayers for Rosh Hashanah, when it also served as the Torah portion that was read. It might, of course, have been the Torah reading of the Sabbath morning, in which case it would have been heard both in the original Hebrew and in an embellished Aramaic version in the *Targum*, and there also would have been *piyyutim* (liturgical poems) recited on the themes of the story. Overall, Saint Augustine's observation about the ubiquity of the Akedah in his own fourth-century Christian society must have held true for the Jews of the time as well:

> [The story of the Akedah is] so famous, that it recurs to the mind of itself without any study or reflection, and is in fact repeated by so many tongues, and portrayed in so many places, that no one can pretend to shut his eyes or his ears to it.[4]

That the Jews, like the Christians, were exposed to the Akedah is clear. Augustine does not tell us, however, how people digested the story. What did it *mean* to them? *Why* was it so ubiquitous? These questions are more difficult to answer.

Interpreting the Story

Despite the lack of narrative details, both in the foreground and in the background, the Akedah is not a Rorschach test, in which readers see themselves, and it is not a blank canvas, onto which lives are mapped. Interpreting this story, like any other story that matters, is a dialogue between text and life, or, more accurately, a conversation — sometimes a heated one, sometimes a desperate one — between the text, the previously seen meanings of the text (the "tradition"), and life. It may be that the gaps in the narrative are so great that interpreters wind up reading it as they would like to read it, even when they profess to not be interpreting it.[5]

The text does constrain interpretation, though, even if it does not speak on its own. There are readings that are more and less faithful to the text, but there are also readings that are more and less meaningful to readers. The interplay between text and life is the grand story of scriptural religions.

A fascinating example of this three-way interplay is seen in the medieval *piyyuṭ* published by Shalom Spiegel first in a long Hebrew article and then translated into English by Judah Goldin, in a book that quickly became a classic, *The Last Trial*.[6] This twelfth-century poem by Ephraim of Bonn retells the story of the Akedah but, when it gets to the climactic moment, contains a shocking twist:

> He made haste, he pinned him down with his knees,
> He made his two arms strong.
> With steady hands he slaughtered him according to the rite,
> Full right was the slaughter.

Down upon him fell the resurrecting dew, and he revived.
(The father) seized him to slaughter him once more.
Scripture, bear witness! Well-grounded is the fact,
And the Lord called Abraham, even a second time from
    heaven.
The ministering angels cried out terrified:
Even animal victims, were they ever slaughtered twice?
Instantly they made their outcry heard on high,
Lo, Ariels cried out above the earth.[7]

The poet relays that Isaac was in fact slaughtered and then miraculously revived. Abraham was girding himself to slaughter his son *for a second time* when Isaac was saved, only through the intervention of the angels.

This shocking understanding of the story is the result of the three factors mentioned as conversation partners: the text, the history of interpretation, and real life. First, the biblical text does report that the angel called out to Abraham "a second time from heaven," hinting that a twofold intervention was required. Second, Spiegel masterfully shows that there is a long, although quiet, current of thought that Isaac was actually slaughtered by his father and then miraculously resurrected. Third, finally, this reading was resonant for Ephraim of Bonn because of the tragedies to which he was witness, in particular the massacre of the Jews of York in 1190. These three sources of thought—the text, the tradition, and life—collaborate or conspire to produce a multitude of possibilities of meaning.

About This Book

Broadly speaking, there are two ways in which "life" can contribute to this conversation. This book will concentrate on interpretations that result from thinkers thinking about the Akedah from a philosophical or theological vantage point: what does it say about God, believers, faith? As we will see, such thoughts have accompanied the reading of the story throughout the history of reading. But alongside such questions, there have also been questions such as "How does the Akedah speak to me about the trauma I just witnessed?" These questions have, tragically, most often accompanied examples of parents who witnessed the deaths of their children, or, even more horrifically, participated in the deaths of their children. At such times, the Akedah becomes a textual touchstone for people of faith.

In particular, this book investigates the ethics of the story, asking, "What is the ethical teaching this story offers?" Pre-modern Jewish readers tended not to ask about the ethical problem, but about the emotional problem, asking more "how could he do it?" rather than "should he do it?"[8] Much of our discussion will therefore take its structure from modern thinkers, although classical Rabbinic literature, and even more so the medieval thinkers, will play prominent roles in the discussion.

The core argument of this book is that the one reading of the Akedah that has become very popular in the past two centuries, most often identified with the Danish philosopher Søren Kierkegaard, is deeply problematic. Kierkegaard and others have claimed that the essence of the story, if it can be boiled down to a single lesson, is that true faith may necessitate the violation of the ethical on occasion and that the person of faith may in fact defy what she knows to be ethical for her faith, on rare but real occasions.

This book will argue that this reading of the Akedah ought to be rejected *as biblical interpretation*. We will question whether his reading, which is essentially unprecedented in the history of interpretation of Genesis 22, does justice to the text; it will be argued that it actually ignores not only other narratives in Genesis, before and after the Akedah itself, but even the second half of this very story. Furthermore, it will be argued that this reading runs counter to some of the core values of biblical thought, including the need for companionship and community. Finally, the ethical implications of this reading will be explored, and the dangerous implications of faith unchecked by ethics, especially when such faith is taken as license to harm others, will be unpacked, leading to the conclusion that this needs to be rejected.

Chapter 1 will set the stage for the discussion by surveying some of the many ways in which readers, primarily Jewish readers, have understood, responded to, and used the Akedah. The themes that will be highlighted are merit, martyrdom, love, and critique: the merit the Akedah generated for future generations of Jews; the significance of Isaac as the first (potential) Jewish martyr for his faith; the love that was, perhaps surprisingly, felt to animate the story; and the critique of Abraham's willingness to kill his son, and sometimes of God for demanding that he do so. The current of critique that runs through Jewish thought, from ancient poems and midrashim to contemporary Israel, will also be explored.

With the groundwork having been laid, the second chapter will discuss Kierkegaard's masterful essay *Fear and Trembling*, which in many ways set the stage for the modern discussion of the story, especially when it comes to an ethically oriented approach. Kierkegaard famously argued that the central conflict in the story was between ethics—universal principles of correct behavior—and faith—a private experience of revelation not subject to verification or even to conversation.

A closer look at how Kierkegaard reads the story will reveal that while his approach was subtle and sophisticated, and his essay quite brilliant, other thinkers of his era read the Akedah in similar directions—although none developed the ideas to the extent or depth that Kierkegaard did. Chapter 3 will look at these comparisons, which often come from surprising places, and in particular from deep in rabbinic culture, from figures such as Moses Sofer (the "Ḥatam Sofer") and Mordechai Joseph Leiner of Izbica (the "Izbicer") in the early nineteenth century and Meir Leibush ben Yehiel Michel Wisser (the "Malbim") in the middle of that century.

Seeing these comparisons will lead us to the question: why did the nineteenth century give rise to the particular reading of the Akedah offered by these thinkers, and in particular by Kierkegaard? The development of the modern world, and the modern nation-state, complicated questions of personal identity in the late 1700s and early 1800s, and it is this tension that most animates Kierkegaard's thinking about the knight of faith, and about Abraham at the Akedah in particular.

We will then turn in chapter 4 to two of the great Jewish thinkers of the twentieth century, the German-Israeli philosopher Yeshayahu Leibowitz and the Lithuanian-American rabbi and existentialist Joseph Ber Soloveitchik. Both were profoundly affected by Kierkegaard's thought in general, and his approach to the Akedah in particular. I will argue that Leibowitz's approach to the ethical problems of the story is simplistic and proves to be unsatisfactory. Soloveitchik attempted to combine a Kierkegaardian approach with other voices from the Jewish tradition to arrive at a more nuanced approach to the central problem.

Still, even the more nuanced approach of Soloveitchik cannot, in the end, produce an ethically defensible reading. Building on critiques by thinkers such as Buber, Levinas, and Hartman, chapter 5 will offer a critique of the approach to the story taken by Soloveitchik, following Kierkegaard. I will argue that, ethically speaking, there is little separating Abraham in this reading from some of the horrific acts committed in the name of religion in the contemporary world. I will also argue that the notion of faith propounded by Soloveitchik and Kierkegaard, which is solitary and silent, runs counter to much of the Jewish tradition of religious experience, which tends toward the communal.

Chapter 6 will turn to the task of developing a different ethical understanding of the Akedah. We will begin with a discussion of the practice of child sacrifice in the land of Canaan. Since, as will be seen, it was not considered clearly unethical to kill one's child as a sacrifice, Abraham would not have couched his dilemma in those terms.

Instead, the "test" in the first part of the story is whether Abraham would be willing to sacrifice a child whom he loves profoundly, who is also his most precious possession, one in whom all of his hopes and dreams are vested, to God, for no apparent reason and in violation of God's own promises.

However, I will also argue that this does not mean that the story is ethically irrelevant. On the contrary, I will suggest that the *second* part of the story—the *non-sacrifice* of Isaac—is one of the primary ethical teachings here, as one central question must be: Why did God *not* want the sacrifice of Isaac in the end? Chapter 7, then, will develop the understanding of the story that I take to be that of Maimonides (twelfth century) and Joseph ibn Kaspi (fourteenth century), according to which the command to *unbind* Isaac is a more profound understanding of God's will than the command to bind him in the first place. I will argue that God *partially*—but only partially—desired the sacrifice of Isaac, while God *fully* desired that Abraham not sacrifice him. This divine dynamic will be explored in a broader context as well, as it is an important linchpin in thinking about the divine will in the Bible.

Chapter 8 will then turn to the implications of this, in two directions: first, the notion that God may partly desire human sacrifice will be re-situated in its biblical context; second, the core question of why God does *not* desire human sacrifice will be addressed more fully. Finally, I will develop what I take to be the central ethical teaching of the Akedah when seen in this light: the crucial teaching that each person, even a child, is an autonomous and independent human being, rather than a being primarily defined by his or her relationship to someone else. In other words, the central lesson is that Abraham cannot sacrifice his son because his son needs to be recognized as an autonomous person, not merely "Abraham's son." It will be seen that in many contexts, the Bible broke with its ancient context in asserting that a child was not the parent's property, but an independent and autonomous human being; this lies behind a number of biblical laws and stories. In the Akedah, too, this is the primary radical lesson: one's religious experience must never come through sacrificing someone else.

The conclusion will draw on some of Levinas's writings, including his comments on the Akedah itself, to bring together the earlier chapters and spell out a way of reading the whole story that is both textually cohesive and ethically defensible, as well as in accord with much of what I see as a Jewish tradition of ethical thinking. We will see that the Akedah can be a foundational text for thinking about the place of the religious individual in the modern world, although in very different ways than what Kierkegaard and Soloveitchik articulated.

This different way of approaching the story allows us to take the best of a number of older approaches and combine them into a compelling synthesis. The core claim, put as concisely as possible, is that the biblical God would like to want child sacrifice—because it is in fact a remarkable display of devotion—but *more* does not want child sacrifice, because it would violate the autonomy of the child as a person. This last point is crucial for the meaning of the story, which is that an authentically religious act cannot be done through the harm of another.

This argument is particularly important in the twenty-first century, as the mode of thought that emerges from Kierkegaard's approach to the Akedah dominates much religious thinking. The contemporary scholar of Jewish law and theology Ronit Irshai has charted the ascendance of what she calls "Akedah theology" in the Jewish—especially Orthodox—world.[9] This mode of thinking is straight out of Kierkegaard, as channeled by Leibowitz and Soloveitchik: it argues that a divine command must be obeyed even if it is immoral, not because God must really be moral, but because divine commands take precedence over morality.

In the broader Western discourse of law and social policy, we also live in a Kierkegaardian world. The courts have exempted religious organizations from providing their employees with health plans that even so much as authorize a third party to provide contraceptives; this is said to violate their freedom of religion. The New York City Board of Health announced an insistence on vaccinations for all children attending preschool and daycare programs. "Children with a valid religious exemption," however, "will not be required to be vaccinated."

Such an understanding of the freedom of religion derives from Kierkegaard's notion that for a religious person alone on the mountaintop, even ethics must be put aside for faith. For Kierkegaard—and, as we shall see, other readers of the nineteenth and twentieth centuries—Abraham being alone with God on the mountaintop is critical to understanding the religious point of the story: the fundamentally personal nature of faith, the incommunicability of religious devotion, the zealousness of the faithful that takes precedence even over one's own moral compass.

One major claim of this book, however, is to urge readers to recall that, of course, Abraham was *not* alone on the mountain. Isaac was there as well, and despite the praise of Abraham as the knight of faith, it was Isaac whose actual life was on the line. Here is where these readings falter and where the social policies and Jewish philosophies derived from such a reading become untenable. It is all well and good to celebrate the personal and individual faith that animates a person's life. But a society cannot afford to allow individuals' sense of religious devotion to lead to the harm of others.

The assumption underlying this book is that the way we read texts—especially texts vested with power, with religious and moral authority—*matters*. Texts, especially sacred texts, can serve as lenses through which people view the world, and the various ways of reading these texts have different hues and tints; they can bring different aspects of the contemporary world into focus or out of focus. Some readers see the Akedah as a story primarily about submissiveness and then wear lenses tinted this shade as they look at the religious landscape of the twenty-first century. But submissiveness needs to be counterbalanced by other values, and the Akedah has profound lessons to teach here as well. For readers who wish to take the Bible seriously in the modern world without abandoning the tenets of modern values, my aim is to turn the Akedah from a distorting set of lenses that leads some people to see "submissiveness" as the dominant element in religious thought, to a pair of the clearest lenses possible, through which the centrality of interpersonal ethics will be plainly perceived.

UNBINDING ISAAC

1

Jewish Experiences of the Akedah

Jews more often experienced the Akedah than contemplated it. What is now a philosophical challenge was, over the last two millennia, primarily a story of faith and devotion. What is now a moral problem was a tragic and inspiring story of love and sacrifice.

This chapter highlights some of the many ways in which the Akedah was used by Jews over the past two and a half millennia. First, it was an awe-inspiring display of faith, the story of a devoted father who had no choice but to sacrifice his only son, and this had to result in merit accruing to the son and his descendants. Second, Isaac was seen as the first Jewish martyr. Tragically, many later Jewish martyrs, and those who wrote about them, had the opportunity to look back to Isaac. We will then turn to a third, related theme: love as the animating factor in the Akedah—and in later martyrdoms as well.

While many Jews absorbed the Akedah as deadly serious and unimpeachable in its value, others looked at it with cynicism or even outright criticism. While this is often thought to be a modern response, we will see that for as long as Jews have been responding to the biblical story, critical and cynical voices have been among them. Thus, the last section of this chapter will turn to some representative texts over the past two millennia.

The two colossal events of twentieth-century Jewish history, the Holocaust and the rise of the Jewish state, affected Jews' readings of the Akedah as well. Given the multiplicity of ways in which Jews had always responded to the Akedah, no new paradigms needed to be created, but some were bent and others broken. These are not linear processes, but important and fascinating ones.

Some of the attitudes we will explore here worked in concert; other times they clashed. In some situations, taking the story to be exemplary led to the belief that it should be repeated. Others angrily rejected that implication and then turned that wrath against the story itself. In all cases, throughout Jewish history, the story could not be ignored.

The texts discussed here are necessarily selective and representative. Others could be added, and other themes could be highlighted as well. But merit, martyrdom, love, and critique have long been central to the Jewish approach to the Akedah, and they deserve our renewed attention.

Merit of the Akedah

Perhaps most basically, the Akedah was invoked as a source of great merit for the Jewish people and sometimes for all of humanity.[1] There are at least three different, perhaps overlapping, ways in which this motif has been broached:

> (1) It was Abraham's insight to turn the Akedah into a source of merit for all generations.
> (2) It was the divine plan to orchestrate the Akedah to serve as a source of merit.
> (3) The Jewish people call on the Akedah as a source of merit.

A fifth-century poem on the Akedah, whose major theme is Abraham's haste in fulfilling the command—"he rushed to fulfill the command; he lost no time at all"—turns at the end to the question of merit, as well:

> Turn, God, to his ashes,
> Recall for us his covenant
> Guard for us his sacrifice [*Akedah*],

Answer our self-affliction,
Redeem us, O powerful Redeemer![2]

These lines all begin with the letter *tav* (תפן-תזכור-תנצר-תען-תגאלינו)
and are all found after the alphabetic acrostic that structures most
of the poem. The complicated poetic structure may seem daunting,
but a line from this poem is cited in the Babylonian Talmud,[3] which
suggests that these liturgical poems may have been remarkably powerful vehicles for the circulation of religious ideas. And of the genres
of literature preserved for us from antiquity, liturgical poems may
have been the most popularly influential, having their home in the
synagogue rather than the study hall.[4]

That this notion was a popular one, extending beyond elites to the
understanding of the Akedah among other Jews as well, is also suggested by its presence in the *Targumim* from the Land of Israel. These
Targumim occasionally contain substantial narrative expansions, and
in Genesis 22:14, the *Targum Neofiti* adds the following:

Abraham worshiped and prayed in the name of the Word of the
Lord, and said: Please, with the mercy that is before You, Lord!
All is revealed and known to You, that there was no division in
my heart in the first time You told me to sacrifice my son Isaac,
to make him into dust and ashes before You. Instead, I rose early
in the morning, and rushed to do Your word with joy, and I fulfilled Your command. And now, when my children will be in a
time of affliction, You should remember the binding of Isaac their
father, and hear the voice of their prayers, and answer them, and
save them from all affliction.

In other texts, this result was actually God's plan from the very
beginning of the story. The *Tanḥuma* midrashim express this in a number of ways, both before and after the Akedah itself. One passage has
God explain this to the angels at the beginning:

When the Holy One, blessed be He, wanted to create the world, the angels said to Him, "What is humankind that You should remember him?" (Psalm 8:5). The Holy One said to them, "You say, 'What is humankind that You should remember him?'! This is because you are looking at the [idolatrous] generation of Enosh. But let me show you the glory of Abraham, 'whom You should remember,' as it says, 'God remembered Abraham' (Gen. 19:29). You say, 'And humanity that You should take notice,' but it says, 'The Lord took notice of Sarah' (Gen. 21:1)." He said to them, "You will see the father slaughtering the son, and the son slaughtered for the sanctification of My name."[5]

Here, the Akedah is what makes the entire world worthwhile.[6] To those detractors who questioned why God would create such a flawed humankind, the midrash responds by pointing to the Akedah: "the father slaughtering the son, and the son slaughtered for the sanctification of My name." This single act redeems the entire cosmos.

In light of the Akedah's significance, it is not surprising that the midrash returns to this theme after referring directly to the Akedah. A *Tanḥuma* midrash has both Abraham and God reflect on the significance of what just occurred and paints a portrait of Abraham full of pathos in doing so:

Abraham said to God, "*You* swear (Gen. 22:16)?! I, too, swear! I will not descend from this altar until You tell me everything I need to know." God said, "Say what you need to say."

Abraham said, "Did You not tell me that you would establish through me the equivalent of a whole world—as it says, 'Count the stars . . . thus will be your offspring' (Gen. 15:5)?"

God said, "Yes."

"Through whom?"

"Through Isaac."

"And did You not tell me that You would multiply my children like the dust—as it says, 'Your offspring will be like the dust of the earth' (Gen. 28:14)?"

"Yes."

"Through whom?"

"Through Isaac."

"Just as I could have responded to You, but I held my tongue, Master of the world—for You said yesterday, 'Through Isaac will your offspring be called' (Gen. 21:12), and now You told me, 'Offer him as a burnt offering' (Gen. 22:2)—but I quashed my impulse and didn't respond to You, so You, when Isaac's children sin before You and get into trouble, recall for them the binding of Isaac, forgive them, and redeem them from their trouble."

God responds, then, that this was, in fact, his plan as well:

You have said your piece, now let Me say Mine. Your children will, in the future, sin before Me, and I will judge them on Rosh Hashanah. But if they ask that I forgive them, and they blow the shofar before Me . . . I will forgive their sins.[7]

This last line introduces another common motif: the connection between the Akedah and Rosh Hashanah, and in particular to the commandment to blow the ram's horn on that day.[8] For example, Rabbi Abbahu asked, "Why do we blow with the horn [shofar] of a ram? The Holy One, blessed be He said, 'Blow before Me with the shofar of a ram, so that I will remember for you the Binding of Isaac, son of Abraham, and I will consider it as if you bound yourselves before Me.'"[9] In the prayers for Rosh Hashanah, too, Jews entreat God:

May the Akedah, where Abraham bound his son Isaac on the altar, and conquered his mercy[10] in order to do Your will with a whole heart, be seen before You, and thus may Your mercy conquer Your anger away from us. . . . Remember the Akedah of Isaac for the sake of his descendants, today, mercifully. Blessed are You, O Lord, who remembers the covenant.[11]

Finally, other texts connect the Akedah not to merit needed once a year, but to every day. "Thus when the Jews sacrifice the daily offering on the altar . . . God remembers the Akedah of Isaac."[12] On this reading, the world is sustained on a daily basis by the eternal merit of the act of Abraham and Isaac untold centuries ago.

The Martyrdom of Isaac

Despite these promises of merit, troubles did often afflict the Jews. These, too, led back to the Akedah, and particularly unfortunate events led others to think of the Akedah as merely the first Jewish martyrdom—or would-be martyrdom.

The story of the woman whose seven sons are killed, one after the other, because of their refusal to abandon the God of Israel is first told in the second-century BCE book 2 Maccabees.[13] The narrator of the tale in 4 Maccabees comments that the woman has steely resolve: "Sympathy for her children did not sway the mother of the young men; she was of the same mind as Abraham" (14:20).[14] In the Rabbinic version of the story, the mother (whose name would be Hannah only in the Middle Ages) says—calmly, but with rage and pathos just below the surface—at the end of the ordeal, "My children, go tell Abraham your father: You offered one child on the altar, but I offered seven!"[15] This is the first time we hear of Jews commenting that the Akedah pales, as sacrifice, in comparison with what they have experienced. Unfortunately, it won't be the last.

A millennium later, many Jews who lived through the First Crusade saw their lives through the lenses of the Akedah. The suffering they experienced, especially in 1096—a year forever seared in Jewish consciousness—could not be explained as punishment for sins.

This was not because the suffering was qualitatively or quantitatively greater than previous tragedies (it was not, in fact), but because the Jews in Germany and France were, overall, confident in their community's righteousness.[16] This was, therefore, a paradigm-shattering experience: suffering that could not be explained through the normal categories of suffering. The community thus turned to the Akedah for an explanation.

Many of the stories in the Crusade chronicles are emotionally difficult to read. The following one, like many others, is absolutely heart-wrenching. At the same time, it is suffused with biblical allusions, primarily to the Akedah but to other biblical texts as well. The result is a disconnect between the intellectual interpretation necessitated by the sophisticated use of textual allusions and the raw emotions being narrated.

There was a young man named R. Meshullam, son of R. Isaac. He called out in a loud voice to all those standing there, and to Mrs. Tzipporah, his wife: "Listen to me, old and young! This son, whom God gave to me and Tzipporah my wife bore in her old age, whose name is Isaac, I will now offer him as a sacrifice, just as our father Abraham did with his son Isaac!"

Tzipporah answered, "My lord, wait a bit, do not yet stretch out your hand against the lad whom I have raised and nourished, whom I bore in my old age. Slaughter me first, and let me not see the death of the child!"

But he answered and said, "I will not wait even a second! The One who gave him to us should now take him back to his portion, and give him a seat in the lap of our father Abraham."

He bound his son, took the knife [*ma'akhelet*, the rare word for knife used in Genesis 22] in his hand to slaughter his son, made the blessing on ritual slaughter, and slaughtered the lad.

He then took his screaming wife. The two of them went outside together, and were immediately killed by the Crusaders.[17]

As the historian Yosef Hayim Yerushalmi noted, the chroniclers of the Crusade "show a marked tendency to pour new wine into old vessels. Confronted with the intolerable . . . the chronicles of the Crusades turn repeatedly to the image of Abraham ready to slaughter Isaac at Mount Moriah."[18] Historians debate how closely the chronicles of the events reflect the way things unfolded in the last years of the eleventh century.[19] For our purposes, this matters very little. The lenses are the important thing. Jews saw tragedy through the lens of the Akedah.

It is worth dwelling on the claim that Meshullam "made the blessing on ritual slaughter" before killing his son. This equates the sacrifice of a child with a ritual slaughter, a practice not limited to the Temple, but familiar throughout the Jewish world. Interestingly, already in Rabbinic literature the Akedah had actually been mobilized as a source for laws of ritual slaughter; in two passages (*Bereshit Rabbah* 56:6 and B. Ḥullin 16a), the *ma'akhelet* is proposed as the source for the rule that the knife for slaughtering an animal may not be a plant still attached to the ground.[20] This construes the Akedah existing within the category of sacrifice: it may be a unique sacrifice but can still be compared to other sacrifices. For our chronicler, this means that Meshullam has to make the blessing before the slaughter of his child.

The Akedah provided the vocabulary not just for description, but for theological outrage as well:

Ask and see! Has there ever been an Akedah like this in all the generations since Adam? Were there ever eleven hundred 'aḳedot on one day, each one like the sacrifice of Isaac, son of Abraham? For the one bound on Mount Moriah the world shook, as it says, "Behold the angels cried out and the skies darkened."[21] What have they done? Why did the skies not darken, the stars not collect their light,[22] the small light and the great light not grow dark because of clouds,[23] when on one day—the third day [Tuesday], the third day of Sivan—eleven hundred holy souls, including children and babies who never sinned or did anything wrong, and the clear souls of the poor, were killed and slaughtered?[24]

Poets of the era described the Akedah repeatedly and never left it as "mere history." Instead, the poems conclude with explicit equations of the sublime religiosity evident in the Akedah with that on display in 1096.[25] One poet ends his poem by turning plaintively to God:

> Recall to our credit the many offerings
> The saints, men and women, slain for Thy sake,
> Remember the righteous martyrs of Judah,
> Those who were bound of Jacob.[26]

Similarly, the chronicle adds that merit for the horrific martyrdoms during the Crusade should be equivalent to the merit of the Akedah—and should, like the merit of the Akedah, accrue to the descendants of the martyr: "May the blood of his pious stand as a merit and an atonement for us and for our generations to come, and for our children's children, forever, just as the binding of our father Isaac, when our father Abraham bound him on the altar."[27]

Perhaps as a natural result of the belief in the merit of the Akedah, some Jews also expressed their desire to perform this very act of faith and devotion. Such a stance may be religiously understandable (as we will discuss in the next chapter). This manner of thinking appears in midrashim about both Abraham and Isaac.

In one midrash, Abraham is frustrated by his inability to slaughter Isaac. The knife, the midrash asserts, was melted by the tears of the angels, so Abraham declared, "I will strangle him!" The angel said, "Do not stretch your *hand* out against him." Abraham tried to salvage something: "Let me at least draw some blood." But he was stymied again: "Do not do anything [*me'umah*] to him—do not make even a blemish [*mumah*]."[28] Having come all the way to the mountains of Moriah, Abraham did not want to leave empty-handed. But can there be merit with no act? (To this question we will return.) So he offered the ram in place of his son. Thus he earned the merit, without harming Isaac.

Isaac, too, is said to have wanted the Akedah. In the days when Christianity was young, there was a strange sort of competition between Jews and Christians as to who sacrificed more for their faith. Since Christianity, but not Judaism, was illegal for the first three and a half centuries of the Common Era, Christian martyrdoms were common, but Jewish martyrdoms were not.[29] The martyrdoms that the Jews talked about were concentrated in the time of Hadrian, who was, of course, reacting to the catastrophic revolt of Bar Kokhba. Because of this imbalance — which obviously was good for the Jews in mundane terms — Jews experienced what we might call "martyr envy."[30] The Akedah was seen as the right corrective to this, and the following dialogue was imagined as a prelude to the story told in the Bible:

> It was after these words, the argument of Isaac and Ishmael: Ishmael would say, "It would be fitting for me to be Father's heir, as I am the first-born son." And Isaac would reply, "It would be fitting for me to be Father's heir, as I am the son of Sarah, his wife, whereas you are the son of Hagar, my mother's maidservant!"
>
> Ishmael answered, "But I am more deserving than you, since I was circumcised at the age of thirteen and, had I wanted to, could have protested and not submitted myself for circumcision. But you were circumcised when you were eight days old! If you had been conscious of what was happening, you might not have submitted for circumcision."
>
> Isaac replied, "But now I am thirty-six years old, and if the Holy One, blessed be He, asked for *all* of my limbs, I would not hesitate!"[31]

One can hear the Jews' protestations here: we are fortunate to not have to martyr ourselves, but let that not for a moment impugn our faith! The lack of sacrifice is only because no one is asking. If there is a need, we are no less faithful than our ancestors. Were God to ask, we would sacrifice everything; we are prepared to go to our deaths for our God.

The question of whether the Akedah was primarily about faith or action, and the split between Jews and Christians on the issue, was long a contested issue, generally dividing Jews from Christians (as we will discuss in the following chapter). The medieval Spanish Jewish tradition, represented by Naḥmanides in the thirteenth century and R. Nissim of Gerona in the fourteenth century, focused explicitly on Abraham's *actions*. Also in fourteenth-century Spain, R. Nissim's student Ḥasdai Crescas took the Akedah in a different, more concrete direction. A sermon of Crescas's on the Akedah is preserved, which is itself interesting, as not many medieval sermons on the text exist: sermons were usually on the beginning of the weekly Torah reading, whereas the Akedah is at the end.[32] It may be that tragic events forced Crescas to turn his attention to this story.

In the summer of 1391, violence against Jews broke out in Seville, then spread northeast over the coming weeks to Córdoba, then Toledo, eventually reaching Barcelona. The riots of 1391 caused thousands of Jews to convert to Christianity. Many others died in order to avoid that fate. Once again, there were tragic cases of adults who killed their own children in order to prevent them from being forcibly baptized. One documented case is that of R. Judah, who had been married to the daughter of R. Jacob b. Asher, author of the *Arba'ah Ṭurim*. A poem written after the events records that he was among the first killed:

> Rabbi Judah first
> who was a man of distinction
> who first sacrificed his wife
> and his children in the midst of Israel.[33]

Like the German Jews in earlier centuries, the Spanish Jews of the late fourteenth century faced a terrible choice: martyrdom or apostasy/conversion. Many thousands of Spanish Jews converted, but many others chose death over life as Christians.[34] The net result was that entire Jewish communities throughout eastern Spain simply disappeared.[35]

Crescas was a Barcelona native who had moved to Saragossa to serve as the rabbinic authority and royal appointee there.[36] His only son still lived in Barcelona when the riots of 1391 erupted. King Juan I and Queen Violant of Aragon, whom Crescas was then serving in the royal court, explicitly intervened to ensure the security of Crescas's family, but the intervention was ineffective.[37] Crescas wrote a letter to the Jews of Avignon narrating what had transpired in each city over the year. When describing the events of Barcelona, he wrote:

> Many sanctified the name of God, among them my son, my only one, a bridegroom, a perfect sheep whom I offered as a burnt offering.[38]

The Akedah imagery in this line is clear and painful. This suggested to some that Crescas may even have had a hand in his son's death to prevent his apostasy,[39] but there is no direct evidence for this.[40] Still, the line between educating a child to accept martyrdom rather than forced conversion and the actual sacrifice of a child to avoid forced conversion is not all that sharp.

Crescas went on to say that many Jews in Barcelona killed themselves. Many jumped from the tower and thus died, and a few went out to the streets to submit to the mobs and die at their hands. The rest of the Jews of the city converted. The exact fate of the younger Crescas is not recorded.

This brings us back to Crescas's sermon on the Akedah. It is hard not to hear autobiographical overtones in Crescas's teachings:

> All Jews should think that, being from the seed of Abraham, they should be prepared to take the lives of their children, and the children should be prepared to be bound by their fathers and

to bind them, as Abraham did to perform the will of his Heavenly Father.[41]

Whatever the precise background to these lines, Crescas does seem to give credence to the possibility of filicide as religiously legitimate and even necessary.[42] There is no reason to detach this from the reality of martyrdom that his community lived through.

In the fifteenth century, Jews likely retold the story as a *romancero*, a Spanish folk ballad; such a tradition has been reconstructed based on later traditions found among Jews and Christians of Spanish origins.[43] The version preserved in the Crypto-Jewish community sings of the dedication of Isaac and the heroism of his actions: "He who dies for his Lord / in heaven is he crowned." There is little doubt that the Crypto-Jews were inspired by Isaac's heroism.[44] We can reverse the point as well and say that in their search for heroic models, they created an Isaac in the image of their ideal.

Love as Driving the Akedah

If Abraham of the midrash and in the Spanish mind wanted to perform the Akedah for the merit it would earn for his descendants, another strain of thought takes the motivation to be love. This is perhaps most famously expressed in a pair of ancient texts:

Rabbi Shimʿon b. Yoḥai said: Love upsets normal behavior, and hatred upsets normal behavior. Love upsets normal behavior, as it says, "Abraham woke early in the morning and saddled his donkey." Did he not have a few servants [to saddle his donkey for him]? But love upsets normal behavior. (*Bereshit Rabbah* 55:8)[45]

For God so loved the world that he gave his one and only Son, that whoever believes in him shall not perish but have eternal life. (John 3:16)

The midrash emphasizes that Abraham woke up in the morning, moved to rapid action by love. The object of this love is not specified. It may be love for God and the passionate desire to fulfill God's will. But it may also be love for his son, whom he loves so deeply that he can think of no better fate for him than to be a flawless sacrifice to God.[46] John, too, emphasizes giving the beloved child as an act of love. Here, though, God—playing the role of Abraham—acts out of love not for the child being offered, but for the world that will benefit from the sacrificial act.

Shockingly, some parents living during the Crusades spoke of the joy of killing their children as an act of religious martyrdom, thus fulfilling the divine command to Abraham:

> Bound on the sweet mountain, his father tied him tight
> For the offering to work, he said, the sacrifice could not
>   fight.
> But we without any binding are slaughtered just for His
>   love,
> Our souls rejoice in God, revel in the salvation above.[47]

A desire for the "privilege" of the Akedah did not die in the Middle Ages. In the poem "The Morning Sacrifice," the Israeli poet Uri Zvi Greenberg (1896–1981) wrote:

> Oh, that the day will come, that this will come, promised,
>   blood to blood like the carrying of the sea!
> It is from the east, in the image of the sunrise. All the
>   prayers of those who long for his arrival with out-
>   stretched arms!
> Then my father will arise from his grave, as should happen
>   at the Resurrection
> And God will command him, as on the other occasion he
>   commanded Abraham

To sacrifice his only son: that he should be a sacrifice—
And this my father will do.[48]

As the literary scholar Yaakov Bahat observes, there is no hesitation about the Akedah in Greenberg's lines.[49] The narrator *wants* to be tested, *wants* to be sacrificed. He dreams of the chance to offer himself on the altar.

To Greenberg, the altar was not one of faith or religion, but of land and Zionism. The Akedah was being fulfilled in the twentieth century by the pioneers in the land. Greenberg made this link explicit in "1923," part of a poem-cycle about living homeless, wandering the streets and the beaches of Tel Aviv instead of settling down like his (former) friends who live comfortably in other countries.

> I was living and singing under the sky
> How good it was then for me to sleep
> On a bench on Rothschild Boulevard
> Like Isaac on the altar . . .
> And my mother's face in the moon.[50]

The parallels between the Akedah story and the Zionist movement— the parents who came and were prepared to sacrifice their children for a greater cause—invited many reflections. As we will soon see, however, many other Israeli writers were unconvinced that they wanted to be Isaacs.

Cynicism, Criticism, and Humor

Already in antiquity, some readers were voicing discomfort with the Akedah. Criticism of biblical texts can be trenchant and cutting, and, especially in modern times, constitute the front edge of religious rebellion. These earlier critiques were far different, however. They were uttered by people who took the authority of the Akedah for granted. Despite this, they were prepared to mutter about the father who would kill his son, or the God who would demand such a thing. Far from rebellion, their protests were in fact acts of piety, not just in form, but in effect.[51]

Sometimes it is not possible to know with certainty how much protest is being registered. An Aramaic poem from the Byzantine era has Isaac say to his father:

> This is the day that they will say,
> A father had no pity, and a son did not delay.
> How will you go and tell my mother Sarah,
> How will you leave me and go home?
> Isaac kissed his father Abraham,
> Commanding him, saying to him:
> Sprinkle my blood on the altar,
> Gather my ashes and bring them to Mother.
> My life and my death—all is in his hand,
> And I thank him for thus choosing me.
> Fortunate are you, Father, that they will say,
> That I am the lamb for the offering to the Living God.
> Let your anger triumph over your mercy,[52] Father
> Be like a man who has no mercy on his son!
> Like a cruel man, take your knife
> And slaughter me, do not defile me....
> Why should you cry? Said Isaac to his father Abraham.
> Fortunate is the one whom the Lord of the world chose.[53]

Despite the protestations of piety, there are no blinders on here; the poem is cognizant of the great religious value of the sacrifice and equally aware of the great human tragedy unfolding. There is the riff on the conventional prayer "Let your mercy triumph over your anger," here reversed to ask that Abraham's anger triumph. There are the similes of Abraham, about to act "like a cruel man" and admonished to be like a man "who has no mercy on his son." There is the pathos of the father, shedding tears as his son displays steely resolve and urges him on. There is also the re-centering of the drama, as Isaac becomes the dominant figure and Abraham recedes to a passive role.[54] Most of all, there is the sense that Abraham is wavering, torn between his will to perform God's will and his love for his son, and that the encouragement he gets from his son—the intended victim—continually reminds him of the horror of what he is about to do.[55]

The merit accruing is also found here, especially in the first lines quoted. Isaac himself foretells that future generations will be telling his story.[56] Thus the poem manages to simultaneously express bewilderment at the human father who would slaughter his son and marvel at the religious value of such a sacrifice.

The same motif is found in many *piyyuṭim* in a section written for the holiday of Shavuot, in which the Torah explains why she did not want to be given through the Patriarchs and had to wait for Moses. In the poem by the great El'azar be-Rabbi Qillir, the Torah explains:

> The young man with whom you graced him when his
>   strength was spent
> he bound on the wood of the altar . . .
> He forgot how a father is supposed to have mercy on a son
> a prayer or plea he should have offered.[57]

Other poets went further in their criticism: "He stretched out his arm like a cruel person, to murder"; "he should have beseeched you, to ask for mercy / to spare his only child from a fire of coal"; "he did not pity, but you pitied, full of mercy / he did not have mercy, except that you did, Lord of mercy!"; "rushing to return a gift to its master / he turned cruel, sharpened his knives / refrained from beseeching or raising a prayer."[58]

Interestingly, other readers, troubled by the lack of prayer, chose not to criticize Abraham, but to simply provide the prayer. A mishnah already quoted dictates a prayer: "May He that answered Abraham our father on Mount Moriah answer you and hearken to the voice of your crying this day" (*Mishnah Ta'anit* 2:4). But what did Abraham ask, that he was answered? The mishnah appears to assume that Abraham prayed he would not have to sacrifice his son, and this prayer was answered.[59] Thus, for the mishnah, the criticism of the *piyyuṭim* is undercut: Abraham *did* pray. It also seems that Isaac was spared *because* Abraham prayed.

Another midrash, however, picks up the theme of criticism. Isaac calls to his father, "My Father" (*avi*)—and repeats it. "Why 'my father' 'my father'? So that he would have compassion on him."[60] The intent is to force the reader into compassion and sympathy when confronted with Isaac's innocent call to his father. The speech cited in the Aramaic poem cited above exacerbates this. The slaughter *is* cruel. It does privilege *anger* (not faith!) over love. It does mean Abraham has no mercy on his son. With such encouragement from Isaac, who needs Satan?

Satan does have a role to play in this story as well, however. The midrash tells that Satan, here called Samael, worked hard to convince Abraham of the folly—indeed, of the wickedness—of his ways. First, he asks him, "Have you lost your mind?! Will you slaughter the son given to you when you were one hundred years old?" After another query, he hurls at him the sharpest challenge: "Tomorrow, you will be considered[61] a murderer, and you will be guilty." Abraham has no answer to any of these questions, other than to affirm his willingness to tolerate it all. Some readers understand the character of Satan as a projection of Abraham's own questions.[62] It is clear the midrash uses Satan as a mouthpiece for asking the hard questions the Rabbis want to ask but dare not do so in their own voices.[63] The Rabbis clearly thought that Abraham could indeed be labeled a murderer.

One character who is not utilized in Jewish texts as a voice of criticism or doubt is Sarah. But Sarah does play this role in Christian texts, especially Syriac ones. A fifth-century poem retelling the Akedah includes this scene toward the beginning:

Sarah saw and her heart groaned, and she began to speak
   to Abraham:
"Why are you sharpening your knife? What do you intend
   to slaughter with it? . . .
You are so drunk with the love of God, who *is* the God of
   gods,
And if He so bids you concerning the child, you will kill
   him without hesitation!"

In this poem Sarah turns out to be Abraham's equal in faith.[64] She asks
only to accompany him, to be a full participant ("If you are going to
bury him in the ground, I will dig the hole with my own hands / If
you are going to build up stones, I will carry them on my shoulder"),
and then encourages Isaac to submit absolutely to his father's will.[65]
Despite this, the echo of the doubt rings clearly in our ears. Abraham
is drunk with the love of God, so he would not hesitate. Cooler heads
would at least hesitate.

An interesting tradition within early Christian poems is to explain
why Abraham did *not* share his plans with Sarah by quoting what
Sarah *would have* said in response.[66] This has the effect of reifying the
gender roles in the story, but also, on another level, allows the poet to
voice the arguments against obedience without affecting the plot. For
instance, a fourth-century poem imagines that Sarah would have said:

Do not cut off this single bunch of grapes,
The only fruit we have produced; . . .
Do not break the staff on which we support ourselves.

Other Syriac poems take these speeches out of the realm of the
imagination and give Sarah a more robustly critical voice:[67]

"You are not aware of how much I endured
—the pains and birth pangs that accompanied his birth.

Swear to me that he will not come to harm,
For he is my hope. Then take him and go."[68]

But again, these passages are striking as a foil for the Jewish texts, where, to my knowledge, Sarah is never the voice of reason or criticism against Abraham's willingness to rush into the sacrifice—and more broadly, Sarah's role *during* the story of the Akedah is not developed. The voice of doubt is primarily that of Satan, and sometimes Isaac, but Sarah remains silent in her tent throughout. When she is introduced into Jewish versions of the Akedah, it is only at the end, and it is only to die.

Another midrash says that Abraham declared to God, "I *could have* challenged You": after all, God, You had promised that Isaac would be the link between Abraham and a grand nation, so how could You then ask for him to be sacrificed? But, says Abraham, "just as I could have challenged You but did not challenge, so when the children of Isaac give way to transgressions and evil deeds, remember for them the Akedah of Isaac and atone."[69] While the form is pious—Abraham did *not* in fact challenge God, and technically all he does is plead for mercy—the content is in fact a challenge, and an unanswered one at that. It can be uttered aloud because of the form.

The semi-critical attitude toward the Akedah is found in medieval texts as well. A medieval Yiddish epic poem, *Yudisher Shtam*, is fascinating in that it emerges from the same culture that writes about the Akedah with great devotion in *piyyuṭim*, but this story takes a very different tone.[70] In this telling (rendered here in English in prose), after Isaac understands from Abraham's great despair that he is to be the sacrifice, the two of them break down:

Isaac's face was covered in hot tears: "Dear father, what are you going to say to my mother, when she does not see me returning with you?" "After your death, your dear mother, Sarah, and I will not long remain on earth, for who could comfort me in my misery and your mother in her grief and pain?" ... The weeping of both of them was great.[71]

Alongside this pathos, there is also some nervous humor in the poem. When the angel instructs Abraham not to slaughter Isaac, Abraham rejects the order, on talmudic logic: "Even if you are the angel Raphael, it nonetheless does not seem proper to me that I should act according to your commandment: the Holy One, blessed be He, Himself commanded me to do it. If there is a teacher and a student, it is proper that the rabbi's command be followed."[72] (This last line is indeed a talmudic principle.[73]) This delay makes the reader somewhat nervous, but I think the primary effect is actually nervous laughter; the reader knows, of course, how the story is going to end, and the only tension is how the situation will be defused. The angel explains to Abraham that no angel can issue commands without being instructed to do so by God.

Finally, the poem ends with a wry—and crushingly depressing—commentary on the nature of humanity and the value of acts such as the Akedah. After the pious conclusion praying that the Akedah should serve as a source of blessing for everyone involved—including the thorns that held the ram—the poem moves to a meta-conclusion:

Nonetheless, no one should hold me to that. If you want to know the truth, I do not think much of people. I swear to you as a true Jew: they are only so pious that they indeed need another Binding just about every day. Now, be that as it may, I cannot change it. I will ask His name, blessed be He, that He hasten and end it and soon send us the Redeemer. And with that I will conclude and make an end.[74]

The Akedah may seem to be transformative in its power, but in fact the world post-Akedah is much the same as it was beforehand. Even an event such as the Akedah is quickly forgotten; people, resilient as always, will soon forget and return to routines. An Akedah would be needed "just about every day" to create a real change in humanity's nature. Let us just pray for the Messiah.

The Akedah in the Twentieth Century: The Holocaust and Zionism

Over the course of the twentieth century, the import of the Akedah kept shifting, even as its relevance remained.[75] This is most prominently seen in Holocaust literature. The task of the modern critic of this literature, according to literary scholar David Roskies, is "to chronicle the break, the point at which analogies no longer hold and the Tradition is radically altered for all time to come."[76] With regard to the way that writers relate to the Akedah, the Holocaust certainly broke the paradigm for many thinkers. Let us look at two.

Haim Gouri, the poet of the 1948 generation, ended his poem "Inheritance," a retelling of the Akedah story, with these cutting lines: "But he bequeathed that hour to his descendants / they are born / with a knife in their hearts."[77] The "knife" (in Hebrew, *ma'akhelet* again) is apparently the fate to which the Jews are condemned, the inescapable martyrdom that follows them everywhere. In the context of the early State of Israel, this clearly refers to the Holocaust.[78]

Gouri's portrayal of the knife in the hearts of Isaac's descendants deprives the Holocaust of any redemptive quality. It is simply, tragically, another instance of the Akedah, another episode of horrific martyrdom that is the lot of the Jews. Other post-Holocaust thinkers, including ultra-Orthodox thinkers, saw things similarly. The Polish-born rabbi Simcha Elberg, a refugee in Shanghai in 1946, for instance, wrote a short pamphlet called *'Akedat Treblinka*,[79] arguing that the Akedah was definitional to Jewish existence: starting with Abraham and reaching through Treblinka; the sacrifice of millions of holy souls was the ultimate Akedah.[80] Again, no redemptive quality to the sacrifice is in evidence. It is tragic through and through.

Rabbi Kalonymous Kalman Shapira, the Piaseczner rebbe, who later served as the rebbe of the Warsaw Ghetto and was shot by the Nazis in 1943, turned to the Akedah in a sermon. On the second day of Sukkot, October 1940—the first anniversary of the death of his son, who had died in the Nazi bombing of Warsaw—Shapira argued that the Akedah was just the beginning: it contained the *intent* to sacrifice without the consummation of that sacrifice. The Akedah was therefore just the start of a continuously unfolding drama. In fact, he glossed the first line of Genesis 22, "God continued to test, even after these things," as follows: "Every act of Jews being killed by idolaters, which is the opposite, action with no intention, is the fulfillment of the Binding of Isaac." To Shapira, the killing of Jews for no reason was in fact that fulfillment because then there was *consummation* with no *intention*—completing the process begun with Abraham's intention that did not lead to action. "Thus the Binding and all Jews who are murdered later is one action."[81]

In effect, to Shapira, the Akedah was a dagger in the hearts of the Jews. It might not have killed them yet, but it might still. All it would take is some thoughtless wicked person to turn it a bit, and the death that had been the Jews' destiny since that day on Mount Moriah would finally arrive.

The Holocaust thus occupied a distinctive place in this story. In the years to follow, as Shapira watched the unimaginable murder of millions of Jews, he argued that this was the end point of the story that had been slowly unfolding over the past four millennia. The Holocaust completed the process and therefore shattered the Akedah paradigm in Jewish history.

The two world wars of the twentieth century also prompted Jews' self-identification and self-reflection on the Akedah. Poets and philosophers saw the Akedah as an apt metaphor for parents sending their children off to die for a cause that they—the parents—believed in profoundly. Just as no one asked Isaac if he wanted to climb the mountain, no one asked the children what they wanted. Wilfred Owens, the

English poet of World War I who died fighting in France just before the Armistice, wrote "The Parable of the Old Man and the Young" in 1918, the year of his death:[82]

> So Abram rose, and clave the wood, and went,
> And took the fire with him, and a knife.
> And as they sojourned both of them together,
> Isaac the first-born spake and said, My Father,
> Behold the preparations, fire and iron,
> But where the lamb for this burnt-offering?
> Then Abram bound the youth with belts and straps,
> and builded parapets and trenches there,
> And stretchèd forth the knife to slay his son.
> When lo! an angel called him out of heaven,
> Saying, Lay not thy hand upon the lad,
> Neither do anything to him. Behold,
> A ram, caught in a thicket by its horns;
> Offer the Ram of Pride instead of him.
> But the old man would not so, but slew his son,
> And half the seed of Europe, one by one.

Once Owen has Abram bind Isaac with "belts and straps," and especially once he introduces parapets and trenches, the parable is clear. And yet, the last line has the force of a blow to the gut. The old man refuses to slay the "Ram of Pride" (the capital letters accentuating the allegorical significance). The statesmen of Europe ("the old man") deem the sacrifice of the Ram of Pride too high a price to pay. Unwilling to sacrifice their own pride, they kill half the children of Europe.

Owen's choice of Abraham's original name Abram in this context was likely driven by metrical considerations. Still, it is worth contemplating that the biblical Abram is renamed Abraham because he was to be the "father of many nations" (Genesis 17:5). Owen may have deliberately stripped him of this title. In the poem, rather than being the progenitor of millions, Abraham is responsible for the massacre of millions.

Such a sentiment does not fit easily within this discussion, because there is nothing pious or wry about it. It is a blanket repudiation of Akedah thinking, a trenchant critique of those who would sacrifice the youth for a supposedly greater cause.[83] A variation, more in keeping with the Jewish tradition, was voiced by a Diaspora Jew, Leonard Cohen, in his song/poem, "The Story of Isaac." Writing in 1969—in the shadow of Vietnam—Cohen compared the Akedah, which he allowed as legitimate, with contemporary Abrahams. The real Abraham actually had a vision; he was responding to the call of God:

> You who build these altars now
> To sacrifice these children,
> You must not do it anymore.
> A scheme is not a vision
> And you never have been tempted
> By a demon or a god.[84]

The sense of the Akedah being a metaphor for generations, rather than individuals, was particularly strong within the Zionist tradition.[85] Already the 1910s, with World War I and the Hebrew Brigade, were a key decade in Zionist thinking about "heroic death" and how the Akedah could be used, positively and negatively.[86] In Palestine itself, the generation that settled there before 1948 saw themselves as Abraham: when war broke out, those early *olim* were typically too old to fight, their sons were sent out to die,[87] and this sacrifice of the sons was understood as an Akedah. Specific episodes were understood in this paradigm. The fall of Gush Etzion in 1948 was often described as an Akedah, for instance.[88] A book published as a chronicle of that battle, *Siege in the Hills of Hebron*, has Genesis 22:2 ("And he said, Take now thy son, thine only son Isaac, whom thou lovest, and go thee unto the land of Moriah; and offer him there for a burnt offering upon one of the mountains which I will tell them you") as one of its epigrams; the other is a midrash on this verse.[89]

Retaining this paradigm, but reversing the judgment, the critical voice got much louder after 1967 and 1973. The developments were not, of course, linear,[90] but there are certain evident trends. As the wars multiplied, and became bloodier, not all the "Isaacs" in the story were happy with the role assigned to them. The following decades saw many of them react explicitly to the Akedah, re-conceptualizing it or rejecting it altogether. At the beginning of the twenty-first century, the Israeli poet Adam Baruch wrote a poem that begins:

> Several dates about the Akedah:
> Until '73 the hero of the Akedah was Abraham (the parents).
> Since '73 the hero of the Akedah is Isaac (the sons).[91]

The year 1973 was, of course, the Yom Kippur War, in which Israel suffered high casualties—more than 2,500 dead and 7,500 wounded—and came to realize that its military supremacy was more tenuous than it had believed in the wake of the 1967 Six-Day War. Thus, according to Baruch, this year, and this war, marked the point at which the victim, the son, Isaac, became the focus of attention, with profound effects.

We see these effects in full force in the classic piece by the dramatist Hanoch Levin (1943–99).[92] "The Binding" was written in 1969, just two years after the Six-Day War, which both enthralled Israelis with their own military successes and gave rise to the anxiety of repeatedly sending "our boys" out to kill or be killed.[93]

After a few minutes of passive-aggressive dialogue between father and son, we hear the following "encouragement" from Isaac, reminiscent of the Byzantine-era Aramaic poem we saw earlier:

ISAAC: I don't understand you, Dad—you see that from my side it's fine. If you're ready to murder in cold blood *me*, the child of your old age, your precious child who was given to you as

a gift at age ninety,[94] the only consolation you have ever had
in life, if you are ready—then am I the person who would
say "no" to you? They tell you to slaughter, Dad, so jump up
on your feet and slaughter, and there shouldn't be, heaven
forbid, any hidden compunctions. Because what, after all, is
really happening here? We are just slaughtering a child. Is it
really such a big deal to slaughter a small weak child? What
is it, in the scheme of things, to slaughter a child? What is a
child, after all? Especially if the slaughterer is his father, who
is a reliable slaughterer and anyway just a messenger! Get up
and drive the blade of the knife into my young flesh, Daddy,
and slice open my throat until the blood erupts and sprays
out on the ground like the blood of a cow. Make me a cow,
Daddy, and when my eyes open wide and nearly pop out of
their sockets, and my tongue is like sick, and hangs out with
my final mangled scream—then, Daddy, turn the knife in my
throat while I, blood of your blood and bone of your bones,
limp legs floundering on the altar as death approaches. *Nu*,
Daddy, they told you to slaughter—so slaughter.

Levin also plays with the notion that the "voice from heaven" that saves
Isaac may be entirely in the heads of the characters—as, of course,
the original command may have been as well:

ISAAC: A voice! A voice! I hear a voice!
ABRAHAM: What voice?! Lie down!
ISAAC: A voice from heaven!
ABRAHAM: What voice from heaven?! Lie down!!
ISAAC: I don't know. It's speaking: "Don't harm the boy."
ABRAHAM: I didn't hear a thing.
ISAAC: For a long time you already don't hear well. Look, it's
saying it again: "Don't harm the boy." Didn't you hear?
ABRAHAM: No.

ISAAC: I swear! "Don't harm the boy."
　　[Pause. Abraham releases him.]
　　Dad, I swear I heard a voice from heaven.
ABRAHAM [after some time]: All right, if you heard then
　　apparently you heard. Like you said, I'm a bit hard of
　　hearing.

Levin is hurling around a dizzying array of questions and challenges. Who is the sacrifice? Who is the hero, and who is the victim? Did father and son see eye to eye, figuratively, when they saw eye to eye literally? Was Abraham inclined to hear a second voice—or inclined not to hear a call to desist? Although in a sense these questions are timeless, much of their raw emotional power derives from the societal context in which they are raised.

Conclusion

Jews have long lived under the shadow of the Akedah. This has often consisted of simple awe at the faith of Abraham and Isaac and perhaps even more often has reflected the community's hope of being the beneficiary of this awesome act of devotion. But this does not mean that Jews were blind to the monstrous side of the story. For as long as there have been retellings, there have been comments on the cruelty and heartlessness of a father who would do such a thing to his son. These criticisms were couched within texts of piety, however, and so they did not rise to the level of modern critiques unfettered from devotion to the text or its characters. Fascinatingly, modern Jewish culture, too—ostensibly free from any such fetters—continued to grapple with the Akedah. A cultural artifact of great power, if not an authoritative divine text, the Akedah provided lenses through which intergenerational life could be understood.

Understood—and embraced or rejected. The Akedah's power remains.

2

Kierkegaard

Søren Kierkegaard was a youthful twenty-eight when his life took a decisive turn. A son of a well-to-do family in Copenhagen, where he was born in 1813, he had become engaged to a young woman named Regine Olsen. A life of comfort lay before him. An inheritance from his father, who had passed away just a couple of years earlier, allowed him to pursue studies and leisure as he pleased—and he pleased primarily study, and occasionally leisure. Regine, who was nine years younger, came from a family of some means as well. A bourgeois life in the Danish capital beckoned to the two of them.

In 1841, however, Kierkegaard broke off his relationship with Regine, completed his degree at the University of Copenhagen (eleven years after having begun), and traveled to Berlin, where he attended the lectures of the Berlin Academy of Sciences' newest member, the philosopher F. W. J. Schelling. Kierkegaard had come to Berlin with high hopes of making sense of the individual's place in the world, but left with the conclusion that he would have to figure this out on his own.

Kierkegaard's actions of 1841 were part of a crisis of identity. The notion of being a bourgeois husband, an upstanding member of Danish society, part of a "system," terrified him. He wrote to Regine that with his melancholy character, he would be an unsuitable husband. While perhaps this was true, more crucially he seems to have been thoroughly unsure whether he was truly living his life or just acting it as he was expected to do.

Schelling had held out great promise to him. Kierkegaard was looking for a way to acknowledge the individual apart from and unsubsumed by the universal/society. By this time, Schelling had come to oppose the philosophy of his former friend and collaborator Wilhelm Hegel, who had advanced *Sittlichkeit* as the ultimate in human ethics. Literally "customariness," *Sittlichkeit* was supposed to encompass everything, from the family to the state.[1] Furthermore, for Hegel, large institutions necessarily had to swallow up smaller ones — the state encompassing the family, history encompassing the great individual. The individual was fundamentally just a cog in the giant wheels of society and history. After Hegel's death, Schelling had come to Berlin, and it was expected that he would offer a different way of viewing the world. And Kierkegaard was looking for a way to bring the individual back into the story, un-subsumed by the universal. For Kierkegaard, being "customary" was a good start, but no more than that. The goal of life was something else entirely: to be oneself.

But Schelling did not offer any alternative Kierkegaard could come home with. Disappointed, Kierkegaard wrote in a letter, "Schelling talks endless nonsense both in an extensive and an intensive sense."[2] He was still in Schelling's debt, if for unexpected reasons: "I do owe Schelling something. For I have learned that I enjoy traveling."[3] Rather than finding a viable alternative to Hegel in Berlin, Kierkegaard realized he would have to craft his own.

It is not unreasonable to say that much of Kierkegaard's subsequent career was shaped by the quest to find an alternative to Hegel, and especially to Hegel's concept of ethics.[4] Kierkegaard spent much of his time opposing the notion that the system reduced every individual to sameness.[5] In the thirty-six books Kierkegaard would publish before his death in 1855 (including six in 1843 alone), perhaps no theme recurs as insistently as the quest for the significance of the individual.

The Author of *Fear and Trembling*

One of Kierkegaard's early essays, *Fear and Trembling*—one of the six published in 1843—addresses this theme through a meditation on Abraham and his "sacrifice" of Isaac. The book is not signed by Søren

Kierkegaard, however; the author is named as Johannes de Silentio, "John the Silent."

Kierkegaard wrote many of his books under pseudonyms. These were generally not meant to hide his identity—in fact, he occasionally listed himself as the editor of a book supposedly authored by a pseudonymous character. Typically, the works written under other names addressed themes central to Kierkegaard's thinking and yet did not exactly represent his thought. Using fictitious authors enabled him to write in other people's voices, exploring themes he cared about deeply but without committing himself exactly to the perspective offered in the work. Kierkegaard would later ask that what he had published under other names not be cited as his own.[6] While he gladly took legal responsibility for the views expressed under other names, he denied that they represented his own views and therefore implored that they not be attributed to him.

In our case, there is good reason not to trust that this book reflects Kierkegaard's thought. Its epigraph is the enigmatic line "What Tarquinius Superbus said in the garden by means of the poppies, the son understood but the messenger did not." The reference is to an old story of Tarquinius, the final king of Rome, whose son Sextus had recently come into power in a different city. He sent a message to his father asking what to do with the people, and his father took the messenger to the garden, where he silently walked around, cutting off the tops of only the tallest poppies. The messenger returned to the son perplexed, but the son understood the message: get rid of the leading members of the city's society, and leave the rest.

Thus the import of the epigraph is clear, though only to a point. Still, the messenger does not understand. To whom does this refer? Who is this clueless messenger? One school of thought points to the average reader as the non-comprehending messenger and posits that only Regine herself could fully understand what Kierkegaard was up to. On this theory, *Fear and Trembling* is really a coded message to his former fiancée, an allegorical explanation meant for her of why

Kierkegaard had to break the engagement. This, however, does not do justice to the richness of the analysis and the centrality of the ideas to Kierkegaard's thought. More compelling is the theory that Johannes de Silentio, the book's "author," is the somewhat obtuse messenger. As we will see, what prevents him from understanding is not a lack of intelligence, but a lack of faith. The book is (really) written by a man who *does* understand faith and is aimed at others who do or wish to. The ostensible author, Johannes himself, is not a man of faith, as he repeatedly emphasizes, and therefore cannot understand his own subject.[7]

For our purposes, the significance of this analysis is twofold. First, when reading *Fear and Trembling*, we always have to keep in mind that Johannes does not speak fully for Kierkegaard. Kierkegaard may in fact use the character of Johannes in different ways, and we have to be attuned to these possibilities. Second, we can relate *Fear and Trembling* to other writings of Kierkegaard's, but we cannot assume that these will fully agree.[8] To the extent that this book addresses themes central to Kierkegaard's writings, it may approach those themes in different ways.

Understanding *Fear and Trembling*

Despite Johannes's confession that he is not a person of faith, he marvels at faith, since faith provides redemptive meaning to life. He finds this modeled in the person of Abraham, in the story of the Akedah. Abraham here serves as the archetype of the "knight of faith."[9] Johannes writes that although he marvels at the faith of Abraham, he does not *understand* it: Abraham's faith keeps Johannes up at night. He cannot sleep out of a burning desire to see what true faith looks like.

Johannes warns against being jaded in looking at faith; true faith, he argues, is a wonder of the world and must be appreciated. "There were countless generations who knew the story of Abraham word for word by heart, but how many did it make sleepless?"[10] People do not dwell sufficiently on what Abraham did.

Johannes tells of a (hypothetical but eminently realistic) preacher who speaks of the faith of Abraham as a model for all—but then is horrified when he meets a congregant so moved by the sermon that he has decided to sacrifice his son to God. Why, Johannes asks the preacher, distinguish between Abraham and this congregant? It cannot be that Abraham gets a free pass since he is "a great man." This, says Johannes, is a shallow avoidance of the real issue, which is that Abraham had faith: "The ethical expression for what Abraham did is that he intended to murder Isaac; the religious expression is that he intended to sacrifice Isaac."[11]

Faith means that Abraham did not rush and yet did not delay. He was perfectly balanced, ready to act but not overeager. He walked up the mountain to sacrifice Isaac and yet believed, "by virtue of the absurd," that somehow he would return with Isaac as well. As a result of this balance, while Abraham was absolutely prepared to sacrifice Isaac, he was simultaneously absolutely prepared to receive him back. "What came easiest for Abraham would have been difficult for me— once again to be joyful with Isaac!—for whoever has made the infinite movement with all the infinity of his soul, of his own accord and on his own responsibility, and cannot do more, only keeps Isaac with pain."[12]

This "double movement" is what strikes Johannes as faith worthy of wonder. The ability to sacrifice Isaac is impressive, but for this alone, Johannes says, "I do not need Abraham." Instead, Johannes lauds the "double movement": the faith that allows Abraham to be prepared to sacrifice Isaac and to accept him back.[13] Some people in Abraham's position may dismiss the demand to sacrifice their child, perhaps arguing that God would never command something so obviously immoral or that God could not seriously mean it, as God had already promised Abraham that Isaac would be his heir. Some might bring Isaac to the altar with a heavy heart, resigned to the unfolding tragedy. But the knight of faith continues to believe fully, approaching God gracefully, presenting the sacrifice, and offering, "Here, O Lord, is my best; do as you will with it."[14]

For Johannes, resignation is a far cry from faith. "Infinite resignation is the last stage before faith, so that whoever has not made this movement does not have faith." Both the knight of faith and the knight of infinite resignation can sacrifice their children. But only the knight of faith can receive her or him back.[15]

Finding knights of infinite resignation is not difficult. Johannes invokes three examples, each poignant in its own right, but each—according to Johannes—altogether inferior to the faith of Abraham. The three cases are parallel in their outlines. First is Agamemnon, the Greek king waiting to lead his naval force to war against Troy. He is unable to do so, in Euripides's play, because there is no wind at sea. Agamemnon soon learns that this is a punishment from the god Artemis, who can only be appeased by the sacrifice of his daughter Iphigenia. The second case, similar in many ways, concerns the biblical Jephthah, who vowed to offer to God the first creature to come out of his home to greet him should he be victorious in battle. This first creature turns out to be his daughter, whom he then prepares to sacrifice in fulfillment of his vow. The third case is Lucius Junius Brutus, one of the founders of the Roman Republic and among its first consuls, whose sons were caught conspiring to restore the monarchy. Brutus, according to the Roman historian Livy, stoically passed judgment on his sons, condemning them along with their co-conspirators to death.

All of these cases involve parents who were prepared to kill their children. What, then, is special about Abraham? This question is raised over and over in the book and answered: "The difference between the tragic hero and Abraham is obvious. The tragic hero still remains within the realm of the ethical."[16]

To make sense of this, we have to recall Hegel's concept of the ethical, of *Sittlichkeit*. Agamemnon can make sense of his decision. Under normal circumstances, it is obviously wrong—unethical—to kill an innocent daughter. But these were not normal circumstances; the fate of the Greek war depended on this sacrifice. And the war itself was justified, since (according to the Greeks) the Trojans had abducted Agamemnon's sister-in-law Helen. Are the needs of the nation profound enough to warrant the murder of a teenage girl? We may or may not be persuaded by the logic that leads to her death; we may disagree at some point along the ethical way. But the decision is an ethical one, made in ethical terms. Agamemnon is therefore within the realm of the ethical.

The same is true for Jephthah and Brutus. Again, we may disagree with their judgments; we may consider their ethical reasoning unsound. But their reasoning can be explained and, if rejected, rejected with counter-arguments. None of these characters has claimed to have left the realm of the ethical.

Abraham has, though. He has no defense, no explanation in ethical terms for the sacrifice—or is it murder?—of his son. He has *suspended* the ethical. This does not mean that the realm of the ethical is gone or no longer important. Normally it is. But sometimes, for reasons that cannot be explained to anyone else, the knight of faith has to depart from it.

As Johannes perceives it, the question is not just about "ethics," but also about the role of the individual. "The tragic hero resigns himself in order to express the universal; the knight of faith resigns the universal in order to become the single individual."[17] For Johannes, this is a far higher level. Anyone can become the universal. Accepting Hegel's universalism is easy. But transcending Hegel for faith—that is something to marvel at.[18]

Leaving the realm of the ethical is not itself difficult. But this is not what the knight of faith does; this is a *teleological suspension* of the ethical. The ethical is suspended for some purpose (*telos*). Johannes then asks: So what is this purpose?

Why then does Abraham do it? For God's sake, and what is altogether identical with this, for his own sake. He does it for God's sake because God demands this proof of his faith; he does it for his own sake so that he can prove it.[19]

This is not a helpful statement, and it is intentionally unhelpful. According to Johannes, there is no way to articulate Abraham's motivation. If there were, we would not have left the realm of the ethical at all. In fact, the story implicitly makes this claim: Abraham speaks to no one about his actions. He does not reveal his plans to Sarah, and even his attendants are left at the bottom of the mountain. Abraham is all alone, and as Johannes understands him, this is because he cannot communicate, a point Johannes approaches a number of times in the book:

Abraham cannot be mediated, which can also be expressed by saying that he cannot speak. As soon as I speak, I express the universal, and if I do not do that, then no one can understand me.[20]

Abraham keeps silent—but he *cannot* speak. Therein lies the distress and anxiety. For if I cannot make myself intelligible when I speak, I do not speak even though I go on talking incessantly day and night. This is Abraham's situation. He can say everything, but one thing he cannot say, and yet if he cannot say it, that is, say it in such a way that another person understands it, he does not speak. The relief in speaking is that it translates me into the universal. Now Abraham can say the most beautiful words any language can procure about how he loves Isaac. But this is not what at heart he has in mind to say, it is something deeper, that he is willing to sacrifice Isaac because it is a trial. No one can understand the latter, and thus everyone can only misunderstand the former.[21]

In a sense, then, we must stop talking, too. There is simply no way to *articulate* Abraham, to *explain* his faith or its greatness.[22]

Although Johannes can say no more about the content of Abraham's faith, he can say something about its importance. He is acutely aware of the possibility for abuse. After all, who is to stop me from killing someone and claiming it was an act of faith? Many have criticized *Fear and Trembling* for this problem. The philosopher Brand Blanshard, for example, writes:

What are we to say of a rhapsody (in forty thousand words) in praise of pure and holy murder, of a defense of the humanly immoral on the ground that it is religious duty?[23]

Johannes is acutely aware of the problem and makes no attempt to resolve it. Instead, he explains, this is a matter for the person of faith to navigate on her or his own. This is not a problem *with* faith, but a problem *for* faith.[24] While "for the single individual this paradox can easily be confused with a temptation . . . one ought not for that reason to conceal it."[25] The potential for abuse does not mean that all faith should be abolished or quashed; it means that "those who have faith ought to be prepared to post some criteria by which to distinguish the paradox from a temptation."[26] Johannes is exempt from this task because, as will be recalled, he does not have faith.

Throughout the book, Johannes has no way of establishing that Abraham truly was a knight of faith. Both theoretically and practically, this seems to be an impossible task. There is simply no way for anyone else to ascertain whether faith or temptation motivated Abraham. All Johannes can offer is a choice: If we are not willing to grant the *possibility* of individual faith, then Abraham is a murderer and must be condemned. And since Johannes thinks it is clear that Abraham is not to be condemned, the possibility of individual faith must be reckoned with. The final verdict offered by Johannes thus expresses this: "Either then there is a paradox, that the single individual as the particular stands in an absolute relation to the absolute, or Abraham is lost."[27]

The phrase "stands in an absolute relation to the absolute" returns us to the question of the individual. How does the individual find meaning in life? As we have seen, Hegel's view, among others, was that meaning is to be found within systems. If the state is religious, by being part of the society, I too am religious. Or perhaps I have joined the state church. Surely this is religion![28]

But the notion that I am Christian because I take part in a Christian society offended the real Søren Kierkegaard's most sacred notions of religion and religious faith, and Johannes expresses this in *Fear and Trembling* with the claim: "The idea of the church is not qualitatively different from that of the state." The person of faith has to find her or his faith *outside* of such institutions. Both church and state subjugate the individual to the collective, which is the opposite of faith:

> Faith is exactly this paradox, that the single individual is higher than the universal, but in such a ways, mind you, that the movement is repeated, so that after having been in the universal he now as the particular keeps to himself as higher than the universal. If this is not faith, then Abraham is lost and faith has never existed in the world.[29]

In a different book (written under a different pseudonym), Kierkegaard mocks the notion of religion being somehow automatically acquired, "a given." He imagines a man who wonders, legitimately, whether he is truly a Christian. This man may have a wife, and the wife may say:

> Dearest husband, how can you get such notions into your head? Aren't you a Dane, and doesn't the geography book tell us that the prevailing religion in Denmark is Lutheran Christianity? You aren't a Jew, or a Mohammedan; so what can you be? After all, a thousand years have gone since paganism was replaced, so I know you are no pagan. Don't you attend to your duties at

the office as a good civil servant should; aren't you a good subject of a Christian nation, a Lutheran Christian state? Then you must be a Christian.[30]

There is nothing wrong with being a Dane, but—the argument goes—there is something terribly wrong about confusing "Dane" with "Christian."[31] In his posthumously published book *On Authority and Revelation*, Kierkegaard again distinguishes between "geographical Christendom" and actually being a Christian.[32] There he contends that those who are unthinkingly "Christians" are actually "pagans," since they have no real faith at all. Interestingly, here Kierkegaard argues that not all religions are the same in this regard: Judaism, in particular, is as much a matter of birth as a matter of faith, and therefore "one can be a Jew and yet not be a Jew." This is not the case for being a Christian, however, which is an all-or-nothing proposition.[33]

On Authority and Revelation is subtitled *The Book on Adler*, and it is particularly interesting for Kierkegaard's discussion of some of the same issues as those raised in *Fear and Trembling*. "Adler" was Adolph Peter Adler, a Danish churchman one year younger than Kierkegaard who had been a devoted follower of Hegel until the early 1840s.[34] Then he experienced some sort of revelation, burned his philosophical books, and published a theological treatise that he said had been dictated to him by Jesus himself.[35]

Here was a perfect trial for Kierkegaard to work out his thoughts on individualism and group-think.[36] Clearly Adler had broken from the conventional wisdoms of the day, charting his own path in response to a perceived call from above. Soon after the affair broke, Kierkegaard began writing about the case of Adler. He continued to work on the book over the next decade, but he never published it. There are many possible explanations for his failure to bring the book to publication, but likely one problem was that he never worked out the dilemma presented by Adler to his own satisfaction.

In the volume Kierkegaard explains that "Magister Adler proclaimed that he had had a revelation, and thus came into collision with the State-Church." This, of course, reminds Kierkegaard of Abraham.[37] But how to distinguish the true knight of faith from the madman? "In case, for example, the individual in the peculiar sense loves the universal, thinks lowly of himself in comparison with the universal, shudders with fear and trembling at the thought of being in error, then he will make everything as good and easy as possible for the universal. And this conduct is a sign that it might be possible that he was a real extraordinarius."[38]

Unfortunately for the questions at hand, Kierkegaard ducks the real issue by concluding that Adler was no prophet, not the recipient of a true revelation, and in fact not a knight of faith at all. This is not, Kierkegaard avers, because revelations could not take place in Copenhagen in the 1840s! "That a man in our age might receive a revelation cannot be absolutely denied."[39] In fact, Kierkegaard *wishes* to meet a person with revelation. The alternative is the genius, creative and brilliant but from within, not from above. "With geniuses," says Kierkegaard, "I can hold my own fairly well."[40] (This distinction between "revelation" and "genius" is comparable to that employed by Abraham ibn Ezra between "tradition" and "reason."[41] For Ibn Ezra, too, reason/genius may be impressive but can be disputed, whereas when faced with tradition/revelation, one can only submit to its authority.) Adler, in any event, turns out to be neither genius nor revelation, but nonsense.[42]

This does not, however, strip the book of its philosophical significance. Despite his dismissal of Adler the person, Kierkegaard has to grapple with Adler the case as a test of his approach to authenticity. He admires the quest for individuality and even seems envious of it at times.[43] At the same time, he is unprepared to simply tip his hat to the man who claimed to have received a revelation. The line between a knight of faith and a victim of temptation is a fine one, and there does not seem to be any way for an outsider to adjudicate.

In all, Kierkegaard walks a fine line. On the one hand, following the crowd is rarely correct and never sufficient. For Kierkegaard, the crowd is the ultimate amoral authority.[44] Resisting the crowd or, better, simply ignoring the crowd and responding to the individual call is a necessary step to authentic faith. On the other hand, it is clear to Kierkegaard that the individual knight of faith will never break outside the norms of Christianity. This claim, of course, is the reflex of Kierkegaard's own faith. All moments of true faith hark back to the coming of God in Jesus Christ.[45] Kierkegaard is—as twentieth-century writers will claim—the father of existentialism, whose goal is authenticity and genuine individuality, but for him this always involves "authenticity with respect to God." And when the knight of faith leaps off the precipice of the plane of ethics, seemingly into an unknowable abyss, in fact he must be leaping into true Christianity.[46]

Individualism in *Fear and Trembling*

We now return to *Fear and Trembling*, and to Abraham. The universal obligations incumbent on Abraham are clear: "Abraham's relation to Isaac, ethically speaking, is quite simply this, that the father must love the son more than himself."[47] But faith may be shocking in its demands. As Johannes notes, Luke 14:26 contains this remarkable teaching:

> If anyone comes to me and does not hate his own father and mother and wife and children and brothers and sisters, yes, even his own life, he cannot be my disciple.

According to Johannes, learned exegetes water this down, by patiently explaining that "hate" does not mean "hate," but "love less" or something of the sort. Through such arguments, the exegete hopes "to smuggle Christianity into the world," by persuading people that Christianity is unoffensive. He may succeed so well, however, that he will demonstrate the utter banality of Christianity, and therefore its absolute superfluity. This exegete will "also succeed at the same time in convincing the same person that Christianity is one of the most pitiable things in the world."[48]

Johannes understands why people do not want to look this passage from Luke square in the eye. First, people operating outside the constraints of the universal may do all sorts of things, and we are not willing to take the chance on individuals unfettered by social norms. Second, why *would* we want to? Being an individual, say others, is *easy*. The difficult task of civilization is to persuade individuals to become like each other.[49] For Johannes, however, this is fundamentally mistaken: to join the universal is the easy task, and becoming the individual is the difficult challenge.

A last point about the argument in *Fear and Trembling* must be emphasized. The "single individual" does not turn his back on the ethical upon entering the world of faith, and also (which is the same thing) does not turn his back on the rest of humankind in finding his meaning in God. To recall a passage already cited, Johannes says that Abraham's love for Isaac continues throughout the narrative, unabated: "Now Abraham can say the most beautiful words any language can procure about how he loves Isaac. But this is not what at heart he has in mind to say, it is something deeper, that he is willing to sacrifice Isaac because it is a trial. No one can understand the latter, and thus everyone can only misunderstand the former."[50] The love he has for his son is part and parcel of the sacrifice.[51] Without that love, Abraham becomes cold, a killer in the name of God. With the love for Isaac burning hot, he is Our Father, the knight of faith and the bearer of the ultimate sacrifice.

Christian Lenses on the Akedah

On the theological level, this is a deeply Christian reading of the Akedah. That Kierkegaard approaches Abraham as a Christian hardly needs to be noted. But it perhaps bears emphasizing that this does not only relate to the terminology he uses or the trappings of the presentation; it is the most fundamental part of his understanding. Focusing on Abraham's *faith* rather than his *actions* takes sides on a millennia-old dispute, going back to Paul and the Rabbis.

For Christians, faith had long been supreme, and Paul had already singled out Abraham as the model of being "justified by faith," rather than by works. Drawing on Genesis 15:6, Paul wrote in his letter to the Romans:

What then are we to say was gained by Abraham, our ancestor according to the flesh? If, then, Abraham was justified by works, he has something to boast about, but not before God. For what does the scripture say? "Abraham believed God, and it was reckoned to him as righteousness" (Rom. 4:1–5).

It is true that this had been a matter of debate among the early Christians and that the author of the book of James had focused on Abraham's *actions* in Genesis 22 in conjunction with it: "Was not our ancestor Abraham considered righteous for what he did when he offered his son Isaac on the altar? You see that his faith and his actions were working together, and his faith was made complete by what he did" (James 2:21–22). Within classical and later Christianity, though, Paul's vision was clearly the dominant one. An author in the style of Paul also turned to the Akedah as proof of Abraham's faith, in a famous passage from Hebrews 11:

By faith Abraham, when put to the test, offered up Isaac. He who had received the promises was ready to offer up his only son, of whom he had been told, "It is through Isaac that descendants shall be named for you." He considered the fact that God is able even to raise someone from the dead—and figuratively speaking, he did receive him back. (Heb. 11:17–19)[52]

Some early Christian readings of the Akedah essentially give us a quite similar version to that developed by Kierkegaard. Consider, for instance, Saint Augustine:

> Not for a moment, of course, could Abraham believe that God took delight in human sacrifices, although he knew that once God's command rang out, it was his not to reason why, but to obey. What Abraham is to be praised for is his faith in the immediate resurrection of his son as soon as the sacrifice was over—faith in God's promise, given when Abraham refused to yield to his wife in the matter of casting out the maid-servant and her son: "In Isaac shall thy seed be called" (Genesis 21:12). . . . It was to this promise, then, that the father, inspired by faith, held firm, because it was to be fulfilled by him whom God commanded to be slain. That is why he had no doubt that the boy who could be given to him after his own hope was dead could be given back to him after his own hope was dead.[53]

Augustine, too, has Abraham "to be praised" because of his faith, and specifically his faith in the absurd: that despite the divine command to offer Isaac as a sacrifice, God's promise would be fulfilled through Isaac. He goes on to cite the passage from Hebrews 11.

Like many Christian writers, Augustine saw Isaac as typologically foreshadowing Jesus.[54] One earlier example is Melito, the bishop of Sardis (western Turkey) in the second century CE. Living among a vibrant and perhaps even powerful Jewish community, Melito claimed the Akedah as a Christian story.[55] Jesus, he said, "was bound like a ram, shorn like a sheep, crucified as a lamb; he carried the wood on his shoulders as he was led up to be slain like Isaac by his Father." But Jesus goes beyond Isaac:

> But Christ suffered, whereas Isaac did not suffer;
> For he was a model of the Christ who was going to suffer.[56]

In this regard, Kierkegaard breaks with the tradition. Isaac is hardly mentioned in *Fear and Trembling*, and he plays no role in the retelling of the Akedah there. Instead, the hero of the Akedah is Abraham, who is not just the sacrificer, but the sacrificed. The ethical person of Abraham is sacrificed; he finds resurrection, so to speak, in the realm beyond ethics.[57]

For the Jew, however, the opposite is clear: faith is not sufficient; works are necessary. The Mishnah makes this claim in a clear polemic against Paul's theology:

> Rabbi Ḥannaniah b. 'Aqashia says: "The Holy One, blessed be He, wanted to justify Israel, so He gave them many laws and commandments, as it says, 'The Lord wanted to justify him; he multiplied Law and glorified it' (Isa. 42:21)."[58]

The mishnah's implicit, but very clear, argument with Paul is how someone can be "justified" before God. Paul rejected the idea that Abraham could be "justified by works," but the mishnah says that this is precisely how God expects people to be justified. For Paul, of course, this makes no sense: "But law came in, with the result that the trespass multiplied" (Rom. 5:20). For the mishnah, law is the only way to salvation; for Paul, it is the sure path to perdition. For Paul, Abraham was justified by faith. For the Jews, faith is never sufficient; the *actions* of Abraham were needed.

Jews could, of course, point out that the verse Paul cites, that Abraham "had faith in the Lord, and it was accounted to him as righteousness" (Gen. 15:6), appears in the biblical text long before the Akedah. What was the need for the Akedah if only faith was needed, and that was already accomplished? Yet God is not willing to let Abraham rest on those laurels! "After these things, God tested Abraham" (Gen. 22:1): after all that faith, God asked him to *do* something.

This line of thought is expressed in an anonymous late medieval Judeo-Spanish poem, part of which reads:

[For] as to the trial
By which God tested him:
What was the reason that,
Without having to draw a conclusion,
He commanded him such a thing?
For we declare based on the commentaries
It is a most erroneous view
That it was to test him
Without bringing anything else about for him
[Since] He already knew his mind.
He rather showed that acting
On something perfect
Causes it to be much more noted,
[More] meritorious and choice
And [deserving] of great reward.[59]

By the time this poem was written in the fifteenth century, there was a venerable Spanish Jewish tradition of understanding that the Akedah was intended to bring Abraham from a position of faith alone to one of action. In the thirteenth century Naḥmanides had written, "The tester, may He be blessed, commands [the one being tested] in order to actualize the potential, so that he will merit reward for a good action, and not only a good heart."[60] A century later, R. Nissim of Gerona generalized this idea into a theory of righteousness: as one completes one commanded task, the person gets religiously stronger, and the tasks get more difficult, creating a cycle of righteousness.[61] It is for this very reason, our anonymous poet concludes, that God ordained the Akedah: God thus "showed that acting on something perfect causes it to be much more noted, [more] meritorious and choice, and [deserving] of great reward."

All this is to say that when Johannes approaches Abraham as a knight of *faith*, we are in clearly identifiable Christian territory. At the beginning of *Fear and Trembling*, we read of a man who was obsessed with the story of Abraham. "That man was not a learned exegete, he did not know Hebrew; if he had known Hebrew, he perhaps would have easily understood the story of Abraham."[62] It is not clear who this man is (Kierkegaard himself did know some Hebrew), but it can be said that Johannes does not know the Jewish tradition of the Bible at all. He approaches it profoundly shaped by Paul's vision. He expects to see faith in the story of Abraham and unsurprisingly finds it there.

The notion that the Akedah is about faith, then, can be and has been debated for many centuries. Kierkegaard's faith-oriented reading is a defensible approach with a distinguished pedigree, even if it has never been the only possible reading.

Unpacking "Sacrifice" and "Received Isaac Back in Love"

In other ways, however, the reading of the story offered in *Fear and Trembling* does less justice to the biblical text. Let's consider, for now, the multivalence of the word "sacrifice," which obfuscates a crucial point in this presentation, and whether in fact Abraham "received Isaac back in love."

Abraham is prepared to sacrifice Isaac; this is true. But does that mean he was prepared "to surrender" Isaac or that he was prepared to "offer Isaac as a sacrifice"?[63] In some passages in *Fear and Trembling*, the former seems to be key, but in the biblical story the latter looms largest. In Johannes's telling, the story primarily "involve[s] the giving up of a person who represents the highest earthly love for the sake of a higher love."[64] This point is emphasized even more profoundly if we understand that Kierkegaard was working out his own need to break with Regine Olsen through his explication of Abraham's story. (Regine, of course, was not physically harmed in the episode and went on to marry another man relatively soon.)

The violence in Genesis 22 is beside the point in *Fear and Trembling*. But this does not seem like a good reading of the biblical text: it is not enough to speak of Abraham "giving up" on Isaac or "surrendering" him. In the biblical narrative, the crucial point is not just the end of the relationship between Abraham and Isaac that constitutes the trial, but the *killing* of Isaac. It does this by juxtaposing Genesis 22 to Genesis 21. In that earlier chapter, Abraham was forced, by his wife and by God, to surrender his first-born son, Ishmael.

The two stories are strikingly parallel. In both, God tells Abraham that he needs to get rid of his son—banish in the case of Ishmael, kill in the case of Isaac (Gen. 21:12–13, 22:1–2). In both, Abraham "wakes up early in the morning" and takes his supplies (21:14, 22:3). In both, the end draws near: Ishmael, about to die of thirst, is left under a bush by his mother (21:15–16), and Isaac is about to be slaughtered by his father (21:9–10). In both, at the last minute, an angel appears to offer a reprieve (21:17, 22:11–12) and then follows that with blessings for the future (21:18, 22:16–17). In both, the salvation is tied to the parent seeing something new—a well of water in the case of Hagar (21:19) and a ram in the case of Abraham (22:13). Both stories finally end with notices related to the children's marriages (21:21, 22:20–24).[65] And in both stories, "the central issue," as biblical scholar Jon Levenson puts it, "is whether the first-born son of Abraham will survive the ordeal into which he has been placed by a father preeminently obedient to God's command."[66]

There are, of course, differences between the two, some of which relate to the most basic story of Genesis, the covenant with the Patriarchs. Ishmael is saved with his mother, the Egyptian slave-woman, and married to an Egyptian girl; Isaac, we understand at the end, will inherit his father's blessings and marry within his father's family. Strikingly, Hagar, but not Abraham, prays for the welfare of the child in her care; the angel appears in Genesis 22 unbidden.[67]

For our purposes, however, the most important contrast is in the role of Abraham vis-à-vis his son. While both are stories of Abraham's being forced to sever his relationship with a son, the first one takes place through banishment and the second through slaughter.

The violence cannot, then, be marginal in the story. It is what makes Genesis 22 into the Akedah and Genesis 21 into an oft-forgotten episode in the life of Abraham.

What is more, while the claim that Abraham received Isaac back in love is central to Abraham's portrait in *Fear and Trembling*, the biblical text never indicates this—and there are apparent indications to the contrary. The story ends, jarringly, "Abraham returned to his servants. They got up and walked together to Beer-sheba. Abraham dwelled in Beer-sheba" (Gen. 22:19). As readers have long noted, Isaac has disappeared. As the midrash and later exegetes ask, "Where was Isaac?"[68] And it is not just that he has become invisible; he has also been replaced. The phrase "they walked together," referring to Abraham and Isaac, has already appeared twice in the story (22:6,8). But now Abraham is walking "together" with others, with his attendants. As far as we know from the biblical text, Abraham and Isaac never speak again.

This is sufficient to convey that the text is quite distant from the notion that Abraham "received Isaac back in love." But some Jewish readers pushed this point further, arguing that in fact Isaac did not return with Abraham at all, because the Akedah had irreparably ruptured their relationship. The late fifteenth-century exegete Don Isaac Abarbanel, for instance, noted that the following chapter opens with Sarah's death in Hebron and continues, "Abraham came to lament Sarah and to cry for her" (Gen. 23:2). Abarbanel argues that from this we learn two facts: first, that Abraham and Sarah lived in different locations, he in Beer-sheba and she in Hebron, and second, that Isaac—who did not have to "come to Hebron with his father"—was already in Hebron with his mother.[69] Although Abarbanel does not say so, it seems reasonable to put these observations together with the fact that father and son never again speak and conclude that their relationship was forever altered by the events in the land of Moriah.

In conclusion, while Johannes's awe-filled appreciation for the faith of Abraham cannot but fill readers with awe as well, the portrayal is not a particularly good interpretation of the text of Genesis 22. It does not adequately grapple with two critically important points in the text—the violence at the heart and the lack of a reconciliation at its end. It is also a deeply Christian understanding of Abraham. It would therefore seem unlikely that *Fear and Trembling* could become an influential book in later *Jewish* theology. And yet it did.

In the following chapter, we will turn to Jewish thinkers of the nineteenth century who approached the Akedah in ways reminiscent of, and sometimes strikingly parallel to, how Johannes explained it. Although these readings are far less influential than Kierkegaard's, their existence helps to explain something of Kierkegaard's influence. Far from being an idiosyncratic voice in the wilderness, Kierkegaard was reflecting some of the deepest anxieties of faith communities in the modern world. When navigating modernity, the role of the individual, especially one of a different faith than the surrounding culture, is a fraught question, and the portrait presented in *Fear and Trembling* opens a powerful way of handling that question. Whether or not its theology is a faithful interpretation of the biblical text, then, it nonetheless commands our respect as a modern theology.

3

Jewish Parallels from the Century
of Kierkegaard

If Kierkegaard is profoundly Christian, he is also profoundly modern. Looking at the influences on his thought from earlier times, one grapples with Christian theology, and especially the sources relevant to a nineteenth-century Danish Protestant. But looking at his thought in its *horizontal* setting—within the eighteenth and early nineteenth centuries—there are commonalities with European thinkers of all stripes, including Jewish thinkers, because they are all inhabiting a new intellectual and religious world.

The changes in worldview evident in the late eighteenth and early nineteenth centuries comprise a story profoundly narrated by the philosopher and historian Charles Taylor, who insightfully called the modern world the "Age of Authenticity."[1] In this world, people marry for love, the novel explores the inner workings of the individual's mind, child-rearing becomes a topic for public conversation, and one looks for encounters with the untamed natural world, usually in a garden. Of course, love or children are not new, but only in recent centuries did these feelings begin to be seen as the most important considerations in one's life.

The increased emphasis on the interior dimensions of human beings ran parallel to the emergence of a private sphere distinct from public life. In turn, the demarcation of public and private spheres led to the decreasing authority of state institutions over people's "private" affairs. The breakdown of large orders of proper behavior was accompanied—as the other side of the coin—by a new emphasis on privacy and individual autonomy.[2] No longer was it seen as acceptable for the townsfolk to intervene in the relationship between wife and husband or parent and child.

Taylor tells the story without any reference to nation-states. But this factor, too, played a role in the anxiety over what it meant to be an "individual." As the state consolidated its authority over various sectors of society, the question of the status of the individual became more fraught. The individual was not simply being liberated from feudal or religious regimes, but was also becoming a subject or a citizen of various nation-states. Recall the wife's speech as cited by Kierkegaard when her husband wonders if he really is a Christian: "Aren't you a Dane, and doesn't the geography book tell us that the prevailing religion in Denmark is Lutheran Christianity?" Who I am may be seen as a function of what state I live in.[3]

Of course, Kierkegaard had the theoretical option of going along with this movement, declaring himself to be Christian because he was a Dane. This would have violated all of his beliefs about Christianity, but it would have appeared reasonable. The Jews, on the other hand, had no such choice. They were clearly not part of the nations they lived in. While some states were slowly granting them increased rights, Jews always found it difficult to fully assimilate into the nation-state; they were forever grappling with bifurcated identities: Polish Jews, Danish Jews, French Jews, and so on. Certainly, Jews had been grappling with such bifurcations for millennia; already the biblical villain Haman is quoted as condemning the Jews for being "scattered and yet always separate" (Esther 3:8).[4] Still, the modern era and the unique matrix of the nation-state presented new challenges and provoked new ways of thinking about religion.

The key move was to turn religion inward. If religion were not defined or governed by society, it could be both more authentic and more protected. Let it be a matter of "faith," of "conscience," rather than community or law. The price paid, of course, was that the community no longer had the ability to coerce religion: if true religiosity was inside the religious person—now called "the person of faith"—

then it was for no one else to dictate how that person should be living.[5] The individual faith comes at the expense of the communal cohesion.

The most obvious turn inward in eighteenth-century Judaism was Hasidism, and numerous commentators have seen Hasidism as comparable to Kierkegaard's thought. "In the nineteenth century, in Judaism and Christianity, there occurred two particularly significant turns to 'inwardness,'" wrote the philosopher Jerome Gellman. "One was the movement of Hasidism in Eastern Europe, the other the existentialism of [Søren] Kierkegaard."[6] Both of these movements—if Kierkegaard himself can be called a "movement"—are also parallel in how they viewed their nemesis. In both cases, the target of their criticism was not the state or the community: "The Hasidic turn to inwardness, like Kierkegaard's, emerged in protest of what was perceived as the lifeless stagnancy of formalistic institutionalized religion."[7]

But while it is easiest to see the turn inward in Hasidism, which explicitly presented itself as new within the Jewish landscape, no segment of Jewish thought was free from this profound shift in the way people thought about human life. The great adversary of the Hasidim, the leader of the "opposers" (*Mitnagdim*), was "the Gaon" Elijah of Vilna (1720–97), whose thought is often said to be more traditional, as opposed to the revolutionary thought of Hasidism. But the Gaon, too, was profoundly inward-looking. Personally, he was free of any community responsibilities or even affiliations.[8] Furthermore, his influence led to the birth of the trans-regional yeshiva movement, which both symbolized and concretized the dissolution of communal authorities (the *kehillah*). As a result of the yeshiva movement, the communities of *Mitnagdim* no longer governed themselves religiously; now, in the nineteenth century, authority rested in rabbis who were often physically distant from the community, whose influence was due to their intellectual prowess, as seen in study within the yeshiva, rather than in their standing within the local community.

The third towering religious voice of the era was that of Moses Mendelssohn (mostly Berlin, 1729–86). Mendelssohn's thought, too—

and, it can be argued, his entire persona—was equally a product of the inward turn. His *Jerusalem* argued that Judaism is an ideal religion in that it affects only the heart and mind, not the structure of political power.[9] Furthermore, Mendelssohn contended that not only should the state not be getting involved in religion, but that even within the Jewish community, the rabbinate cannot coerce observance. How could they, when religion is properly the domain of the individual?

The very fact that Mendelssohn could live the life he lived, as a Jew among the philosophers, discussing religion without fear of being coerced to convert, was a function of this inward turn. While some of his friends challenged him to refute Christianity or submit to it, it was assumed that this would be based on inner conviction, never external pressure.

Thus, all segments of eighteenth-century Judaism—the Hasidim, the *Mitnagdim*, and the modernizers such as Mendelssohn—reflected this inward turn.

One reflex of this turn inward was contemplation of the potential—or actual—clash between the societal definitions of proper behavior and one's own faith or conscience. On the one hand, personal faith was now to be respected, and society was not supposed to intervene in such matters. On the other hand, this meant there was no way to rein in deviants or heretics, who could preach whatever gospel they wanted. And how far could this noninvolvement reach? What about someone preaching a gospel of violence and mayhem? Or a person actually *acting* on such a gospel and attributing it to a profound, and inscrutable, faith?

The clash between "the normal" and "uniqueness" was therefore an increasingly prominent theme in nineteenth-century literature. The novelists Fyodor Dostoevsky and Herman Melville (among others) explored this topic, since they, like Kierkegaard, were unimpressed by what passed for religion in the world around them, perceiving it as shallow and conventional, not at all a matter of true faith. What would happen if true faith actually caused people to act in the world? And, all these writers agreed that while most people ought to obey laws, truly extraordinary people had the right to violate them.[10]

Jewish Writers of the Period

In light of all this, it would therefore not be surprising to find that there were Jewish writers of the nineteenth century who, like Kierkegaard, saw the Akedah as a story of individual faith in the face of societal pressures for conformity. Scholars have naturally searched for such analogues within Hasidic works.[11] In general, however, Hasidic writers approached the Akedah in very different ways than Kierkegaard did. In their interpretations, Abraham does not experience any pain, and the "trial" is not whether Abraham would obey God or not—for how could anyone not?—but whether Abraham would successfully obliterate his will altogether, nullifying himself in the face of the divine will. Whereas Kierkegaard stressed Abraham's enduring love for Isaac, the Hasidim denied it.[12]

There were occasional exceptions, however. Some Hasidic writers did strike notes reminiscent of Kierkegaard. One possibly relevant interpretation is that of R. Mordechai Joseph Leiner of Izbica, Poland (1801–54).[13] Rabbi Leiner's argument begins with the claim, already noted, that for Abraham to violate the prohibition on murder in response to a direct command from God is no test at all. For the Izbicer, it is clear that any religious person faced with the direct command of God would hasten to do the divine bidding, whatever the social and ethical costs. For this, Abraham would not have deserved any accolades. What made this an actual *test* was that the divine command was fundamentally ambiguous: the imperative *"ve-ha'alehu* there as a burnt offering" could mean either "offer him as a burnt offering sacrifice" or "lift him up as a burnt offering." And the latter reading allows for the possibility that Abraham is to "lift up" Isaac and then bring him down again.

This ambiguity has a long history in Jewish interpretive history.[14] It is discussed in the classical midrash *Bereshit Rabbah*, where it is used to exonerate God from the charge of inconsistency. God responds to an accusation to that effect in the mouth of Abraham with the defense that God never intended for Isaac to be sacrificed at all: "just lift him up and then bring him down."[15] It is picked up again in the tenth century by Sa'adia Gaon again to defend God's consistency, this time against the accusations of philosophers.[16] It is worth observing that Sa'adia may well have been familiar with the Qur'ān's version of the Akedah story and that there (*Al-Ṣāffāt* [37] 102) Ibrahim does not *hear* God's word, but instead sees a vision: "He said, 'O my son, indeed I have seen in a dream that I sacrifice you.'" Later, Allah stops Ibrahim: "And when they had both submitted and he put him down upon his forehead, we called to him, 'O Abraham! You have fulfilled the vision.' Indeed, this was the clear trial" (103–6).

Rabbi Levi b. Gershom (Ralbag), a Provencal philosopher and exegete of the fourteenth century, also made the alleged ambiguity of the divine command the centerpiece of his interpretation of the Akedah, in a manner strikingly similar to the Izbicer's.[17] For the Ralbag, however, the two interpretations of *ve-ha'alehu* are not equally plausible, but Abraham could have preferred the less compelling interpretation of God's words in order to free himself from the obligation to kill his son. For this, philological improbability is a small price to pay! "God, may He be exalted, tested him to see if it would be difficult in his eyes to do *anything* that God might command him."

Returning now to the Izbicer, Abraham now had to respond to the ambiguity in the divine command. There was no answer key, no way for Abraham to ascertain the intended meaning—and in this case, authorial intent was *all* that mattered. But, of course, given the ambiguity, there are obvious reasons to prefer the understanding that does *not* involve child sacrifice: first, self-interest; second, the principle of charity, assuming that God would not be contradicting himself. "Had he had the slightest affection for Isaac in the ways of the love a father has for his son, he would have resolved the ambiguity for himself that he should *not* sacrifice him, for there were in front of him many considerations, and he was confused by them all."[18] So Abraham has quite a strong case for concluding that despite the ambiguity, God does not want him to *sacrifice* Isaac, but only to "lift him up."

Why, then, does he prepare to sacrifice him anyway? Rabbi Leiner does not answer this directly. He does, however, observe that actually God did *not* want Abraham to offer Isaac as a sacrifice, as we learn as the story unfolds. And yet Abraham is rewarded for being *prepared* to sacrifice him, in line with a plausible but mistaken interpretation of the original command. Gellman suggests that the test was whether Abraham would be able to act against all his self-interest, and in fact all of his rationality, in deciding to go forward with the sacrifice anyway.[19] Abraham knows that this is a sin—murder, after all, was forbidden to Noah already after the Flood—but it is a sin for the sake of Heaven ('*averah li-shmah*).

Elements of this interpretation are reminiscent of Kierkegaard. The phrase '*averah li-shmah* could be translated as "teleological suspension of the law" in the name of individual religious experience,[20] and this is conceptually similar to Kierkegaard's teleological suspension of the ethical. Additionally, Rabbi Leiner portrays Abraham as continuing to believe in the original covenantal promise even as he is on his way to sacrifice Isaac: "He still believed in the first words, as before; this type of belief cannot be rationally understood."[21] This certainly sounds something like Kierkegaard's "absurd" faith.

But the comparison is less than entirely convincing, for two reasons. First, it is not clear whether on closer analysis the teleological suspension of the ethical and the religiously motivated sin can fruitfully be compared, or at least, it is clear that they are not quite the same. For Kierkegaard, religious faith may demand the teleological suspension of the ethical, and the realm of the ethical is outside the religious sphere. The '*averah li-shmah*, on the other hand, is a suspension of the normal rules of Jewish law for the sake of a local transgression that is seen to be more spiritually significant in the moment. This is, then, an inner-religious clash, rather than a clash between religion and more general *Sittlichkeit*.[22]

Second, when the Izbicer's comments are subjected to close analysis, they seem to yield either philosophical incoherence or ethically monstrous conclusions. Can it be that whenever there is even the chance that God might want me to kill someone, I should hasten to do it or that I should always adopt the most radical (i.e., violent? sinful?) interpretation possible of any commandment? It is difficult to imagine that the Izbicer would defend such a position.

Kierkegaardian elements also crop up in the writings of two non-Hasidic nineteenth-century thinkers: R. Moses Sofer (Pressburg, 1762–1839) and R. Meir Leibush Wisser (primarily Romania and Poland, 1809–79). There two rabbis were traditionalists in practice, staunchly opposing various novel elements introduced within European Judaism during their lifetimes. But when it came to the way they saw the Akedah, they were rather novel in and of themselves.

For Rabbi Sofer—better known by the name of his primary works, the Ḥatam Sofer—the test of the Akedah pitted everything Abraham had previously understood about God against the explicit revelation now received.[23] The Ḥatam Sofer's discussion is found in a letter to the Galician rabbi Zvi Hirsch Chajes, upon the publication of the latter's *Torah ha-Nevi'im* in 1836.[24] The letter was written probably the following year, in 1837, six years before the writing of *Fear and Trembling*.[25] Rabbi Sofer lauds a particular interpretation of the Akedah offered by Rabbi Chajes and then shares his own view. He argues that Abraham had previously understood the significance of sacrifices.[26] He also understood that God did not want human sacrifice; had he thought that God did, he would have offered one, Ishmael or even Isaac, without explicitly being told to do so, just as he observed the rest of the commandments because of their inherent value. When the command came to offer Isaac, then, Abraham concluded that he had been mistaken in his understanding of the divine will and began to wonder whether in fact he had been mistaken in other aspects as well, including the foundations of his belief in God.

According to Rabbi Sofer, that Abraham would be prepared to question the foundations on the basis of a direct revelation from God is not actually surprising. How can one's reasoning about the divine possibly take precedence over the explicit divine word itself? Isaac's response is more impressive, since he had only Abraham's word to rely on; despite this, "he did not question the words of the sages, and he listened and extended his neck."[27] In the end, the Ḥatam Sofer argues that Isaac really *was* a sacrifice, because "a person who surrenders himself to be sacrificed and offered, without any hope of escape . . . his soul is in fact a pure offering to God, may He be blessed." For an animal, actual slaughter and consumption are necessary, but not for a human sacrifice, which can be bloodless. Rabbi Sofer even suggests that this point is "obvious to anyone with understanding," and it took a divine miracle to withhold this insight from Abraham and Isaac; had they understood it, of course, the surrender would paradoxically not have been complete.

In effect, the Ḥatam Sofer maintains that the Akedah presented Abraham with a clash between the immediate call of God and the structures of good and evil that he already knew. This is, in a sense, similar to the question of the teleological suspension of the ethical broached by Kierkegaard. For the Ḥatam Sofer, it did not seem possible to Abraham that the command to sacrifice Isaac could be incorporated within the general structures of good and evil known to him, so the choice was between retaining those general structures or admitting that God did not always exist within them. Abraham no longer had any certainty about God and God's will, so he followed God's immediate command, trusting apparently that in the end it would all become clear.

The approach of R. Meir Leibush Wisser—known, because of the Hebrew acronym for his name, as the Malbim—extends the Ḥatam Sofer's interpretation in ways that make it even more Kierkegaardian.

In his commentary on Genesis, the Malbim includes two extended comments on Genesis 22 that describe Abraham and his experience very much the way Kierkegaard does.

The first relevant comment appears on Genesis 22:5. Earlier, Malbim had asked why Abraham had told his attendants to stay behind with the donkey; after all, throughout his life Abraham had always been interested in educating others about God and God's ways. Here Malbim offers an answer:

> "You sit here with the donkey": Thus it is told that this test differed from all else that Abraham did up to this point, since everything Abraham did until now to walk in the ways of God and keeping his injunctions and commandments involved commandments that did not violate his intellect, so every command that he fulfilled, he did publicly for all to see, so that all the people of the land would know God and guard his path, to act justly and righteously. But this command was different. It violated his intellect: until now he had argued against idolaters, who offered human sacrifices, arguing that God did not want such abominations, and that there was no greater abomination in God's eyes than homicide. . . . And now that this command, which violated his intellect *and violated God's good ways*, reached him, he did not want to fulfill it in front of his servants, for he was ashamed to do something in front of them that until now he had held to be an abomination, and he also did not want them to learn to do likewise. Therefore he hid it from them and said, "We will bow down and we will return to you."
>
> This was the core principle in this test, that he did God's command that went *against his intellect* and *against the right and the just and the good ways of God*, and still did not second-guess God. . . . This act, which God in fact did not desire—and had [Abraham] slaughtered Isaac, it would have been an act of murder and an abomination to God, which He despises—this act was opposed by

his spiritual being, which sees the secrets of the higher wisdom, and he was therefore ashamed to do it in front of his servants, just as one is normally ashamed to commit an abominable act where others can see. And yet, the faith in God and his love and fear trumped all these considerations, and he did not refuse to fulfill God's will—which violated the intellect and decency, and which humiliated him in the eyes of men—still, the love of God was more powerful than all these, and he was tested and found to be perfect.

The other (earlier) comment is in Malbim's commentary on Genesis 22:2. Here he responds to a different question he had raised at the outset of the chapter: why does God use the locution "your son, your only one, whom you love, Isaac" in identifying the intended victim to Abraham? Why not just cut to the point and say "Isaac" alone? Here Malbim gives his response:

"He said, 'Take your son . . .'": The essence of the test was to see if the love of God in his heart was great enough to take precedence over all other loves he had, that the rest should all be nullified when compared to this love. Now, the more something is loved by one, if he sacrifices it to God . . . and the more he would be conscious of Isaac's qualities and his own love for him—and still these feelings of powerful love he possessed for his only son would be nullified by the greater love (sparks of flame, torch of God!) for the Creator: so will his love for his God be tested. Therefore He commanded him that at the moment that he offers him as a sacrifice, he must not forget that he is his son—therefore, "take your son." And he must not forget that he is his only son (and think that he does, after all, have another son, Ishmael)— therefore, "your only one." And he must not forget how much he loves him, and that his very soul is intertwined with his son's— therefore, "whom you love." And he must not forget his character, that he is a wise and righteous son—therefore, "Isaac": that at the moment you sacrifice him, you focus on all of these characteristics, and yet you sacrifice him with joy, and rejoice that you have a precious sacrifice, sacred from the womb, from the beginning unique and beloved, to give as a present.

To Malbim, the command Abraham received to slaughter his son was not something he could understand ("this command . . . violated his intellect"). Furthermore, this was not a failing of Abraham's, since the command was in fact incompatible with God's will ("this command . . . violated God's good ways"). Abraham realized that he did not comprehend the command because it was fundamentally incomprehensible ("this act was opposed by his spiritual being, which sees the secrets of the higher wisdom"), and therefore, had Abraham killed Isaac, it would have been murder. Despite all this, Abraham knew he had to carry out the command. This created a conflict between what Abraham knew he had to do and what he knew to be right. Abraham was conscious of this conflict, which pitted his obedience to God against not only his religious and moral senses, but his deep and abiding love for Isaac. Finally, as a result of this conflicted situation, Abraham had to act alone; he realized that although he had to do what God had instructed him to do, there was no lesson for others to learn from this act.

In all its major points, this analysis echoes that offered by Kierkegaard. Both Kierkegaard and Malbim, as well as the Ḥatam Sofer, focus our attention on the drama taking place within Abraham's ethical mind. All three, in fact, claim that the central conflict is between a universal—or at least generally true—system of ethics/religious law and the specific divine command.[28] Malbim and Kierkegaard further agree that it would have been "murder" in universal terms had Abraham killed Isaac and also that part of the test was whether Abraham could sacrifice Isaac despite continuing to focus on his love for him.

Yet, neither the Ḥatam Sofer, nor even the later Malbim could have known of Kierkegaard's thought when writing, even though the Malbim, at least, was actually interested in modern philosophy.[29] No German (or any other) translation of any of Kierkegaard's works appeared until the 1870s, not long before Malbim's death in 1879. Indeed, Kierkegaard's influence throughout the nineteenth century was negligible. Only in the fin-de-siècle and then the early twentieth century did his works and thought become toweringly significant within broader European thought.[30] Further, Malbim did not so much as drop a hint here that he might be drawing on the work of others. Although he was generally reticent to name his sources, he did not usually hide that he *had* sources.

If there was no direct relationship, the shared interpretation is most likely a reflection of a broader shared culture. While some of the commonalities may be coincidental, the common emphasis on the unrelenting drama within Abraham's ethical mind—specifically the clash between the universal and the specific—is explicable as a function of nineteenth-century religious thought. For Kierkegaard and Malbim, what it meant to be "religious" within society was the key issue of the day. Kierkegaard argued that it was not enough to be Danish; one had to be Christian in a personal sense. Malbim's argument was different: to be a Jew in Europe, without a *kehillah*, had to be a function of personal faith. And both found their models in Abraham, who was prepared to suspend the universal for the personal call of God.

In this sense, Kierkegaard, while thoroughly Christian, also provides a way of thinking that may be amenable to being translated into Jewish thought. And while in the nineteenth century no Jews were reading him directly, in the twentieth century Jews had ample opportunity to encounter Kierkegaard's writings directly and grapple with his thought. In the following chapter, we will look at two twentieth-century Jews, Yeshayahu Leibowitz and Joseph Ber Soloveitchik, who did just that.

4

Jewish Followers from the
Twentieth Century

In the early nineteenth century, as we saw, Jewish thinkers from disparate traditions of religious thought had come to think about the relationship between religion and ethics, and thereby about the Akedah, in broadly similar ways to Kierkegaard—most likely because of dramatic developments in late eighteenth- and early nineteenth-century Europe. A century later, when Kierkegaard's influence on contemporary thought had grown and his writings were translated into many languages and studied around the world, Jewish theologians and historians of Jewish thought in the twentieth century sought an appropriate reaction to his piercingly individual reading of the Akedah. Was his reading entirely idiosyncratic? Was it unprecedented? Did it find any echo in—indeed, could it even be accommodated within—a traditional Jewish framework?

Numerous Jewish thinkers addressed these issues from the perspective of intellectual history, with the implication that intellectual history may sometimes be normative as well. The British scholar and rabbi Louis Jacobs diplomatically suggested that "there is more than one Jewish interpretation," and that "in this and similar matters of biblical interpretation there is no such thing as an 'official' Jewish viewpoint."[1] Others argued that although there were a variety of pre-modern Jewish approaches, there was an unbridgeable gulf between Kierkegaard and Jewish thought.[2]

Jewish philosophers and theologians also responded to Kierkegaard in varied ways. Buber could not tolerate the radical individualism of Kierkegaard's man of faith.[3] To him, such individualism was nothing more than self-righteous egotism and was both an ethical and a religious abomination. The prominent American rabbi Milton Steinberg reacted violently to the idea that God could ever command the suspension of the ethical: "Nor does anything in Judaism correspond to Kierkegaard's teleological suspension of the ethical. From the Jewish viewpoint—and this is one of its highest dignities—the ethical is never suspended, not under any circumstance and not for anyone, not even for God. *Especially not for God!*"[4]

At the same time, other Jewish thinkers—among them Yeshayahu Leibowitz and Joseph Ber Soloveitchik—were profoundly influenced by Kierkegaard. Furthermore, as we will see, they were not operating in a vacuum: unlike the nineteenth century, when a rabbinic scholar such as Malbim could be entirely ignorant of Kierkegaard's thought, in the early twentieth century, Kierkegaard's influence was immense. This was especially true in the German philosophical circles in which Leibowitz and Soloveitchik traveled in their university days.

Leibowitz

Yeshayahu Leibowitz (1903–94) was a professor of biochemistry and neurophysiology at the Hebrew University but was most famous as a teacher and expositor of Jewish thought. He taught the subject in both small academic circles and—via the radio and his voluminous publications—in broader Israeli society, from the middle of the twentieth century until his death near its end.[5] Although his thought is, in my view, not consistent with most of the Jewish tradition,[6] and possibly not even internally coherent,[7] he offers a bracing approach to the Akedah, which serves for him as the template for all that is authentically religious in religion.

Much of the central content of Leibowitz's thought, including his thinking about the Akedah, was in place in the 1950s. Most centrally, his lifelong insistence that history, including the Holocaust and the founding of the State of Israel, was religiously meaningless was likely a reaction to just those events, born in the years immediately follow-ing them.[8]

We begin with an essay that allegedly has nothing to do with the Akedah—which makes the Akedah's centrality in the essay all the more striking. The topic of the essay is the image of Maimonides, a subject of lifelong interest to Leibowitz, and it was written in 1955. In that year, the philosopher and political scientist Leo Strauss served as a visiting professor at the Hebrew University. Strass taught that Maimonides was primarily a philosopher, and a political philosopher at that, and that his halakhic work was marginal in understanding what Maimonides was primarily interested in. Leibowitz's short arti-cle, published in Hebrew in 1955 and in English in 1957, was entitled "Maimonides—the Abrahamic Man,"[9] and Leibowitz argued that on the contrary, Jewish law was central to Maimonides' thought and to any proper understanding of his oeuvre.[10] This essay, penned when Leibowitz was relatively unknown in broader circles, represents well his thoughts on the Akedah and on the nature of religious devotion.[11]

To make his case, Leibowitz portrays Maimonides as one who opposed the importation of other value systems into Judaism and instead built a picture of Judaism—and in particular, of divine worship—derived inductively from the Jewish texts. The crucial text for true religious worship, as Leibowitz understands Maimonides, is the Akedah. On this reading, the Akedah is the epitome of the worship of God: "Only for a god who is 'a true being' and not one who provides people's needs is it conceivable that a person would take 'the fire and the knife' in his hand and go, with no complaint or response, 'to the place that God told him' to sacrifice his only son and thus to cancel not only his personal aspirations but also all of the aspirations for the future that are bound up in this son." This leads Leibowitz to an understanding of the Akedah that is reminiscent of Kierkegaard's: "For Maimonides, who only conceives of God as 'true being' and does not attribute any independent value or purpose to humans (as opposed to Kant!), morality has no inherent or independent value."[12]

It should be emphasized that this is a tenuous reading of Maimonides, but this does not matter for our present purposes. In fact, the very tenuousness is what makes this noteworthy: what is reflected here is not really Maimonides' interpretation of the Akedah, but Leibowitz's. It is Leibowitz who insists that worship of God renders all other considerations obsolete and that following the divine command must be independent of critical or moral thought.

The essay from 1955 already represents the core of Leibowitz's thought on the Akedah, but he wrote much more about the topic elsewhere, and in ways that flesh out some of his thinking. Particularly worthy of attention from the perspective of biblical interpretation is a short piece called "Abraham and Job," published in 1974,[13] in which Leibowitz situates the story of the Akedah, and the (a)moral lessons it teaches, within the narratives of Genesis. He observes that many biblical characters speak about the "fear of God" in the book but that God explicitly credits only Abraham with properly fearing God, and this commendation is offered solely in the wake of the Akedah, not for anything else in his biography.

This leads Leibowitz to suggest that the Akedah is a *corrective* to earlier *mis*-understandings of what the fear of God truly is. Abraham had earlier (in Genesis 18) argued with God over the ethics of wiping out the towns of Sodom and Gomorrah. Abraham had exclaimed, "Far be it from You to do such a thing—to kill the righteous with the wicked!" He made the basis of his claim clear: "Will not the Judge of all the earth act justly?!" (Gen. 18:25). As Leibowitz accurately perceives, Abraham here assumes that God, *at least* as much as humans, ought to act ethically. But whereas readers have generally followed Abraham's lead in making this assumption, not so Leibowitz: he reads this as a major conceptual error committed by Abraham, for in truth God is not bound by ethics or by anything else.

Abraham repeats this error in Genesis 20. After Abraham (again) passes off Sarah as his sister rather than his wife, the king challenges him to explain what could have possessed him to claim such a thing.

"I saw," says Abraham, "that there was no fear of God in this place, so they would kill me because of my wife!" (Gen. 20:11). In Abraham's parlance, "fear of God" clearly means "basic morality," for no more than that is needed to prevent people from murdering visitors to abduct their wives.

This error, as Leibowitz has it, is corrected in the story of the Akedah. Here God asks Abraham to do something grossly immoral; no sophisticated moral philosophy is needed to reach the conclusion that one oughtn't kill one's son (or most anyone else). When Abraham fulfills the immoral divine command, showing that he understands that obedience to God necessitates the abandonment of all ethics, God commends him as one who fears God. The Akedah, then, is the episode in which Abraham learns the lesson that for Leibowitz is the archetype of all true religion: true devotion to God takes no heed of human considerations, even of basic moral judgments.

It is clear that this reading of the Akedah has much in common with Kierkegaard's.[14] Both Kierkegaard and Leibowitz see the story as fundamentally about the conflict between religion and ethics, and both read the lesson as submission is the essence of religion.[15] There are also differences; Kierkegaard's exposition of the faith reflected in, and demanded by, the Akedah is more subtle and paradoxical than the simplistic portrait drawn by Leibowitz.[16] As Israeli philosopher Avi Sagi explains, all humanism is idolatry for Leibowitz, and therefore antithetical to religion. For Kierkegaard, however, relinquishing the world is the first step, but this allows for a deeper connection to the rest of humanity. Additionally, while Kierkegaard spoke only of a *suspension* of the ethical, Leibowitz seems to think that the ethical has been *permanently* canceled by religion.[17] Both readings yield the claim that faith is "absurd" and highly personal and are open to the criticism—to be developed at length below—that religion can allow for ethical monstrosities if the Akedah is taken as a paradigm.[18]

Leibowitz does not just read the Akedah in this mode, however, but builds his entire picture of Jewish life on it. Far from being a unique occurrence in the life of the patriarch, the Akedah is, according to Leibowitz, the model for all authentic Jewish acts. In his 1953 essay "Religious Praxis: The Meaning of Halakhah," Leibowitz writes:

> Not everyone is Abraham, and not everyone is put to so terrible a test as that of the Akedah. Nonetheless the daily performance of the Mitzvoth, which is not directed by man's natural inclinations or drives but by his intention of serving God, represents the motivation animating the Akedah.[19]

It is unprecedented in Jewish thought, however, to take the Akedah as the paragon of halakhic observance within the Jewish tradition.[20]

Textually speaking, Leibowitz's claim about the "fear of God" seems to be contradicted by subsequent biblical narratives.[21] Later on in Genesis, Joseph tells his brothers that they can trust him, "for I fear God" (Gen. 42:18). The reference here is clearly to basic morality, not theocentric devotion. Even more, the biblical narrator uses the expression to editorialize in describing the actions of the midwives in Exodus 1: "The midwives, however, *feared God* and did not do what the king of Egypt had told them to do; they let the boys live" (Exod. 1:17). Here no mistake can be ascribed to the biblical character; it is unmistakable that the "fear of God" means, and continues to mean, morality. Thus, Leibowitz's analysis is falsified — but the problem of the Akedah becomes more serious.

The most crucial problem with Leibowitz's analysis, though, is not textual but philosophical. Leibowitz takes a massive step beyond Kierkegaard in building the entirety of religion on the foundation of the Akedah. What for Kierkegaard was a one-time *suspension* of the ethical becomes for Leibowitz a permanent *divorce* from the ethical. There simply is no room for ethics in religion, according to Leibowitz, whereas for Kierkegaard, normally ethics and religion go quite nicely together. It is important to emphasize, however, that Leibowitz does not think that religion is fundamentally immoral; it is simply amoral. In general, people should be moral—but not because of religion. They should be moral because morality is binding; they should be religious because religion is binding. They should not, however, conflate the two and claim to be moral because of religion or religious because of morality. Such conflation leads to the deterioration of both religion and morality.

The notion that Judaism demands an abdication of moral thinking is, in fact, contrary to nearly the entirety of Jewish thought.[22] One set of classic texts in this regard are the comments of Naḥmanides on a series of biblical passages.[23] He introduces the notion of "common ethics" already in his commentary on Genesis 6, in explaining why the generation of the Flood deserved punishment. Many sins were being committed, he says, such as adultery and other sexual misdeeds. But the people were punished only for theft, "for that is an intuitive matter, which needs no Torah."[24]

More generally, Naḥmanides writes in a number of comments that the Torah is, perforce, incomplete; there is no way that any text could contain all of the rules and regulations needed to describe a "well-lived" life. Therefore, the Torah itself, according to Naḥmanides, indicates the need for human ethical thought to supplement what is written explicitly. This is how he understands, for instance, the injunction in Deuteronomy 6:18, "And you shall do what is good and what is just in the eyes of the Lord":

> What is here is that first it said that you must obey His statutes and laws, which He commanded you, and now it says that even regarding what He did *not* command you, you should set your mind to do what is good and what is just in His eyes—for He loves the good and the just. This is a great matter, because the Torah could not mention all the practices that a person should undertake with his neighbors and friends, all his business dealings and civil service, and all politics. Instead, after it mentioned many of them . . . it simply reiterated: Do what is good and just in every matter.[25]

This comment would be rendered nonsensical by Leibowitz's insistence that what humans consider good is irrelevant to religious thought.

In his approach to the Akedah—as, perhaps, elsewhere as well—Leibowitz emerges as an ultimately unsatisfying thinker.[26] Although he takes his lead from Kierkegaard, the vision he offers is, upon close inspection, less complex than Kierkegaard's. Gone is the paradox that is so central to Kierkegaard's understanding, and with it is gone the sense of dread that one feels upon encountering a person of faith such as Abraham. In its place is the possibility of a self-assured complacency: complacency in the *halakhah* as a source of obligation that is self-contained and therefore unaffectable by other realms. Gone, too, is the extraordinary nature of the Akedah as Kierkegaard (and pretty much everyone else) understood it. Now every act of halakhic observance is something like an Akedah. This seems to me to be both a trivialization of the Akedah and a mis-construal of the halakhic life. Neither Kierkegaard himself nor the other major twentieth-century exponent of a Kierkegaardian approach to the Akedah, Soloveitchik, is open to these criticisms, as we will see now.

Soloveitchik

A more nuanced voice is that of Rabbi Joseph B. Soloveitchik (1903–93), the most prominent Orthodox rabbi of the twentieth century outside of the *haredi* community. There are many reasons to link Soloveitchik with Leibowitz. The two met in Berlin in the 1930s and followed each other's work—and occasionally met—throughout much of the rest of the century. Soloveitchik sent some of his published books to Leibowitz. Leibowitz is said to have described Soloveitchik as one of the greatest modern philosophers, and Soloveitchik returned the favor, calling Leibowitz the only interesting religious thinker in Israel (in the 1950s).[27]

It is not surprising that the two most prominent Jewish thinkers who channel Kierkegaard in their religious worldview are Orthodox.

For Leibowitz and Soloveitchik, competing claims of modernity and religion were central to their religious lives and thought; on the one hand, the creation of a modern society requires individuals to check their differences at the door, while on the other, the logic of religion demands that individuals be free to act on their own deeply held beliefs. This tension is central to Kierkegaard's thought, of course, and lends itself particularly well to a religious worldview that is centered on action, as the halakhic life is. One could even say that Kierkegaard's analysis is more fitting for a Jewish (or Islamic) religious person, for whom law is central, than for Kierkegaard himself, whose religion was primarily focused on faith rather than actions.

There are deep and relevant parallels between the thought of the two men as well. For both, modernity was the central challenge to traditional Jewish faith, and both built their views of Judaism, meant to counter this challenge, on *halakhah*.[28] Since for both *halakhah* was the primary focus of Judaism, it is not surprising that "both discern the antinomy between the assertive and the submissive themes in the tradition, [and] both take the Akedah to be a paradigm."[29] As we will see below, there is also good historical reason for these thinkers to have focused on Kierkegaard as a source of influence: philosophical circles in 1920s Berlin, and Germany more generally, were deeply interested in Kierkegaard as a remedy for perceived flaws in other modes of thought. Both Soloveitchik and Leibowitz reflect this influence profoundly, as we will soon see.

Soloveitchik's dissertation was on the thought of Hermann Cohen, the neo-Kantian philosopher—and Jew—who towered over much of the philosophical establishment in Germany at the time.[30] The short work (110 pages) does not address Judaism at all, even though Cohen himself spent the end of his career teaching in a rabbinical seminary, the Academy of Jewish Sciences in Berlin, and his last, posthumously published book was *Religion of Reason Out of the Sources of Judaism*; nothing of Cohen's later, religious thought is even cited in the dissertation.[31]

Soloveitchik's treatment of Cohen does point the way to understanding the attraction Kierkegaard held for Soloveitchik's own religious thought.[32] For Cohen (as analyzed by Soloveitchik), a person's psychological stance is "not real"; only the objective world is real, not the internal life of a human. This then leads to "the degradation of mental activity" and "the removal of the mental world from reality."[33] But for Soloveitchik himself, the inner mental world was not just real, but of paramount significance. This is the gap that Kierkegaard fills: Kierkegaard takes the person's psychological stance and mental world to be equivalent in import to ethical and other worldly facts. (The dangers of doing so, of which Soloveitchik was acutely aware, will be discussed below.) Soloveitchik perceived that this allowed for the re-entry of personal religion, something crucially important for him. The combination of Cohen with Kierkegaard allowed for the amalgamation of an objective approach (derived from the neo-Kantian Cohen) with an emphasis on subjectivism (from the proto-existentialist Kierkegaard). Whether this combination is possible is a different question.

In his writings throughout his life, then, Soloveitchik built on Kierkegaard, although he also often diverged from the Danish Lutheran. Nowhere is the influence of Kierkegaard more evident than in Soloveitchik's classic essay "The Lonely Man of Faith," published in 1965.[34] At times in this essay, one could be forgiven for forgetting that the writer is a rabbinic thinker; the existentialist voice[35] of Kierkegaard rings clear:

"To be" means to be the only one, singular and different, and consequently lonely. For what causes man to be lonely and feel insecure if not the awareness of his uniqueness and exclusiveness? The "I" is lonely, experiencing ontological incompleteness and casualness, because there is no one who exists like the "I" and because the *modus existentiae* of the "I" cannot be repeated, imitated, or experienced by others.[36]

In other passages, although the voice is clearly a Jewish voice, the texture and tone are that of Kierkegaard:

> Abraham, the knight of faith, according to our tradition, searched and discovered God in the star-lit heavens of Mesopotamia. Yet, he felt an intense loneliness and could not find solace in the silent companionship of God whose image was reflected in the boundless stretches of the cosmos. Only when he met God on earth as Father, Brother and Friend—not only along the uncharted astral routes—did he feel redeemed.[37]

But individual quotations are almost superfluous: the entire essay "The Lonely Man of Faith," from its title, through its opening paragraph, and through to the end, channels Kierkegaard.[38] The essay opens (after a brief preface) with Soloveitchik's statement "I am lonely." He explains that although he is surrounded by comrades and acquaintances, he is lonely "because . . . I am a man of faith for whom to be means to believe."[39] Kierkegaard's Abraham, similarly, knows that "it is beautiful to be born as the particular individual who has his home in the universal," but "he knows as well that higher than this there winds a lonely trail, narrow and steep," where he "walks without meeting a single traveler."[40]

Loneliness is one major facet of Kierkegaard's Abraham, of the knight of faith. The other is the submissiveness that exemplifies the faith itself. No body of ethics, no independent reasoning, no emotions or attachments—no matter how reasonable and indeed inescapable they may be—can stand in the way of the knight of faith's submission to God. "If anyone comes to me and does not hate father and mother, wife and children, brothers and sisters—yes, even their own life—such a person cannot be my disciple," said Jesus (Luke 14:26), and as noted, Kierkegaard takes this to be the definition of faith.[41] In a sense, then, faith consists of a prerequisite *voluntary* isolation, followed by a *resulting* isolation.

Soloveitchik, too, goes in this direction. In fact, he extended Kierkegaard's claim of the existential isolation of a person of faith, and the act of submission that defines this faith, in two interesting directions. First, he took this to be not just the meaning of certain rare but exemplary acts, such as the Akedah, but as the meaning and content of *religious life in general*. Second, he argued that not only are *individuals* isolated by virtue of their faith, but so too are communities of faith.

In a number of essays, Soloveitchik describes religion in general as exemplified by retreat, recoil, sacrifice, and self-defeat and describes all of these as exemplified by the Akedah. Interestingly, this is not a major theme in his early writings from the 1940s. But in his writings from the early 1960s and on, suffering and sacrifice take on profound religious significance in his thought.[42] For Soloveitchik, every Jew practicing the *halakhah* is already a knight of faith. One example he turns to repeatedly is the bridegroom who has to withdraw from sexual relations with his new bride for halakhic reasons:

Bride and bridegroom are young, physically strong and passionately in love with each other. Both have patiently waited for this rendezvous to take place. Just one more step and their love would have been fulfilled, a vision realized. Suddenly the bride and groom make a movement of recoil [when a drop of menstrual blood is seen]. He, gallantly, like a chivalrous knight, exhibits paradoxical heroism. He takes his own defeat. There is no glamor attached to his withdrawal. The latter is not a spectacular gesture, since there are no witnesses to admire and to laud him. The heroic act did not take place in the presence of jubilating crowds; no bards will sing of these two modest, humble young people. It happened in the sheltered privacy of their home, in the stillness of the night. The young man, like Jacob of old, makes an about-face; he retreats at the moment when fulfillment seems assured.[43]

The male is painted in "conquering" images: the knight conquers but paradoxically does not vanquish the other, or evil, or danger; he vanquishes his own, very natural and nearly overwhelmingly powerful carnal desire for his bride. By withdrawing he demonstrates great heroism, but of course there is no one there to cheer. It is also fascinating that although both the bride and groom are "passionately in love with each other," and "both have patiently waited for this rendezvous," and both "the bride and groom make a movement of recoil," the focus then shifts entirely to him.[44]

Soloveitchik generalizes this point: "Self-defeat is demanded in those areas in which man is most interested. . . . It is precisely in those areas that God requires man to withdraw."[45] (If taken to the extreme, this implies that the religious ideal is that the bride begin to menstruate on her wedding night, so that the young lovers have the opportunity to display their religious heroism.) Of course, the model for this is Abraham:

> What was the most precious possession of Abraham; with what was he concerned the most? Isaac. Because the son meant so much to him, God instructed him to retreat, to give the son away: . . . "Take your son, your only son, whom you love—Isaac."[46]

Thus far the picture is somewhat one-sided, from Kierkegaard's perspective. The submission is the first part, but the true knight of faith submits with an "absurd" faith that somehow he may emerge victorious. Soloveitchik does not exactly follow Kierkegaard in this regard, but he does argue that the submission is not the final act in the drama. After the knight retreats, "God may instruct him to resume his march to victory and move onward in conquest and triumph." Again, Abraham is the model: "Abraham found victory in defeat."[47]

In a remarkable footnote appended to this sentence, Soloveitchik explains why he cannot really follow Kierkegaard: many acts of heroic retreat are not, in fact, followed by a renewed march to victory. He could have pointed to the bride and groom, who will simply have to wait another week to consummate their relationship, but he chooses a more canonical, and perhaps for that reason more dramatic example: "Moses was less fortunate. He withdrew; he gazed upon the land from afar; but his prayers were not fulfilled. He never entered the Promised Land, which was only half a mile away. His listened, though his total obedience did not result in victory. God's will is inscrutable."[48] No solution is proffered, no explanation attempted. "God's will is inscrutable." Retreat *may* lead to victory, but it may not. A knight of faith cannot be defined by the absurd belief that submission will lead to redemption, because *it may not*.

In an important sense, then, Soloveitchik's knight of faith is more sacrificial than Kierkegaard's and may in fact be better compared to Kierkegaard's tragic hero. Whereas Kierkegaard imagined the faithful responding to God with submissiveness but simultaneously with faith that God would come through for him, Soloveitchik imagines no certain redemption at all. The key for Soloveitchik, then, is the submissiveness itself, whether or not it proves to be a step on the road to victory. It may not be, at least in this world. "Only God knows how to reconcile; we do not. Complete reconciliation is an eschatological vision."[49] In the meantime, retreat may not be a step on the way to redemption; it may simply be retreat. But this, too, is faithful.

The influence of Kierkegaard on Soloveitchik's thought is evident in much of the latter's writing about the Akedah. The deep Kierkegaardian strain running through his thought led Louis Jacobs to write that Soloveitchik "is the most determined exponent of a Kierkegaardian interpretation" of the Akedah.[50] And to some extent, of course, this is true, but only to some extent. There are in fact two themes that continually reappear when Soloveitchik discusses the Akedah: the need for Abraham to actually kill Isaac, whether physically or emotionally; and the shift from Abraham sacrificing Isaac to Abraham, and more generally, every religious person, offering themselves as a sacrifice. Only the second of these is really from Kierkegaard.

To Soloveitchik, Abraham had to kill Isaac because the "breakage of human will" was the whole purpose of sacrifice and of the Akedah in particular.[51] And indeed, elsewhere he writes that the fact that the only reason Isaac was not slaughtered was because he was, from Abraham's perspective, already dead. There was simply no reason to kill him again:

> Of course, the idea of sacrifice is a cornerstone of Judaism, and the [Akedah] has inevitably introduced sacrificial action as part of our historical drama. . . . There are two ways in which the total sacrifice is implemented—the physical and the experiential. . . . Abraham implemented the sacrifice of Isaac not on Mount Moriah but in the depths of his heart. . . . Abraham asked no questions. He did not point out the contradiction between God's promise to be with him and his children and the paradoxical command to kill Isaac and burn his flesh. . . . Had Abraham engaged the Creator in a debate, had he not immediately surrendered Isaac, had he not experienced the [Akedah] in its full awesomeness and frightening helplessness, God would not have sent the angel to stop Abraham from implementing the command. Abraham would have lost Isaac physically.[52]

Soloveitchik makes the truly radical move of generalizing the religious experience of the Akedah to all of religious life. This is most pronounced in some of Soloveitchik's writings on prayer. The longest and most developed is found in a 1979 essay called "Thoughts on Prayer," in which Soloveitchik writes:

> The ram was sacrificed, but Isaac was cloaked in its form and was offered with it. The command of the Akedah was never cancelled by God. When he sent his angel to warn Abraham not to harm the child, Abraham had already completed the act of sacrifice. It was fully completed at the moment that he grasped the knife.

The external drama changed, but the internal drama remained the same. Isaac, bound on the altar, turned into a ram, and Isaac was a ram, slaughtered, his blood sprinkled, his body burnt, the ashes were piled on Mount Moriah for generations. The binding of Isaac, which plays such a prominent role in the Jewish liturgy and world-view, means: the binding of man and the sacrifice of him. The law of sacrifices demands the sacrifice of a human, in the form of an animal. The spirit of man, clothed in the body of an animal, is sacrificed to God. . . . Build an altar. Arrange the pieces of wood. Kindle the fire. Take the knife to slaughter your existence for My sake—thus commands the awesome God Who suddenly appears from absolute seclusion. This approach is the basis of prayer. Man surrenders himself to God. He approaches the awesome God and the approach expresses itself in the sacrifice and Akedah of oneself.[53]

For our purposes, four critical comments on this approach to prayer are relevant. First, Soloveitchik's student and critic David Hartman argues compellingly that this model of prayer does not reflect the rabbinic view of prayer, since the Jewish tradition has always taken it as central that the human has the ability and the right, and perhaps even the responsibility, to approach God with her or his needs and requests and be taken seriously.[54] In fact, rabbinic law allows for "voluntary prayer" (*tefillat nedavah*) and does not worry overly much about the legitimacy of a worshiper approaching God. On the contrary, the covenantal relationship may level the apparent imbalance, so that the worshiper can approach as a partner, albeit an infinitely inferior one.[55]

Second, Soloveitchik himself elsewhere describes the experience of prayer as entirely different.[56] This is true in much of "The Lonely Man of Faith," for example, where the prayer community is the continuation of the prophetic community and presupposes a covenantal relationship between humans and God.[57] Consider the following emotional passage from an essay from the 1970s entitled "Majesty and Humility":

Eleven years ago my wife lay on her deathbed and I watched her dying, day by day, hour by hour; medically, I could do very little for her, all I could do was to pray. However, I could not pray in the hospital; somehow I could not find God in the whitewashed, long corridors among the interns and the nurses. However, the need for prayer was great; I could not live without gratifying this need. The moment I returned home I would rush to my room, fall on my knees and pray fervently. God, in those moments, appeared not as the exalted, majestic King, but rather as a humble, close friend, brother, father: in such moments of black despair, He was not far from me; He was right there in the dark room; I felt His warm hand, *kivyakhol*, on my shoulder, I hugged His knees, *kivyakhol*, He was with me in the narrow confines of a small room, taking up no space at all.[58]

Here the pray-er needs no special invitation, no special permission. On the contrary, there is nowhere he more belongs than in the bosom of God. Far from being a source of anxiety, the act of prayer is a comforting act of communion, not spiritual as much as emotional. The act of prayer is the act of one who is *otherwise* alone—in this case, because his spouse is dying—and desperately in need of the comfort of companionship. No questions can be asked; all that is needed is unconditional presence. This is a profound, and profoundly different, vision of the nature of prayer.[59]

Third, the extension of the Akedah to an act that a Jew is commanded to perform three times each day is not only unfaithful to Kierkegaard's thought in a technical sense, but conceptually pushes the idea to, and perhaps past, the breaking point—as Leibowitz did, as well. "Build an altar. Arrange the pieces of wood. Kindle the fire. Take the knife to slaughter your existence for My sake—thus commands the awesome God Who suddenly appears from absolute seclusion." But the Akedah was, for Kierkegaard and for the book of Genesis, a singular, epoch-making event. Never before had Abraham been tested in this way, and never again would anyone else have to endure this trial. And yet Soloveitchik turns this into the meaning of the most mundane of religious acts: "This approach is the basis of prayer. Man surrenders himself to God. He approaches the awesome God and the approach expresses itself in the sacrifice and Akedah of one-self." Of course, Soloveitchik would respond that prayer is far from a mundane act and that each prayer is tantamount to an Akedah. This is not only an unprecedented claim to make, however; it is also psychologically and spiritually impossible, and thus seems like an unfortunate application of Akedah theology. If every act of prayer is an Akedah, then what Abraham did on a mountaintop is not all that awe-inspiring after all.[60]

Finally, conceptualizing prayer as an act of Akedah elides what is perhaps the most important fact that we must keep in mind about the actual Akedah: the sacrificer was not the sacrificed. Abraham did not "take the knife to slaughter [his own] existence," and did not "surrender himself to God," and his action was not "the sacrifice and Akedah of oneself." It was the sacrifice of *another*. As we will see below, this elision in Soloveitchik's thought has had damaging consequences on subsequent Jewish thought.[61]

As mentioned, the second surprising twist that Kierkegaard's Akedah undergoes in the thought of Soloveitchik is the claim that not only are *individuals* of faith isolated from humanity because of their faith, but *communities* of faith are similarly isolated. In his 1964 essay "Confrontation," Soloveitchik begins by discussing the individual: "In each to whom I relate as a human being, I find a friend, for we have many things in common, as well as a stranger, for each of us is unique and wholly other. This otherness stands in the way of complete mutual understanding. The gap of uniqueness is too wide to be bridged. Indeed, it is not a gap, it is an abyss."[62]

How lonely individuals can unite was addressed by Soloveitchik in a later essay, "The Community," published in 1978.[63] In this presentation, each human being again starts as a "single, lonely being, not belonging to any structured collectivity," but here this is nuanced by the claim that he or she is simultaneously "a thou-related being, who co-exists in companionship with somebody else."[64] For a person to accomplish anything worthwhile, that first aspect must be emphasized: "Lonely man is a courageous man; he is a protester; he fears nobody; whereas social man is a compromiser, a peacemaker, and at times a coward. . . . Social man is superficial: he imitates, he emulates. Lonely man is profound: he creates, he is original."[65] Not surprisingly, the biblical heroes were "lonely": "Who was Abraham? Who was Elijah? Who were the prophets? People who dared rebuke society in order to destroy the *status quo* and replace it with a new social order. . . . At first man had to be created *levado*, alone; for otherwise he would have lacked the courage or the heroic quality to stand up and protest, to act like Abraham, who took the ax and shattered the idols which his own father had manufactured."[66]

Of course, at some point the person has to overcome this loneliness. This necessitates the fundamental recognition of an other, the concession that the person is not the only person and that indeed there is another person with equivalent, if different, singularity. Remarkably, Soloveitchik calls this recognition "a sacrificial act." It is, of course, an act of *self*-sacrifice, and he explains: "The mere admission that a thou exists in addition to the I, is tantamount to *tzimtzum*, self-limitation and self-contraction."[67]

Returning now to the community of faith discussed in "Confrontation," we have to deal with the problem of a community comprised of many singular persons or, alternatively, of many lonely individuals who have sacrificed enough of themselves and their uniqueness to forge a community. Soloveitchik is never able to escape this paradox. On the one hand, "each faith community is engaged in a singular normative gesture reflecting the numinous nature of the act of faith itself, and it is futile to try to find common denominators."[68] At the same time, "the great encounter between God and man is a wholly personal private affair incomprehensible to the outsider—even to a brother of the same faith community."[69]

The same paradox animates Soloveitchik's thought when he turns to the practical aspects of prayer. In a letter written in 1954, he strongly opposes entering a synagogue where women and men sat together. Among other considerations, he argues:

> The entire concept of "family pews" is in contradiction to the Jewish spirit of prayer. Prayer means communion with the Master of the World, and therefore withdrawal from all and everything. During prayer man must feel alone, removed, isolated. He must then regard the Creator as an only Friend, from whom alone he can hope for support and consolation.[70]

This, of course, glosses over the obvious point that when in a synagogue praying, a woman or man is emphatically *not* alone. Since Soloveitchik presumably had men, more than women, in mind here,[71] let us focus on that side of the ledger for a moment. It may be true that sitting next to another man is not as distracting as sitting with one's family, but not only is the pray-er not physically alone, he is halakhically defined as not alone: the fact that there are other pray-ers with him changes his own prayer experience. Now there is the repetition of the *Amidah*, there is *Kaddish*, the Torah is taken out and read. The pray-er cannot feel alone when participating in the call and response of the communal prayers. If it is a holiday, he will chant *Hallel* aloud; if it is one of the many days that the Torah is read, he will hear this performance of learning, made possible by the fact that he is not alone.

Communal prayer is not, then, designed to produce a feeling of individual "aloneness." There may, however, be a sense of communal aloneness, that the community stands alone—but stands alone together.[72] The lonely men, gathered together physically and defined as a unit halakhically, nevertheless require solitude, which must not be punctured by the presence of families. I do not think there is a way out of this paradox. "Loneliness" must remain, by definition, the realm of the individual. Communities cannot be lonely.[73]

A very different—and yet no less Kierkegaardian—interpretation of the Akedah is found in Soloveitchik's fascinating but incomplete essay *Emergence of Ethical Man*, published posthumously but probably written in the 1950s.[74] The vision of humanity, and religion, sketched here differs sharply from some of what Soloveitchik wrote elsewhere; as part of his quest for a view of Judaism that was both faithful to the tradition and that could draw on the best thinking of the modern world, Soloveitchik continuously refined and revised his approach to some of the most important issues. Unlike Leibowitz, then, there is no single text of Soloveitchik's that can epitomize his thought about the Akedah or religion more generally.

In the *Emergence of Ethical Man*, the ideal religious person is the charismatic person, but this should not be taken to mean that his or her insight comes from God. "The charismatic person discovers the ethos himself. As a free personality, he goes out to meet the moral law with his full collected being; he chances to find it in himself and to consciously adopt it. . . . Only later does he find out, to his surprise, that with the moral law in himself he has discovered the God of morality beyond himself, and at a still later date he becomes acquainted with this unique being."[75]

This, of course, has a profound effect on this charismatic person's relationship with God. She is not dependent on God for guidance, but only more recently discovered that her own intuitions agree with the divine will, at the same time that God discovered that the divine will was intuited by this charismatic person. Without the dependence, the relationship is nearly one of equals. "There is no imposition of divine authority upon the charismatic person. Only a bilateral covenant, which binds both man and God, was concluded."[76] This ideal religious type does not give up personal autonomy in entering into a covenant with God. She does precisely what she would have done anyway, but now with the knowledge that what she chooses to do is *also* what God wants her to do. In fact, God does not desire servitude or obedience: God just wants her to be God's friend.[77]

Soloveitchik's prime example of this type of religious figure is, somewhat surprisingly, Abraham. Rather than emphasizing the *divine command* to Abraham to leave his father's house and homeland (Gen. 12:1), Soloveitchik credits Abraham with the initiative: "The first prerequisite for prophecy is loneliness. A lonely man finds the Lonely God, and this very loneliness creates the charismatic bond between them."[78] I do not think it would be wrong to hear echoes of Jesus's teaching of the necessity to "hate one's own father and mother and wife and children and brothers and sisters" (Luke 14:26), perhaps channeled through Kierkegaard, here.

But this vision of the relationship between the person of faith and God runs smack into the Akedah. Soloveitchik is undeterred. He argues that the first line of Genesis 22 is not a command, not exactly, but a request. Building on the word *na'*, "please,"[79] Soloveitchik claims that "God entreated Abraham; He implored him to give away his only son. He never commanded. He just uttered a wish, and Abraham complied."[80]

This is remarkable. Rather than the commanding, imperious divine figure who haunts Kierkegaard, demanding faith at the expense of ethics, obedience at the expense of other loyalties, devotion in place of any human love, we have here a solicitous, needy, lonely God, who merely asks—politely—for Abraham to offer his son. It was to Abraham's credit that he complied with such a gentle request, but Abraham's behavior is a far cry from the retreating, submissive knight of faith described so often by Soloveitchik as the hero of the Akedah.

Perhaps because this is transparently far-fetched, Soloveitchik appends to this a two-page-long footnote, which goes in a different direction.[81] Here he concedes that the Akedah does appear to be a different relationship between God and Abraham, not a partner, "but an omnipotent, jealous master to whom man is enslaved and who almost ruthlessly lays claim to the entirety of human existence." To solve this, Soloveitchik argues that although from *God's* perspective the Akedah was an exception, from *Abraham's* perspective the Akedah was not experienced as such. "Abraham did not realize the absurdity and the paradoxality of the divine order, which canceled all previous promises and covenants. . . . Naively, almost irrationally, did he conceive of the demand as somehow compatible with the whole."

In this note we hear the most Kierkegaardian reading of the Akedah within Soloveitchik's writings, although it is still not quite the same. Here, as in Kierkegaard's essay, Abraham acts to fulfill God's command without losing faith in the original covenantal promises. Abraham here is fully covenantal, trusting implicitly in his covenantal partner. This is, then, a different type of submission: not a retreat from one's own specific desire in the face of the awesome divine command, but the more general retreat from an independent, autonomous will, to be replaced by complete, almost childish faith in the goodwill and responsible stance of God.[82]

This is quite different from Soloveitchik's presentation in *Abraham's Journey*, a book published posthumously in 2008, for example, where Abraham responds to the command by immediately killing Isaac in his heart, and he does not ask God about the paradox because the deed has already been done, not because he has faith that it never will be. This portrait emphasizes the absurdity, the faith, and the holistic relationship more than the earlier one, which focused primarily on the retreat and specific submission.

This is still not exactly the same as Kierkegaard's view, however. Kierkegaard never paints Abraham as naïve. The knight of faith is acutely aware of the absurdity of his faith, not ignorant of the absurdity of his actions. The action that Kierkegaard's Abraham takes is bold and decisive *despite* full awareness of the fact that by acting he is suspending the ethical, engaging in murder, and at the same time having faith that the promise of descendants through Isaac will remain inviolate.

The Context: The Reception of Kierkegaard in 1920s Germany

That Soloveitchik was thoroughly influenced by Kierkegaard is far from surprising. As a doctoral student of philosophy in Berlin in the late 1920s, he could not have helped but study Kierkegaard's thought.[83] Kierkegaard, along with his fellow nineteenth-century proto-existentialist Dostoevsky, "found a newly receptive audience in the 1920s."[84] Writing in 1932, Hannah Arendt observed:

> If we were to write a history of [Kierkegaard's] fame, only the last fifteen years would concern us, but in those years his fame has spread with amazing speed. This fame rests on more than the discovery and belated appreciation of a great man who was wrongly neglected in his own time. We are not just making amends for not having done him justice earlier. Kierkegaard speaks with a contemporary voice; he speaks for an entire generation that is not reading him out of historical interest but for intensely personal reasons: *mea res agitur* [it concerns me].[85]

Kierkegaard's influence did not sweep uniformly through the philosophical schools of interwar Germany, however. Heidegger, who had begun teaching at Marburg in 1923 and ascended to the chair of professor of philosophy at Freiburg in 1928, was very much influenced by the Danish philosopher. Heidegger also clearly had an influence on Soloveitchik,[86] at least through his writings and perhaps through personal interactions, as well.[87]

The neo-Kantians, however, were not perceptibly moved by Kierkegaard. This is hardly surprising. The neo-Kantian tradition emphasized the possibility of objectivity and unbiased progress, whereas Kierkegaard—and Heidegger—stressed the inescapably private, individualistic nature of fundamental parts of human existence. The quest for objectivity offended these thinkers, who believed that the human ought to work hard to discover what lies deep within her- or himself, and not simply float along in the situations into which one has been thrown by life. For this purpose, societal expectations and norms are obstacles, not ends in themselves, and the authentic person transcends those expectations and norms, finding and living a life true to oneself.

When the eminent neo-Kantian Ernst Cassirer (who happened to be Jewish) dialogued with Heidegger (who would soon be a Nazi) at Davos in 1929, the unbridgeable gap between their worldviews was caused in part by this issue: Was there any firm ground on which human beings could stand where they could evaluate the progress they had made thus far and from which they could continue to march forward— thus Cassirer—or are humans unavoidably subjective, thrown into life and unable to transcend their "thrownness"—thus Heidegger?[88]

As we discussed earlier, Soloveitchik trained with the neo-Kantians and wrote about Cohen, the most important neo-Kantian, but saw the failure to deal with the mental world—that part of human existence that included religion, among other things—as a major flaw in Cohen's thought. It may therefore not be unfair to see Soloveitchik as attempting to grasp both ends of a dichotomy simultaneously: the mathematical model of the neo-Kantians held out appeal for an objective religious philosophy, while the existentialism of Heidegger and others opened up the possibility of profoundly individualistic faith, not subject to the scrutiny of others. It is increasingly clear that Soloveitchik's thought was very much at home in the interwar German philosophical scene.[89] I hasten to add—as we will see in more detail presently—that this does not imply that Soloveitchik merely adopted the views around him. He criticized and synthesized, attempting to arrive at a set of views that could be both Jewishly and philosophically compelling.

In this context, it may also be unsurprising that some of Soloveitchik's views are far from the earlier approaches within Jewish thought.[90] This is particularly relevant with regard to the Akedah. Both Soloveitchik and Leibowitz share the view that the Akedah is the archetype of religious life—a view quite at odds with earlier approaches, Jewish or otherwise. The major gap was the adoption of the leap of faith, the willingness to act on faith even against everything known to be right, without thereby correcting the view of right and wrong. To do something *wrong* because God commanded it is not something earlier Jewish thinkers would have countenanced—likely because it is not something that they would have imagined possible. For both, the revolution created by modernity and secularism could not be denied, and they both struggled to articulate what role faith could play in the modern world.

Despite the significance that the Akedah has in Kierkegaard's thought, Soloveitchik expands the "Akedah ethos" beyond the restricted way in which Kierkegaard deploys it. Kierkegaard's knight of faith *normally* lived an ethical life, only very rarely, if ever, being asked to suspend the ethical for faith. While Leibowitz extends this to be the foundation of religious life generally, Soloveitchik's expansion is not as radical, but still substantial. For Soloveitchik, the sense of submissiveness in response to the overwhelming and unquestionable voice of God has expanded to become the basis of prayer, as we have seen.

But if the Akedah is a template for everyday religious life, is there any autonomous ethical person left?[91] Would a religious life of this sort ineluctably quash human emotions and experiences? Is there any way to temper the real danger that is present in the radical subjectivity that is so important to Kierkegaard, and which comes through clearly in much of Soloveitchik's writing? And is this subjective experience of faith compatible with Jewish thought more broadly? Does it matter that *Abraham's* submission is about to lead to the *death of Isaac*? Can we tolerate a worldview that countenances a person of faith murdering an innocent other and calling it "sacrifice"? These and other critiques will be taken up in the following chapter.

5

Criticizing Kierkegaard

Kierkegaard's reading of the Akedah was profoundly influential, especially in the twentieth century, as we saw in the preceding chapter. It is also, as we began to see as well, profoundly problematic. In this chapter we will address a number of criticisms of Kierkegaard, each of which provides reason for readers, and especially Jewish readers, to reject his reading. Whether Kierkegaard is a compelling reading of Genesis 22 for other communities may require different treatment. The goal is to understand the story as it has been told by a specific religious community, whose ideals therefore have to be taken as guideposts to the interpretation.[1]

In the context of Jewish thought, Kierkegaard's reading ought to be challenged on four grounds:

(1) the radical subjectivity;
(2) the erasure of Isaac from the narrative;
(3) the focus on the individual rather than the collective as the locus of religious fulfillment; and
(4) the very modern idea of a fundamental idea of a clash between faith and morality, which is without grounding in earlier sources.

Let us take each of these in turn.

Radical Subjectivity

We can return to Soloveitchik as a way of opening our criticism of Kierkegaard, because despite his intense Kierkegaardian streak,

Soloveitchik was also very wary of Kierkegaard's existentialist voice, and in places he was an acute and unrelenting critic of Kierkegaard. In *The Halakhic Mind*, written in 1944 but not published until 1986,[2] Soloveitchik both historicizes and criticizes subjectivity in religion.[3]

The first part of this essay is a study of the philosophy of science. (In general, one of the remarkable aspects of the book is that no Jewish sources are quoted until the last few pages of the book, to which we will soon turn.) Soloveitchik's first argument is that modern science is inherently pluralistic; in this he echoes a major theme of his philosophical mentors from the 1920s. The eminent philosopher Paul Natorp and his student Ernst Cassirer had written about Einstein's theory of relativity already in 1921, arguing that Einstein's adoption of a model of space-time different from Newton's did not mean that Newton's model was *false*; there were simply different ways of modeling reality, each of which approached that underlying reality in a different way.[4] Soloveitchik commented that because of this pluralism, this age was more conducive to *homo religiosus* than any other age.[5]

At the same time, pluralism must not be taken to the extreme, but Soloveitchik knew very well that that was in fact one trend in philosophy:

> In particular is this true of philosophical religion where subjectivist gods have reigned since the days of Schleiermacher and Kierkegaard. Here mysticism proclaimed its greatest triumph.[6]

Referring to the thirteenth- to fourteenth-century German theologian of the individual soul who was accused of heresy, Soloveitchik continues in a slightly sarcastic vein: "Meister Eckhardt was proclaimed the philosopher. His non-given God, 'the still desert' (*die stille Wueste*), replaced the God of revelation."[7]

His tone then returns to deadly serious to reflect on the need for objectivity in religious thought:

It need hardly be stressed that this reduction of religion into some recondite, subjective current is absolutely perilous. It frees every dark passion and every animal impulse in man. Indeed, it is of greater urgency for religion to cultivate objectivity than perhaps for any other branch of human culture. If God is not the source of the most objective norm, faith in him is nothing but an empty phrase.... To avert misery and confusion the human mind would do well were it to approach the subjective realm with far greater caution and reserve than it has in the past.[8]

Here Soloveitchik powerfully conveys the danger of a subjective faith. But his claim in the middle of this passage reveals where his own view will founder. God may be the source of objective norms, but in the modern world it is a matter of subjective faith whether to believe that God exists at all.

Soloveitchik returns later in the essay to this topic, and to the hint of sarcasm that he found earlier, to explain the temptation of subjective views of religion in the modern world:

Religious subjectivism was born out of the matrix of faith philosophy (Pascal, Rousseau, Hamann, Herder) which traced religious verities to emotional sources. Schleiermacher, Kierkegaard, Wilhelm Hermann, Auguste Sabatier and others were among the consecrated priests who worshipped God in the temples of inwardness and mental craving.... What is important, however, is the fact that the subjectivist school intrigued many great minds who, sundered by the colliding forces of faith and knowledge, hoped to find quiescence in subjectivism. In freeing religion from any association with an objective performance, be it either theoretical or practical, they hoped to turn religion into an impregnable fortress.[9]

And again, he turns to enumerate the problems with the subjectivist view. One of the problems is internal to religion: Soloveitchik denies that a religious person can have the reflexive view of her own faith as "merely" subjective; the person of faith, on the contrary, wants to share her faith with the world, since she believes that it is objectively correct. This is a point we will return to, but not in a manner that will satisfy Soloveitchik. The other problem is the ineluctable march from subjectivity to the demise of ethics:

> All attempts to divorce objective standards and postulates have been fraught with menace to ethical and cultural advancement. This is singularly true in the case of religion. When intercourse with God is divorced from its social and communal aspects and concrete normative action, religion may develop into a barbaric, deleterious force. The unguided, inward life leads to the renunciation of ethical authority and moral awareness.[10]

Writing in 1944 of "a barbaric, deleterious force" with no "ethical authority and moral awareness," Soloveitchik was clearly thinking of contemporary events. Elsewhere, in a passage also written in the midst of the war, Soloveitchik similarly implies that the inward turn of religion allowed for—and could always allow for—any type of atrocity, without the possibility of correction based on objective standards:

> Experience has shown that the whole religious ideology which bases itself on the subjective nature of religion—from Schleiermacher and Kierkegaard to Natorp—can have dangerous, destructive consequences that far outweigh any putative gains.[11]

Given the connections between Heidegger and Kierkegaard, this argument is very much related to the question of whether there is a deep connection between Heidegger's philosophy and his membership in, and service to, the Nazi Party, especially in 1933–34.[12] Some of his students (such as Hannah Arendt) argued that this political move on Heidegger's part was simply a mistake and irrelevant to an understanding of his work or thought more generally,[13] while others such as Buber went so far as to argue that Heidegger's philosophy, when properly understood, paved the way for Nazism: after all, universal ethics could be set aside to allow for actions of overwhelming significance.[14] Many, exemplified by the Protestant theologian Paul Tillich, took a middle position, arguing that Heidegger's Nazism was not a *result* of his philosophy, but did show that "pure existentialism cannot provide any answers in the area of moral philosophy and ethics."[15]

The problem, already noted, is that Soloveitchik is not willing to forgo existentialism in the face of this problem. He is, ineluctably, existentialist in much of his thought. He wants to follow Kierkegaard (and Heidegger) as far as possible but then introduce a corrective that will prevent this mode of thought from being entirely untethered and amoral.[16]

It is here that Soloveitchik introduces *halakhah* as a remedy.[17] But this is paradoxical, and inescapably so. *Halakhah* may be objective, but the acceptance of this claim is subjective. Only the person of faith will recognize the *halakhah* as binding—but the person of faith does not need this "objective" correction.[18] The problem therefore remains: Kierkegaard's thought untethers religion from ethics and provides no objective basis for deciding on the correct course of action. At best, then, religion and ethics travel two parallel roads; at worst, ethics, divorced from religion, is now free to go in dangerous and indeed horrifying directions.

The Erasure of Isaac

This leads to the next problem with Kierkegaard's reading, which is a textual point but actually profoundly philosophical: in all of his extended meditation on the Binding of Isaac, Isaac is but rarely mentioned and never seriously considered. It is true that in the biblical narrative, too, Isaac is not given a prominent role. But the erasure of Isaac from Kierkegaard's narrative enables a perverse notion of the "sacrifice" involved, raising deep ethical problems.

Over and over Kierkegaard reflects on Abraham's aloneness. "The knight of faith is assigned solely to himself; he feels the pain of not being able to make himself intelligible to others, but he feels no vain desire to instruct others. . . . The true knight of faith is a witness, never a teacher, and therein lies the deep humanity that is worth more than this frivolous concern for the welfare that is extolled under the name of sympathy but is really nothing more than vanity."[19] But Abraham is not, in fact, alone on the mountain, nor could he be. Isaac is there, and it is Isaac who is about to die for Abraham's faith.

It certainly violates many theories of ethics for one person's profound faith to be vindicated through the death of someone else. In Kierkegaard's telling, therefore, the death of Isaac is not so much justified as ignored. Isaac himself is reduced to a mere prop in the story, a necessary prop—because otherwise, how could Abraham kill him? This is a profoundly disturbing aspect of Kierkegaard's reading. It is the trial of Abraham, and Abraham is the sacrificer and the victim. How the victim? He has sacrificed his ethical standards, his standing as a moral human being, his independence of thought. All this is true. But is it not more important that Isaac is losing his life?

To put the matter bluntly, Jews must avoid a reading of the Akedah that leaves no argument against the person of faith who slaughters an innocent other in the desert, or who massacres a whole community, and claims that although this is obviously unethical, ethics had to be suspended—teleologically, of course—by faith. How can we condemn such atrocities without condemning Abraham, as well? Kierkegaard leaves us little room to maneuver.

Observing that "for Kierkegaard, Isaac drops out of the picture altogether, and Abraham *becomes* the sacrifice," contemporary thinkers Tova Hartman and Charlie Buckholtz write, "Placing Abraham at the center of the story animates and perpetuates the sacrificial ethos, making Isaac an appendage to the action and suggesting that his sacrifice — the sacrifice of his life — is incidental to Abraham's all-encompassing encounter with the God who commanded it."[20]

As we have seen, the same is true in the thought of Soloveitchik, in much of his writing on the Akedah. For example, in his passage in "Thoughts on Prayer," he moves from "the law of sacrifices," which "demands the sacrifice of a human," to a climax in the command "take the knife to slaughter your existence," which, in turn, "is the basis of prayer. Man surrenders himself to God."[21] This passage slips from discussing sacrifices, where the sacrificer and the sacrificed are distinct, to *self*-sacrifice, which forms the basis of prayer. Others, too, have seen Abraham as engaged in self-sacrifice:

> Abraham is father of the teaching of annihilation of self as the way of entering into intimate relation with God or union with God. Abraham inspires the religious ideal of self-deprivation embodied in the words, "*Kadesh atsmekha be-mutar lakh.*" Abraham is father to the Medieval Christian mystics who entered upon the "Dark Night of the Soul," of sensory and spiritual deprivation for the purpose of communion with God. And Abraham is father to the Islamic poet who writes, "The lover of God is busy annihilating himself." And he is father of a dominant strand of Hinduism which teaches "complete renunciation" of "worldliness," and of the Buddhist ideal of "emptiness" of the self.[22]

But the Akedah cannot be the model here: Abraham was not engaged in self-sacrifice, but in the killing of another human being.

Strikingly, this version of the idea of self-sacrifice — where another person actually suffers more — has become a major element in contemporary Jewish thought. The basic idea is that the person of faith sacrifices her- or himself on the altar of religion, but in actuality it is often another person who will suffer as a result. Building on a seminal article by Tamar Biala,[23] Ronit Irshai calls this "Akedah theology"[24] and argues that Soloveitchik (as well as Leibowitz) is to be credited, or blamed, with the new focus on the Akedah as the basis for religiosity.[25] Indeed, it is striking in this context to realize that Soloveitchik virtually never deals with the concept of "the other," which is a central element in twentieth-century thought, including Jewish thought, more broadly.[26]

Of course, many religious commands do not conflict with morality, but the cases where they do are thought to be the real tests of faith and commitment. Faithful people pass these tests and demonstrate their fealty, specifically by being willing to quash their own moral thinking and submit to the divine will.[27] Very often, however, those justifying religious devotion even at the expense of the "sacrifice of morality" are not the ones who stand to suffer.

The scholar of gender and religious thought Ronit Irshai draws attention to a contemporary rabbinic letter on the question of whether a Jew may violate the Sabbath in order to tend to a wounded—even gravely wounded—non-Jew. In contemplating the prohibition, the rabbi utilizes Akedah terminology: "Are we not obligated to the Torah's laws even when they appear, in human eyes, to be unethical norms?"[28] In this way of thinking, a religious person who questions a religious command is weak in faith. One who is strong in faith has fully sacrificed his or her sense of "human morality"; the one who suffers, though, will be someone else, such as the wounded non-Jew in this case, who will die for the other's religious accomplishment.

Religious devotion may often ask the believer to forgo some earthly pleasure, some delight otherwise available, whether sexual, gastronomical, social, or economic. The philosopher Moshe Halbertal argues that this asceticism may morph into a more profound sense of self-denial and lead to the notion that the sacrifice of one's own intuitions—including moral intuitions—is a profound religious act.[29] Halbertal appropriately notes, however, that at this point the pain may be felt by another, and he brings us back to the Akedah and the deeper problem inherent in Kierkegaard's analysis of it:

He was willing to sacrifice his moral obligation as a father in order to follow God's will. It is important, though, to stress that in this "sacrifice" of moral conscience, the one who was actually sacrificed (or who would have been sacrificed had God not intervened at the last minute) was another human being. Though Abraham had to overcome his moral conviction, the real victim of the story is Isaac, not Abraham. Isaac would have been slaughtered in the end. More generally, when morality is depicted as a temptation to be surmounted in the name of a higher goal, it is always someone else who pays the price. It is a rather perverse moment in some religious traditions to view the victim as the one who sacrificed his moral principles. In such cases, the very fact of sacrifice purifies a crime with the illusion that the criminal is the victim since he has sacrificed his conscience.[30]

Ignoring Isaac in the story of the Akedah is monstrous. This is the ethically fatal problem with Kierkegaard's reading of the narrative.

If it is immoral to ignore Isaac, we need to pay attention to him. Readers who have done so have perceived two different roles that Isaac may play. The first is reflected in the 1603 painting by Michelangelo Merisi de Caravaggio (Italy, 1571–1610), The Sacrifice of Isaac, which hangs in the Uffizi.[31]

The philosopher J. M. Bernstein draws attention to the single visible eye of Isaac in the painting: "Isaac's pleading eye performs a searing iconoclastic shattering of the Abraham image, leaving just his suffering, his brutalized becoming an animal, a sacrificial ram, to be witnessed. . . . We perceive the true internal connection between the symbolic sacrifice and the literal one." Caravaggio uses Isaac's eye to break the illusion of tranquility that one might otherwise be tempted to imagine. Isaac's screaming gaze forces us to grapple with the fact that as Abraham is becoming "our father," Isaac is being murdered.[32]

The Jewish tradition, as reflected in Rabbinic literature, of course goes in a different direction. The Rabbis rejected the obviously false

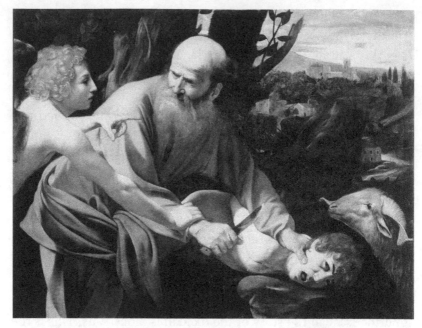

Fig. 2. Caravaggio, *The Sacrifice of Isaac*, Uffizi Gallery, Florence, ca. 1603, https://commons.wikimedia.org/wiki /File:Sacrifice_of_Isaac-Caravaggio_(Uffizi).jpg.

image of Abraham alone on the mountaintop. They, too, pondered Isaac's involvement, but rather than raise the possibility of a rupture between father and son, the Rabbis emphasized the commonality of purpose shared by the two. The midrash goes out of its way to bring Isaac back into the story, as subject rather than object, and thereby to undercut Abraham's detachment. Rather than radical isolation, Rabbinic literature insists that Abraham was walking in lockstep with Isaac the entire way; in Rabbinic tellings, Isaac was not kept in the dark about the purpose of the trek. "God will choose a sheep for Himself," said Abraham, "but if not, you will be the sacrifice, My son."[33] And they continue, in full awareness of the plan, "together" (Gen. 22:8): "this one to slaughter and this one to be slaughtered."[34] "The two of them walked together, with their hearts complete."[35]

The same is true in the Qur'ān's version of the story, which has Abraham seeing a vision that he understands to mean that he must sacrifice his son and then turning to his son to tell him about it. The son replies, "O Father! Do what you are commanded. You will find me, if God wills it, among the patient ones." Both of them, then, submitted (*'aslamā*) to the will of God and then set off to fulfill the vision.[36]

The twentieth-century Jewish theologian Emil Fackenheim argues, therefore, that a Jew cannot accept "Kierkegaard's Abraham." As opposed to the portrait of the solitary lonely man of faith, "the midrashic Abraham, in contrast, communicates with Isaac, and Isaac shares his father's purpose. The two are at one in the love of God."[37] And Fackenheim, too, detects here a difference between faith traditions: a Christian faith centered in the individual and a Jewish faith focused on the community.[38]

Religious Experience as Solitary

This, then, brings us to the third point in criticism of Kierkegaard: the individualism of Kierkegaard's faith experience clashes with the biblical and later Jewish fundamental notion of a covenantal community as the norm. Judaism has rarely focused on the individual's experience in solitude as the religious ideal.

In Kierkegaard's reading, the solitariness of the Akedah is fundamental to its significance. Abraham had to be alone because faith is a lonely experience. It cannot be shared, discussed, or even described. This omits one of the basic ideas of biblical thought, however: the covenantal *community* or *nation*. Abraham was not promised that if he went to Canaan he could commune alone with God; he was promised that he would give rise to a nation. When later Jews approached God, it was not as individual knights of faith, but as heirs to the tradition of Abraham, as members of the community created by him. The idea that Abraham could approach God only by leaving his human relationships behind contrasts with these ideas.

Abraham's human relationships clearly are part of the story. Abraham is the first person in the Bible who is said to "love" someone else.[39] And the context is Genesis 22:2: the command to sacrifice the one he loves. On Kierkegaard's reading, that love is the problem. Abraham may love Isaac too much; he may not be prepared to live without the object of his love, and thus the Akedah teaches that human relationships need to be expunged from a person's consciousness in order to meet God. As many have noted, and as is explicit in Kierkegaard's writings, the theologian saw his own severing of human relationships—and in particular, the relationship with Regine Olsen—as a necessary, Akedah-like move in the direction of faith.

Buber objects to this idea: "Creatures are placed in my way so that I, their fellow-creature, by means of them and with them find the way to God. . . . God wants us to come to him by means of the Reginas he has created and not by renunciation of them."[40] For Buber, human relationships are not obstacles preventing the person of faith from reaching God; they are the way to the destination.[41] Only by deepening human relationships can a relationship with God be forged. Whatever the Jewish background to Buber's idea of the interpersonal relationship, it is clear that his notion leads more naturally to the deeply Jewish notion of community than Kierkegaard's solitude.[42]

Fackenheim, too, sees the isolation of Kierkegaard's Abraham as opposed to mainstream Jewish thought. As he observes, even Kierkegaard does not think that Abraham is fully alone: he is alone *with God*. But Fackenheim protests that Jewish thought envisions not just a bilateral relationship, but a trilateral one:

The revealed morality of Judaism demands a three-term relationship—nothing less than a relationship involving man, his human neighbor, and God Himself. . . . The startling claim of the revealed morality of Judaism is, however, that God Himself enters into the relationship. He confronts man with the demand to turn to his human neighbor, and in doing so, turn back to God Himself.[43]

Unlike some varieties of Christianity, Judaism has rarely idealized solitude as a way of life. This is not to deny the value of some time alone or the possibility of sublime revelations in solitude (consider Elijah on the mountain in 1 Kings 19). These are not models for the ideal life, however, as Kierkegaard wants them to be. There is no general injunction in Jewish thought to abandon human relationships.[44] Marriage has always been the ideal, beginning in Genesis 2:24: "Therefore a man leaves his father and mother to cling to his woman, and they become one flesh." A midrash (*Bereshit Rabbah* 34:14) compares a celibate person to a murderer.[45] Deep human companionship is taken as not just tolerated or even commendable, but commanded.

The prophet is the one type who does seem to exist on a private plane, but even here there are different models—the "prophetic call" experienced by Amos while working and by Jeremiah before birth, versus the "band of prophets" convened around Elijah and Elisha, which Saul joined and where numerous people trained to be prophets. The history of this difference need not concern us now,[46] because the prophet has never been the model for the ideal religious figure. Even Soloveitchik, who often reveled in his loneliness, as we have seen, elided the difference between the person of faith and the *community* of faith. "For Soloveitchik," writes the scholar Daniel Herskowitz, "the individual is never understood as an isolated entity lacking a historical community. . . . In contrast to Kierkegaard's believer (or 'knight of faith'), who stands in his or her individuality in front of God, halakhic man's religiosity is at once personal and communal."[47]

It may be said, then, without any surprise whatsoever, that Kierkegaard's Abraham is not a Jew. The radically individualistic faith experience described by Kierkegaard, in which Abraham could not involve Sarah, much less anyone else, is foreign to most strands of Jewish thought, although it may be home in Christianity, especially

Protestantism. And this is what the French Jewish philosopher Emmanuel Levinas meant when he spoke of "the value of the Kierkegaardian notion of existence and its deeply Protestant protest against systems."[48]

This difference goes far in explaining—if not justifying—some of the harshly negative Jewish responses to Kierkegaard.[49] Of course, as we saw in the previous chapter, there are prominent Jewish thinkers who responded to Kierkegaard very differently. But I would submit that the weight of Jewish thought is against them.[50]

Kierkegaard may have thought that an embedded individual, an individual defined by relationships with other individuals, could not develop on his or her own as a self—such a person, was, in a sense, not an individual at all, but merely a collection of relational fragments. The "atomic" model of the self—self-contained, self-sufficient, without dependencies or even attachments—has also been criticized as opposed to the human need for relationships, and especially with the emphasis on relational identity in modern thought.[51] This is contested by Levinas: "Ethics as consciousness of responsibility toward others . . . , far from losing you in generality, singularizes you, poses you as a unique individual, as *I*. Kierkegaard seems not to have experienced that, since he wants to transcend the ethical stage, which to him is the stage of generality."[52]

Some readings emphasize the loss of all of Abraham's relationships as a result of the Akedah. We have discussed already the view of Don Isaac Abarbanel that from the mountain, Isaac went to his mother at Hebron and did not accompany his father back to Beersheba. This reading emphasizes the cost of the Akedah on Abraham's human relationships.[53] Its poignancy is disturbing. But this is still a far cry from Kierkegaard: for Abarbanel, the loss of a relationship with Isaac was a tragic result of the Akedah; for Kierkegaard, it is the whole point.

One other related objection to Kierkegaard's reading should be addressed here as well. David Hartman often contrasted Abraham's reaction to the command of the Akedah with his actions just four chapters earlier, in Genesis 18. Abraham there stood up to God to stand for the people of Sodom: "Far be it from you to do such a thing, to kill the righteous with the wicked, treating the righteous and the wicked alike. Far be it from you! Will the Judge of all the earth not act justly?" (Gen. 18:25). Leibowitz, we remember, argued that the Akedah was a *corrective* for the Sodom narrative: Abraham acted improperly in Genesis 18, and God used the Akedah to teach him a theological lesson. Whereas Abraham had thought that God ought to act justly, here he learns that actually God is beyond ethics and that "fear of God" is amoral and may be immoral.

Hartman goes in a very different direction, developing the character of Abraham in Genesis 18 as a paradigm of religious faith:

> Yet Abraham, in pleading for Sodom, felt that God was not beyond his own understanding of moral argument and persuasion. This other paradigm, therefore, says: "Bring your moral intuitions, your subjective sense of dignity and justice into your understanding of the reality of God." Not only does it not threaten or undermine religious consciousness, but it is actually necessary for recognizing the validity and applicability of the divine command.[54]

Hartman emphasizes that there is no earlier revelation to Abraham about justice and righteousness, so Abraham is clearly assuming—apparently correctly—that God too (or perhaps God especially) cannot violate the norms of justice.

Of course, Genesis 18 does not stand alone, and in Hartman's reading, it contrasts with—but is not superseded by—the Akedah in Genesis 22. Instead, Hartman argues, Abraham presents us with two different models of how to respond to perceived divine injustice within just a few chapters. On the one hand, the Sodom model allows people to protest, as covenantal partners, holding God to universal standards of justice. On the other hand, when the same Abraham is told that he must personally go murder his son, he responds with "total submission and unconditional surrender."[55] Neither of these models is to be discarded, and both stand as models of faith-full action.

While elaborating these two models, Hartman argues that the Akedah model has been exaggerated, and the Sodom model needs to be invoked more often in Judaism. This is for theological reasons: the Akedah model threatens the very idea of a covenant. How can a covenant exist if one partner cannot be sure that the other will not, at any moment, violate the most basic norms in the most horrific way? What kind of covenant can Israel have with God if God may slaughter innocents whenever God wishes?[56]

Hartman's argument is not compelling, however, for two reasons. First, it should be noted that he leaves the "Akedah model" entirely intact, taking for granted that indeed Genesis 22 teaches a mode of religiosity of "total submission and unconditional surrender." He only offers another model alongside this one.[57] Second, the case of Sodom in Genesis 18 is actually not comparable to the Akedah at all: Abraham did not *respond differently* to the two cases; he was faced with two entirely different cases and reacted appropriately for each one, on its own terms. Let us look more closely at the Sodom story, as this will allow us to appreciate when the covenantal relationship empowers Abraham and when it renders him powerless to protest.

After the visit to Abraham from the three divine messengers, God's attention is turned to Sodom.

> Then the Lord said, "Shall I hide from Abraham what I am about to do, seeing that Abraham shall become a great and mighty nation, and all the nations of the earth shall bless themselves by him? For I have chosen him so that he will direct his children and his household after him to keep the way of the Lord by doing what is right and just, so that the Lord will bring about for Abraham what He has promised him." Then the Lord said, "The outcry against Sodom and Gomorrah is great, and their sin very grievous. So

I will go down and see if what they have done is as bad as the outcry that has reached Me. If not, I will know." (Gen. 18:17–21)

At this point, two of the messengers depart for Sodom, "and Abraham was still standing before God" (Gen. 18:22).[58] Abraham, cognizant of his covenantal responsibilities and of God's expectations of him, now steps forward: "And Abraham approached and said, 'Would you destroy the righteous with the wicked?'" (18:23).

Two points bear emphasizing. First, we know that God engaged Abraham here, at least in part, *because* of his sense of justice: "I have chosen him so that he will direct his children and his household after him to keep the way of the Lord by doing what is right and just" (Gen. 18:19). Thus, the reader at least knows that Abraham's invocation of justice—"Will the Judge of all the earth not act justly?" (18:25)—is precisely what God wanted from him.

Second, and more crucially for understanding Abraham, God did not confront him with a command or a statement of any sort. This is, perhaps, even more theologically interesting than what Hartman thinks is going on. There are two ways of understanding the dynamic, one that assumes more about God's knowledge and the other that assumes less. If we assume that God knows the proper way to govern the world, we may understand that on the way to investigate whether the crimes of Sodom are as bad as the reports say ("So I will go down and see if what they have done is as bad as the outcry that has reached Me. If not, I will know" [Gen. 18:21]),[59] God stopped to talk over with Abraham what the results ought to be if the situation really is bad. God wanted to teach Abraham to think about governing, to think about governance, because after all, Abraham himself will be in charge one day ("seeing that Abraham shall become a great and mighty nation" [18:18]). God therefore elicits from Abraham thoughts on justice and righteousness, in an ongoing project of educating Abraham for future leadership.

An alternative is that God, too, is unsure of how to handle the situation. The previous divine attempt at punishment was collective (Genesis 6–8), so God is struggling to formulate rules for the punishment of a town where the vast majority of people—but perhaps not every single one—is wicked. "There is no reason," God may reason, "that I have to struggle with this on My own. After all, I have entered into a covenant with Abraham for the specific goal of him instructing his descendants in the ways of justice and righteousness." God therefore visits Abraham, reveals to him the dilemma, and awaits the opinion of the covenantal partner.

Abraham then approaches and begins with what he sees as the overarching principle: "Will the Judge of all the earth not act justly?" (Gen. 18:25). He then begins to negotiate, to work out the ground rules for the collective punishment. If there are fifty righteous people, that should be enough to save the cities (although presumably the wicked individuals would still be punished); God assents. Abraham then pushes a bit harder, deferentially: what if there are only forty-five? Then too, agrees God, collective punishment seems unjust. And so, too, with forty, thirty, twenty, and ten: the rule is laid down that if there are ten righteous people, the cities will not be wholesale destroyed. After agreeing on those rules, Abraham returns to his tent to await the results of the divine fact-finding mission.

This story has profound things to say about the covenantal relationship between God and humanity, about Abraham, about justice. But it cannot be compared to the Akedah. In the story of Sodom, God engages Abraham with a question: "So I will go down and see if what they have done is as bad as the outcry that has reached Me" (Gen. 18:21). Abraham then, indeed, takes the initiative, involving himself in the planning of the appropriate punishment, ensuring that the divine plans include no injustice. The involvement was invited, however. In the Akedah, God never offers an opening. "Take your son . . . and offer him as a burnt offering" (18:2). There is no uncertainty, no hesitation, and therefore no invitation. Abraham is faced with a blunt and unambiguous command, and he obeys. Sodom and the Akedah are not different models, but different realities.

This undermines Hartman's argument that Genesis 18 and Genesis 22 present two models, meant to stand alongside each other. More generally, this means that the story of Abraham and Sodom cannot in any way serve as an escape hatch, cannot save us from the Akedah. Hartman took the lesson of the Akedah for granted and tried to blunt its force by laying it alongside a different model. In actuality, however, the Akedah itself needs to be rethought.

Anachronistic Clash of Faith and Ethics

The final criticism of Kierkegaard to be discussed here is that it is a modern idea, out of place in earlier religious thought and certainly in the Bible, that faith and ethics may clash. In chapters 2 and 3 we saw how developments in the nineteenth century led to this issue being a central one. The flip side of that argument is that prior to the nineteenth century, few people worried about such a clash. Faith and ethics were assumed to be complementary, if not in fact merely synonyms.

Evidence for this claim lies in the history of ideas: until Kierkegaard's time, no one read the story as a clash between ethics and divine command. It was often, instead, understood as a conflict between natural paternal love and morality, *which was the same as* obedience to God.[60] Other evidence comes from more sensitive attention to the character of Abraham. Philosopher Howard Wettstein writes:

> Were I asked to kill a child of mine, probably only (much) later would I think about morality. Abraham must think: how can I kill my boy. I can't imagine that he is thinking, "How can I violate morality?" To be primarily stunned by the violation of morality would be the proverbial one thought too many. What's at stake is more in the domain of love.[61]

The other part of this criticism is more fundamental. Interpreters did not posit a clash between faith and ethics because the two were meant to agree. The system of Judaism did not set itself up against the ethical intuition, but instead built on it, refined it, and extended it. This is not to say that nothing in the Jewish tradition conflicts with much ethical thinking; there certainly is. It is to say that the Jewish tradition struggled with those cases on a foundation of understanding that religion *ought to* agree with ethics.

The commanded massacre of Amalek is a problem *because* the Torah is presumed to be ethical.[62] Kierkegaard's knight of faith would have to struggle internally, would have to overcome his own natural thinking to suspend ethics and fulfill the command to massacre the Amalekite women and children, but would not struggle with the question of how God could have commanded such a thing. Kierkegaard seemingly has no problem with the fact that God commanded something unethical: this is the essence of faith. Jewish thought does not seem to have any place for such a view.[63]

It may well be that this gap between Kierkegaard and Jewish thought reflects a profound difference between Judaism and Protestantism on the question of the system. There is a Protestant ideal of breaking free of the system, because the system constrains and even corrupts. Judaism has not traditionally had this ideal. This seems to be the import of Levinas's comment on "the Kierkegaardian notion of existence and its deeply Protestant protest against systems."[64] Levinas's point seems to be that for a Protestant, systems are to be challenged; Jewish thought has rarely gone in that direction. Even Soloveitchik, we may recall, who did glorify the charismatic person of faith who independently found the ethical ideals of the world, argued that at a later stage the person of faith would then discover that her intuitions were in agreement with the divine will. This point is also a focal point of Fackenheim's discussion of the Akedah:

In Kierkegaard's account . . . , religious sacrifice threatens morality with destruction. In posing this threat, Kierkegaard and his
knight of faith are in marked contrast with virtually the entire
Jewish tradition. For Kierkegaard, the ethical is actually suspended in the *Akedah*, and potentially suspended for every other
knight of faith after Abraham. In Judaism, the Torah ends the
possibility of any such suspension, and . . . the Midrash denies
that even in the *Akedah* itself it ever had the form that Kierkegaard ascribes to it.[65]

The ethical cannot be purposefully suspended by God because
God aspires to the ethical.[66] The very notion that Abraham would be
forced to choose between faith and ethics, then, is not just anachronistic, but clashes with fundamental Jewish ideas of revelation and
morality. Despite the Jewish thinkers who have been swept up in the
thrall of Kierkegaard's thought, this then is one final reason for his
approach to be rejected, on both Jewish and ethical grounds.

6

On Child Sacrifice

Over the centuries, most Jews have read the Akedah not as a *philosophical* text, but as an emotional-religious text. Still, we *also* must account for it philosophically, and in particular, ethically. Kierkegaard's view having been criticized from a number of angles, it is left to propose a different reading.

One key is to pay careful attention to the whole story: not only act 1, in which the sacrifice of Isaac is commanded, but act 2 as well, in which it is prevented. Strikingly, Kierkegaard's understanding of the story does not include any discussion of act 2. Some other readers have overemphasized act 2, at the expense of an appreciation of act 1, but the corrective to that must be a reading that takes both into account, not downplaying either half.[1] Relegating the command to spare Isaac to a mere footnote in the story, a trivial epilogue, seems literarily unfair; if the story has theological import, both commands issued to Abraham have to be engaged.

One of the more eloquent spokespeople for reintroducing the end of the drama into our thinking about the Akedah has been Levinas. In a stirring passage, he wrote:

Kierkegaard has a predilection for the biblical story of the sacrificing of Isaac. Thus, he describes the encounter with God as a subjectivity rising to the religious level: God above the ethical order! His interpretation of this story can doubtless be given a different orientation. Perhaps Abraham's ear for hearing the voice that brought him back to the ethical order was the highest moment in this drama.

In his evocation of Abraham he describes the encounter with God at the point where subjectivity rises to the level of the religious, that is to say, above ethics. But one could think the opposite: Abraham's attentiveness to the voice that led him back to the ethical order, in forbidding him to perform a human sacrifice, is the highest point in the drama. That he obeyed the first voice is astonishing: that he had sufficient distance with respect to that obedience to obey the second voice—that is the essential.[2]

The goal of this chapter and the following ones is to flesh out what I take to be the crux of Levinas's interpretation: we must account for the "astonishing" command to Abraham to kill Isaac and then the "essential" command to Abraham to desist. And we have to account for this not only textually—clearly, in the narrative, the second command to Abraham supersedes the first—but philosophically: how can we account for the two divine commands, both authoritative and yet one superseded?

In order to do so, we need to try to articulate something of what the initial command would have meant to Abraham, and to Iron Age readers of the narrative. As many have noted, there is a profound anachronism in the notion that the commandment to sacrifice Isaac would have been perceived as grossly unethical, since other people, neighbors of Israel, did just that. Certainly, this does not mean that Abraham was meant to recognize the command as just and immediately comply, of course; within biblical thought, the fact that others did something is certainly no reason to follow. It is also true, however, that other biblical passages, too, entertain the possibility of child sacrifice as desirable. Untangling these issues is the task to which we now turn.

Child sacrifice was long an attractive act of religious devotion. No contextual reading of the Akedah can plausibly claim that the notion of a father sacrificing his "only son" on the altar was simply an abomination to the God of Israel: the evidence of the Bible begs to differ. The burden of this section will be to defend two propositions: first, that for Israel, as reflected in the Bible, the sacrificing of children was thought to be generally positive; and second, that it is rejected in biblical religion. These are not mutually exclusive: many actions that are laudable from some perspective are rejected by religious systems. Child sacrifice may be laudable, yet rejected; this need not be a wholesale rejection of the entire idea of child sacrifice.

Child sacrifice has simple yet powerful religious logic to it. Just as God provided the fruits of the earth, and so should be honored with a gift of the first fruits, and provided the flocks in the field, and so should be honored with a gift of the first of the flocks, God provided the fruit of the womb, and so should be honored with a gift of the first of that fruit, as well. And this does seem to be the implication of two passages in Exodus:

> The Lord said to Moses, "Consecrate to Me every first-born male. The first offspring of every womb among the Israelites belongs to Me, whether human or animal." (Exod. 13:1–2)

> You must give Me the first-born of your sons. Do the same with your cattle and your sheep. Let them stay with their mothers for seven days, but give them to Me on the eighth day. (Exod. 22:28–29)

These passages, especially Exodus 22, could certainly be understood to mandate the sacrifice of the first-born son, *the same* as what is mandated for one's cattle and sheep.

There is another line of religious thinking that leads to the same conclusion, or perhaps a more specific one. If I offer my first wheat to God, I may be actually thinking in the back of my mind of the benefit this will bring to me in the long run: when God sees that I have recognized the divine beneficence, surely God will ensure that next year's crop is even grander! If I offer God my finest sheep, I can be assured that next spring there will be many healthy lambs. But if I offer a child to God, I am asking nothing in return. This child will be gone forever, and even replacement children cannot undo the loss of this one (contrast Job 42:13–15). This is that rarest of religious acts: the gift to God that cannot be reciprocated. This is a sublime moment of religious worship, an act of pure devotion, performed for no material benefit at all.

Rather than emphasizing gratitude, this lays the stress on a profound sense of dependence, and rather than comparing the first fruits, first flocks, and first-borns, one might reflect on the profound difference between them. Only with the sacrifice of the child can a worshiper hope to have offered something that is religiously pure, untainted by thoughts of self-service.[3]

These two lines of thinking—that proper gratitude demands the sacrifice of a child, and that pure religious devotion can be accomplished by nothing less—held a powerful grip on the people in ancient Israel. There was yet another formidable consideration that ensured that this grip could not be easily broken: at least on occasion, the neighbors of the Israelites offered their own children as sacrifices.

Indeed, child sacrifice was practiced, apparently, by the Phoenicians, as has been reported since antiquity and is seemingly confirmed by archaeological and epigraphic data.[4] Tertullian, the early third-century church father who was a native of Carthage, writes:

> Children were openly sacrificed in Africa to Saturn as lately as the proconsulship of Tiberius. . . . And even now that sacred crime still continues to be done in secret. . . . When Saturn did not spare his own children, he was not likely to spare the children of others; whom indeed the very parents themselves were in the habit of offering, gladly responding to the call which was made on them, and keeping the little ones pleased on the occasion, that they might not die in tears.[5]

Tertullian scornfully concludes his description: "And between murder and sacrifice by parents, oh, the difference is great!" This, of course, is the crux of the matter. If it is not a laudable sacrifice, it is murder. This is what troubled Kierkegaard and earlier the midrash. If one does not agree that the sacrifice is religiously commanded, it is a horrific crime.

Far earlier, Cleitarchus, one of the historians of Alexander the Great, who wrote in the late fourth century BCE, described the scene in some detail:

> There stands in their midst a bronze statue of Kronos, its hands extended over a bronze brazier, the flames of which engulf the child. When the flames fall upon the body, the limbs contract and the open mouth seems almost to be laughing until the contracted body slips quietly into the brazier. Thus it is that the "grin" is known as "sardonic laughter," since they die laughing.[6]

Numerous Greek and Latin writers mention the Phoenician, and especially Carthaginian, practice of child sacrifice,[7] and while many of these authors may be suspected of anti-Carthaginian bias, the picture painted is so consistent that it may not be ignored. Furthermore, the practice is amply confirmed by archaeological remains.

Some modern scholars have resisted the notion that we are dealing with an actual practice of child sacrifice. Archaeologist Lawrence Stager paraphrased one sort of objection to this: "How could this great civilization once and for all time give us the gift of the alphabet, which we still use, and engage in the 'barbaric' rites of child sacrifice?"[8] But ten or so cemeteries of cremated children—dubbed "tophets" in deference to Jeremiah 7:31 and other biblical passages about the practice of child sacrifice—are known within the Sardinia–Sicily–Tunisia triangle, perhaps including Malta.[9] The tophet in Carthage, the largest and best studied of them, apparently contains tens of thousands of children, interred from the eighth through the second centuries BCE; in some centuries these were interred at a rate of two per week.[10] Repeated study has shown that this tophet mostly contains children between one and six months old, clustering around a month and a half.[11]

This suggests that the sacrifices were the results of deals made between the parents (often, to judge from the inscriptions, just the father) and the goddess Tanit and/or the god Ba'al Ḥammon, the chief goddess and god of Carthage. Inscriptions throughout the tophet make clear the nature of these burials: "To my lady, Tanit, face of Ba'al, and to the lord, to Ba'al Ḥammon,[12] that which Yakon-Shalom, son of Ivelet vowed."[13] In this and the many other cases, the parents had earlier prayed for something and promised that if the request were granted, they would reciprocate with the gift of their next-born child. When that child came and perhaps enough time elapsed to ensure that the baby would not die on its own, the sacrifice was performed, the corpse cremated, and the ashes interred in the tophet.[14] Animals are buried in the cemetery as well, as substitutes for children, as accompanying inscriptions again make clear: "life for life, blood for blood, a lamb as a substitute."[15]

Such vows are of course familiar from the Levant as well. The Aramaic "Melqart stele" from approximately 800 BCE announces itself:

> The stele which Bir-Hadad, son of 'Attar-hamek, king of Aram, for his lord, Melqart, to whom he vowed [*zy nzr lh*], and he listened to him [*šm' lqlh*].[16]

The erection of a stele for the fulfillment of a vow is reminiscent of the promise made by Jacob:

> If God remains with me, if He protects me on this journey I am making, and gives me bread to eat and clothing to wear, and if I return safely to my father's house, and the Lord shall be my God, this stone, which I have erected as a stele shall be the Lord's house, and all that You give me, I will set aside a tithe for You. (Gen. 28:20–22)

Psalms refers to the same practice: "For You, God, have heard my vows" (61:6).[17] And of course the question of the vow brings us also to the example of Jephthah (Judges 11), who also returns us to the matter of child sacrifice:

> Jephthah vowed to the Lord: "If You indeed give the Ammonites into my hands, whatever comes out of the doors of my house to greet me when I return safely from the Ammonites will be the Lord's, and I will sacrifice it as a burnt offering." . . . When Jephthah returned to his home in Mizpah, lo, it was his daughter who came out to greet him, with drums and dancing! She was an only child. Except for her he had neither son nor daughter. (Judg. 11:30–31,34)

It is implausible that it did not occur to Jephthah that a human may be the first to leave the house to greet him, although to judge from his reaction, it seems clear that he had not counted on it being his one and only daughter: "Oh no, my daughter! You have brought me down and I am devastated. I have made a vow to the Lord that I cannot break" (Judg. 11:35).[18] (In the similar Greek story of Idomeneus, too, child sacrifice was not the intention, and in that case Idomeneus's offering of his son—the first creature to come out of his house when he returns safely from sea—is explicitly said to have angered the gods.) Whatever the original intention, the story does seem to take for granted that the sacrifice of Jephthah's daughter would be appropriate—in fact, necessary—in God's eyes, in fulfillment of the vow uttered on the battlefield.[19] Thus within the Bible itself we have a close parallel to the dynamic behind the many interments in the Carthaginian and other tophets.

Of course, that second to last sentence highlights a crucial difference as well. Within the Levant, in Israel, Phoenicia, and Moab, child sacrifice was, if practiced at all, extraordinary. The absence of tophets in the Phoenician heartland is unlikely to be entirely accidental, and in any event we have the explicit testimony of a Phoenician named Sakkun-yaton, as cited by Philo of Byblos (who was in turn cited by Eusebius):

> It was a custom of the ancients, when great dangers befell them, that, to avoid complete destruction, the rulers of the city or the people should give over to the slaughter the most beloved of their children as a ransom to the vengeful daimons.[20]

This description calls to mind Mesha, king of Moab in the ninth century BCE. When his city was about to fall to an allied force of Israelites, Judeans, and Ammonites, Mesha "took his first-born son, who was to rule in his place, and offered him on the wall as a burnt offering" (2 Kings 3:27). Shockingly, the biblical narrative concedes that this was effective, as the text continues, "A great fury [qeṣef] came upon Israel, so they withdrew from him and went back to their land."

The same was apparently practiced in Judah, at least by Ahaz and Manasseh. About both it is said that "he passed his son through fire" (2 Kings 16:3, 21:6). The slightly later Jeremiah also complains about this practice (32:35), and he may well be referring to actions that took place a generation earlier, under Manasseh. It is not known what led Ahaz and Manasseh to offer their sons as sacrifices,[21] but it would not be unreasonable to presume that extraordinary circumstances led to these offerings.[22] The crucial point for our present discussion is that in particularly dire straits, Phoenician, Moabite, and Israelite parents all thought it appropriate to offer a child sacrifice as a last resort.[23]

Out in the Mediterranean colonies, however, the Phoenicians forged a new culture. Here child sacrifice went from being prominent by virtue of its rarity and drama to prominent by virtue of its common practice. It is possible that this is the result of cultural influence from cultures elsewhere in the Mediterranean, but it is also possible that this is an organic development as the Phoenicians set up communities far from home and without the rituals of their original lands. The construction of a diaspora identity, and specifically diasporic religious practices, is a familiar phenomenon.[24] Could the Phoenician exiles, recently arrived on the distant shores of Libya, have elaborated and extended the practice of child sacrifice, converting something extraordinary into something foundational and regular?

When it comes to religious practices, and especially sacrifice, the practice of one's neighbors is not merely peer pressure. One can imagine an Israelite preacher thundering: It is inconceivable that the Phoenicians, who worship a fictional deity, could be more devoted to him than we are to the Creator of Heaven and Earth! Can it be that our encounter with the One True God does not provoke the devotion that the idolatrous Phoenicians have? How can the Phoenicians sacrifice their precious children, while we suffice with mere sheep?

There is plenty of biblical testimony that such entreaties, whether heard in the streets, at shrines, or in the hearts of men and women, had their effect. A number of biblical texts seem quite aware that Jews would *think* that God wanted them to practice child sacrifice.[25] The most explicit of these texts are from Jeremiah and Micah:

> I am bringing calamity to this place; the ears of anyone who hears of it will ring. Because they have abandoned Me, and made this place foreign—they offered incense within it to other gods, whom neither they nor their ancestors, or the kings of Judah, knew—and they filled this place with the blood of the innocent; they have built shrines to Baal to burn their children in the fire as burnt-offerings to Baal—something I did not command, did not say, and it never entered My mind! (Jer. 19:3–5)

Jeremiah here addresses head-on the presumption on a part of his audience that God ordained child sacrifice. In the name of God, he denies this categorically: this is "something I did not command, did not say, and it never entered My mind!" Jeremiah repeats the denial, and the report of Judean behavior, in 7:30–31:

For the Judeans have done what is evil in My eyes—says the Lord—they have placed their abominations in the house over which My name was called, defiling it, and they built the shrines of the Tophet in the valley of Ben Hinnom, in order to burn their sons and daughters in fire—which I did not command, and it never entered My mind!

These very denials are, for our purposes, precious evidence that some of the ancient Judeans did believe that God had commanded just that. Even more suggestive is the evidence from Micah (6:6–8) a century earlier:

> With what shall I come before the Lord and bow down
>   before the exalted God?
> Shall I come before Him with burnt offerings, with calves a
>   year old?
> Will the Lord be pleased with thousands of rams, with ten
>   thousand rivers of olive oil?
> Shall I offer my first-born for my transgression, the fruit of
>   my womb for the sin of my soul?
> He has shown you, O mortal, what is good. And what does
>   the Lord require of you?
> To act justly and to love mercy, and to walk humbly with
>   your God.

The rhetorical question, "Shall I offer my first-born for my transgression?" is asked alongside other rhetorical questions, all of which involve practices that seem unambiguously to be in fact the will of God (bowing down, burnt offerings, sacrifice of rams). One could argue that Micah is simply meeting the people where they are, arguing that *even according to their view* that child sacrifice is a positive, God rejects it in favor of mercy and humility. It is more reasonable, however, to take this text as face value: Micah presupposes that child sacrifice — more precisely, "the fruit of my womb" — is as desirable as burnt offerings, rams, and libations. All of these are rejected in favor of mercy and humility, however.

Many thinkers assume that God cannot desire child sacrifice, because it is evil. We will argue below that God in the Akedah does *not* desire child sacrifice, despite it *not* being evil. The prophet Ezekiel suggests a way that God *can* desire child sacrifice despite it *being* evil. In the midst of a caustically critical diatribe against Israel's lack of fidelity in chapter 20, Ezekiel says in the name of God:

> I also gave them over to statutes that were not good and laws they could not live by: I let them become defiled through their gifts — the sacrifice of every first-born — that I might fill them with horror so they would know that I am the Lord. (Ezek. 20:25–26)

In this passage, Ezekiel avers that God has in fact commanded the sacrifice of the first-born but that this was done — somewhat in the manner of hardening Pharaoh's heart and other similar biblical cases — in order to lead the Jews to destruction and exile at the hand of the Babylonians.[26] Textually, Ezekiel may be referring to the passage from Exodus 22:28–29 discussed above ("You must give me the first-born of your sons. Do the same with your cattle and your sheep"). It is even conceivable, in such a textually oriented prophet, that he is suggesting that a *mis*-reading of that text is at the root of the practice of child sacrifice. In other words, he may be suggesting that the people are taking the phrase "do the same" overly literally, sacrificing their children the same way they sacrifice their cattle and sheep. Theologically, this is a shocking claim: God has intentionally misled the Judeans into sacrificing their children, despite this being a horrifying evil, in order to condemn them. They are not wrong in thinking that God wants them to offer their children on the shrines of the valley of Ben Hinnom. They simply don't realize that God, against Descartes's claim, may in fact deceive people, and the goal may be to punish the people further, in line with the divine tactics seen when dealing with Pharaoh: "I have hardened [Pharaoh's] heart . . . so that I may perform these signs of Mine" (Exod. 10:1).

Finally, the biblical texts are attuned to the religious thinking that may lead to the desire to perform child sacrifice, in particular the thought that our worship of God must not fall short of the standards set by others. Back in Deuteronomy there is already explicit concern that people will be tempted to sacrifice their children as an act of devotion to God for this reason. Deuteronomy 12 ends with the following warning:

> When the Lord your God has cut down before you the nations that you are about to enter and dispossess, and you have dispossessed them and settled in their land, beware of being lured into their ways after they have been wiped out before you! Do not inquire about their gods, saying, "How did those nations worship their gods? I too will follow those practices." You shall not act this way toward the Lord your God, for they perform for their gods every despicable act that the Lord detests; they even offer up their sons and daughters in fire to their gods. Be careful to observe only that which I command you to do; do not add to it nor subtract from it. (Deut. 12:29–13:1)

Again, rather than just social pressure, religious worship has a logic all its own: since the value of something may be measured by how much people are willing to sacrifice for it, "our" God cannot be served less than other gods. The same dynamic is at work in later responses to the Akedah. A number of Rabbinic sources report that the Akedah was provoked by a dispute between Isaac and Ishmael. For example, the Targumic text cited in chapter 1 has Isaac offering to sacrifice himself, in order to prove his worthiness to Ishmael, and thereby to himself as well.[27] There, as seen, Ishmael is a stand-in for Christians, and Isaac plays the role of the Jews. If it is the case that the more worthy the cause, the more one will be willing to sacrifice for it, does it follow that the more sacrifices made for a cause shows that it is a more worthy cause? And if so, the Jews may conclude, the fact that the Christians had many more opportunities to demonstrate their fealty than they did may, heaven forfend, suggest that their cause is indeed more worthy! The lack of Jewish martyrdoms would then show that the God of the Jews is not worth as much as the God of the Christians. And so the Jews exclaim, "Oh, but would that we had the chance!"

Returning to the Iron Age, there is every reason to think the same religious logic would be at work. Israelites would see the Phoenicians and lament the fact that Ba'al was the recipient of surpassingly powerful gifts—his worshipers' precious children—whereas the God of Israel received only sheep. What did that suggest about the relative values of the deities? Such must not be allowed! Surely the God of Israel deserves children as well . . .

All of this is to suggest that the notion that God desires human sacrifice is not absurd, not historically and not by the logic of biblical religion. To presage the following chapter, it may even be that we can formulate this more precisely, and perhaps more jarringly: there is a part of the biblical God that does desire that worshipers offer their children in sacrifice. After all, God, too, is not immune to the sense of jealousy when other worshipers offer their children to their deities. And God, too, recognizes that the sheep and grain offered on a daily basis on the altars below will always be tainted by self-interest. So perhaps a gift of children would be appreciated?

Moshe Halbertal argues that the purpose of child sacrifice is to overcome this problem, to once and for all give to God selflessly, to give in a manner that can never be recompensed:

> For Abraham, nothing could compensate for his son's loss, since a child has ultimate value. God, in his trial of Abraham, wished to ascertain that Abraham didn't worship him simply because he had given him a son at such an old age. He tested that premise by

demanding that Abraham sacrifice his Isaac. In this way, the same anxiety of instrumentality gave birth to this horrifying request.[28]

Child sacrifice is thus a temptation for worshipers, as well as for God. It is no wonder, then, that God tempted Abraham and told him to offer his only child as a sacrifice. The question, then, is why God turned Isaac away at the last moment.

7

Maimonides and the Complexity
of the Divine Will

If child sacrifice is so admirable, why does Isaac live? This chapter and
the next will address that question. In this chapter, we will see that it
is possible to read the story of the Akedah as rejecting, but not altogether repudiating, the initial command to Abraham to sacrifice his
son. Indeed, such a reading of the story was propounded by a number
of Jewish philosophers over the past thousand years. This will allow
a reading, in the next chapter, in which child sacrifice is rejected in
the final analysis, but sympathetically so.

Maimonides shows us how to understand the two stages of the
Akedah in a way that is both textually and philosophically coherent.
Maimonides did not, of course, write a running commentary on the
Bible, but his *Guide for the Perplexed* is in large measure a book of bib-
lical interpretation.[1] Maimonides addresses the Akedah a number of
times. The most explicit treatment is in book 3, chapter 24.

In that chapter, Maimonides focuses on the topic of the "trial."
He states categorically that "the purpose and the meaning of every
'trial' that appears in the Torah is only that people should know what
is proper to do, or what they are obligated to believe. The meaning of
a 'trial,' therefore, is as if a specific action should be done but not for
the purpose of having that specific instance of the action be done;
rather, the purpose is that it should serve as an example that should
be enshrined and others should follow." After discussing a number
of biblical "trials," he arrives at the Akedah, which, he says, contains
two major themes that are fundamental to the Torah. The first is "to

make known to us the limits of the love for God and fear of Him, to what extent they reach." The second needs to be cited in full:

> To inform us that the prophets accept as true whatever comes to them in revelation. One should not think that because it is a dream or a vision, as we have explained, and mediated through the Active Intellect, it may be that what appears to them or what they hear is taken to be uncertain, or that any wasteful imagination is mixed in. Therefore, He wanted to inform us that all that a prophet sees in a prophetic vision is *certain truth in the eyes of the prophet*. In no way should anyone raise doubts about any of this. It is, in his eyes, the same as physical things, apprehended with the senses and the intellect. The proof is that [Abraham] turned to slaughter his only son, whom he loved, just as he was commanded, even though this command was in a dream or a vision. If the prophets were at all doubtful regarding the veracity of prophetic dreams, or if they had any doubt about what they learned through prophetic visions, they would never do what nature forbids, and [Abraham]'s soul would not have responded to the multiply dangerous deed because of the uncertainty.

There is, of course, something quite striking in this passage. Maimonides emphasizes the veracity of the prophetic experience, but even while doing so, he subtly but explicitly limits it. Nowhere does he make the claim that we expect to hear: prophecy is true. Instead, he repeatedly insists on a more limited claim, that prophecy is subjectively *perceived* as true by the prophet. The proof for this claim is Abraham, who would never have moved to sacrifice his son if he had even the slightest doubt regarding the authoritativeness of the divine command to do so.[2]

This passage is, so to speak, Maimonides' response to a criticism of Abraham offered by Kant:

For if God should really speak to a human being, the latter could still never *know* that it was God speaking. It is quite impossible for a human being to apprehend the infinite by his senses, distinguish it from sensible beings, and be acquainted with it as such. But in some cases the human being can be sure that the voice he hears is not God's; for if the voice commands him to do something contrary to moral law, then no matter how majestic the apparition may be, and no matter how it may seem to surpass the whole of nature, he must consider it an illusion.

We can use, as an example, the myth of the sacrifice that Abraham was going to make by butchering and burning his only son at God's command (the poor child, without knowing it, even brought the wood for the fire). Abraham should have replied to this supposedly divine voice: "That I ought not to kill my good son is quite certain. But that you, this apparition, are God—of that I am not certain and never can be, not even if this voice rings down to me from (visible) Heaven."[3]

Kant's objection to the Akedah is what others have called "the problem of hearing." Whereas Kierkegaard takes the content of the divine command for granted—on Abraham's word—Kant argues that this itself needs to be interrogated. How can Abraham, or anyone else, truly know that it was God speaking?

This view is developed by Buber as well: "the problematics of the decision of faith" must be preceded by "the problematics of the hearing itself." Buber points out that within the Bible, there is sometimes confusion as to whether a voice is God's or not. In 2 Samuel 24:1, God provokes David to take a census of the people; the same act is attributed to Satan in 1 Chronicles 21:1.[4] In the opposite direction, one could point to the narrative in 1 Samuel 3, where the young prophet Samuel thinks the actual divine voice is the voice of Eli. Confusion appears to be possible, and Buber argues that this has to be dealt with before one can discuss obedience.[5]

Other thinkers, as we have already seen, exploit the "problem of hearing" in a different way to reach an altogether different understanding of the test in the Akedah. Sa'adia Gaon and Ralbag, as well as the Izbicer in the nineteenth century, all argued that the divine command was in fact ambiguous, and the crux of the test was whether Abraham would resolve the ambiguity in the way that was comfortable for him or in the way that accurately captured the will of God.[6]

The notion that it is fundamentally unknowable whether it is God speaking seems obvious to us. And yet Abraham did not hesitate. The contemporary philosopher Stephen Evans argues that in modern times, Kant is right, but that Abraham was not in the same (epistemic) situation as modern people with regard to God.[7] Evans's argument is not that Abraham was *more* familiar with God, and therefore certain of God's voice, but that *we* are more familiar with God and therefore know enough to know that God would never command the sacrifice of an innocent person. According to Evans, divine revelation can teach new things about God but cannot overturn everything already known: "It is not conceivable that rape and murder should suddenly become obligatory, while kindness and love would become forbidden."[8] Thus Kant is wrong about the biblical Abraham but right about any subsequent "Abrahams."

Maimonides, too, addresses Kant's challenge by turning the "problem of hearing" on its head.[9] Apparently sharing with Kant the view that nothing other than absolute certainty could have justified the sacrifice of Isaac, Maimonides argues that this very story shows that Kant's assertion that "it is quite impossible for a human being to apprehend the infinite by his senses" is false. To be more precise, Maimonides argues that this story shows that a true prophet would never raise the doubts that Kant thinks he should, because "all that a prophet sees in a prophetic vision is certain truth in the eyes of the prophet." To the outsider it may be hard to understand how this could be so. Not being a prophet, Maimonides cannot attest to the truth of this statement firsthand. Instead, he argues that the shocking willingness of Abraham to act proves that it is so. Maimonides argues, to paraphrase the end of *Fear and Trembling*, that either a prophet is absolutely certain of the veracity of the prophecy or Abraham is lost.

This being said, we are still left to wonder: Why was Maimonides so careful to limit the authoritativeness of the prophetic experience to the realm of subjective truth as experienced by the prophet? Why did he not simply say that "prophecy is true"? Addressing this question will take us to the topic of how prophecy works and lead us to Maimonides' more sustained thinking about the Akedah.

The second passage in which Maimonides engages the Akedah—this time implicitly—is in his discussion of prophecy, and it is therefore worthwhile to first introduce another question. This question is never explicitly asked by Maimonides, but asked by his philosophical predecessors and answered in the *Guide*. When we read the story of the Akedah, we tend to ask questions about Abraham: How could he have been willing to sacrifice his son? What was he thinking about for three days while walking? What were his emotions when he was told to desist? What motivated the sacrifice of the ram? Why is he alone at the end? For many medieval philosophers, however, there was a far more obvious question, not about Abraham but about God. The question is asked by Sa'adia Gaon: How could God change his mind? In Genesis 22:2, God commands Abraham to sacrifice Isaac; in verse 12 God (through the intermediary of an angel) commands him not to. But how could this be?

This troubled the medieval thinkers greatly, and various solutions were proffered. Sa'adia himself reports that there were people who tried to establish from the biblical text that God was inconsistent. He cites ten of the examples brought to make this point, rejecting each one in turn. The fifth example was, "God, may He be exalted, told Abraham, 'Bring him as a burnt offering,' and then told him, 'Do not extend your hand against the lad, and do not do anything to him.'" Sa'adia's solution is that the command "Bring him as a burnt offering" does not entail actually sacrificing Isaac; as soon as Abraham had bound Isaac and prepared him *as* a sacrifice, he had fulfilled the original commandment of God.[10]

This question gains most of its gravity from the way these medieval thinkers understood prophecy to work.[11] For Maimonides in particular, prophecy was not verbal communication from God to a person. "Know that the true reality and veracity of prophecy consist in it being an overflow overflowing from God, may He be cherished and honored, through the intermediation of the Active Intellect, toward the rational faculty in the first place and thereafter toward the imaginative faculty."[12] God did not speak to Abraham directly, and since prophecy is an act of *understanding God*, it seems impossible to understand something misleading. How could Abraham "receive a prophecy" to sacrifice his son if God never desired that?

This question, again, is never explicitly asked by Maimonides. But it is answered, and, I believe, quite deliberately so, in another passage about prophecy, this time in *Guide* 2.45. Here Maimonides introduces a taxonomy of prophecy, dividing all prophetic experiences (that of Moses is excepted[13]) into eleven levels of increasing understanding. He emphasizes that this is not a taxonomy of *prophets*, but of *prophetic experiences*:

> Let us not mislead you with regard to these levels if you find in the prophetic books a prophet who experiences a revelation on one of these levels, but it then turns out that this same prophet himself experienced a revelation in the form of a different level. For with regard to these levels I will note that a revelation may arrive to a particular prophet on a particular level at one point, and at another time a revelation may arrive to him at a lower level than the first revelation.

Following that, Maimonides articulates the eleven levels of prophecy, classified by the mode of revelation. *How* the revelation arrives bespeaks the quality of the revelation. Not all the eleven levels are relevant for our discussion, but the final five are:

> *The seventh level*: that he sees in a prophetic dream as if He, may He be exalted, speaks to him, as it said with regard to Isaiah, "I saw the Lord . . . and He said, 'Whom shall I send?'" (Isa. 6:1,8), and as it says with regard to Micaiah b. Yimla: "I saw the Lord . . ." (1 Kings 22:19).
>
> *The eighth level*: that a revelation arrives to him in a prophetic vision, and he sees symbols, like Abraham at the Covenant Between the Parts (Gen. 15:9–10), for these symbols were seen during the day, as was made clear.
>
> *The ninth level*: that he hears speech in the midst of a vision, as it is written about Abraham, "And the word of God came to him saying, 'This one will not be your heir'" (Gen. 15:4).
>
> *The tenth level*: that he sees a person speaking to him in a prophetic vision, also like Abraham, in the terebinths of Mamre (Gen. 18:1), and like Joshua at Jericho (Josh. 5:13).
>
> *The eleventh level*: that he sees an angel speaking to him, like Abraham at the time of the Akedah. This is, in my view, the highest level of prophets that the books testify about their states.

It is interesting that the four highest levels of prophecy are all exemplified with reference to Abraham.[14] Perhaps this was meant to demonstrate what Maimonides had said at the outset: the very same prophet may experience different revelations at different levels. Beyond the general point being made, however, the use of Abraham opens up a way for Maimonides to solve the problem of God's will changing over the course of Genesis 22. Rather than the change being in God, the change was in Abraham, or, more specifically, in the level of revelation experienced by Abraham. To put it differently, what changed over the course of the story of the Akedah was not God, but how well Abraham understood God.[15]

For Maimonides, the "command" to sacrifice Isaac issued in Genesis 22:2 must have been a "seventh level" prophecy, which, as we saw, he defines as a prophecy rooted on a dream—"[the prophet] sees in a prophetic dream as if [God] speaks to him." That this command was a dream is made clear by the following verse, "Abraham woke up in the morning."[16] The command to desist from this sacrifice issued in verse 12 was an eleventh-level prophecy, as Maimonides explicitly indicates here. What has changed, then, is that Abraham has moved from a lower-level prophecy at the beginning of the chapter to a higher-level prophecy—in fact, the highest level attainable—by the climax of the chapter.

This, then, provides a dramatic example of the development of the prophetic personality. Maimonides said earlier in *Guide* 2.45 that prophets experienced different revelations on different levels, and here we have a graphic example. It is graphic because the two revelations were on the exact same topic and addressed the exact same issue in polar opposite ways. To put this bluntly, then: the first prophecy was flawed. It was not *false*, but it was incomplete. The later prophecy was *more* true; it reflected a fuller and therefore more accurate understanding of God's will.[17]

Recall that in *Guide* 3.24, Maimonides studiously avoided asserting flatly that "all prophecy is true." Instead, he carefully said that prophecy is "certain truth in the eyes of the prophet." It is now evident why. It is not true that all prophecy is "true" without any modifiers. Although true prophecy perhaps cannot be false (although we will revisit this question in the next chapter), it may be incomplete, and the Akedah provides an example of the results of such prophecies.[18] Abraham's initial prophecy was true but incomplete, because all prophecies are "certain truth in the eyes of the prophet," but this incomplete understanding convinced him that God desired that he sacrifice his son, and this was enough to compel him to act on this belief. A Maimonidean outsider may have pointed out that since the prophecy was clear speech in a prophetic dream, it was only a seventh-level prophecy, and (assuming Maimonides was correct in his classification) perhaps even Abraham himself, in a non-prophetic moment, may have been able to articulate that concern. But all prophecies are "certain truth in the eyes of the prophet," so at the time of the revelation, Abraham was entirely certain of what he had to do.[19]

At this point, the conclusion from the previous chapter needs to be brought into our discussion. It is eminently reasonable that a partial understanding of God's will would lead to the sacrifice of Abraham's son. The desire for such a sacrifice, after all, is reasonable: it *does* seem to make good sense to offer one's child as a sacrifice to God. And it can be argued that God in fact actually desires it as the ultimate expression of a worshiper's devotion; Abraham *correctly* understood God's will on this front. Despite this, God in the end does *not* want Abraham to sacrifice his son, and Abraham eventually understands this, too. As his discernment of the divine will increases, he moves from acceptance of the idea of child sacrifice to its rejection.

Some interpreters of Maimonides have concluded that there is another facet to his interpretation of the story, and that is that the entire episode was a prophetic vision reflecting Abraham's thoughts, but that nothing of the sort described in Genesis 22:1–19 ever took place in the physical world.[20] To my mind, there is little positive evidence that this was in fact Maimonides' position and is at least on its face contradicted by some explicit statements he makes.[21]

One of the relevant considerations is Maimonides' view of "trials."[22] This, we may recall, is the topic of *Guide* 3.24. As articulated in a synthetic way by the historian and philosopher James Diamond, trials represent the slow methodical acquisition of intellectual understanding that stands at the center of Maimonides' religious value system.[23] It is no accident that this chapter of the *Guide* concludes with comments on the Akedah; this is the prime biblical example of a "trial."[24] Passing the trial means that Abraham has risen to a "superlative rank of perfection," having grasped the divine view on child sacrifice. Regarding the facticity of the Akedah, Diamond writes, "Abraham's successful passage of this trial manifests itself in the world of the mind and cognition and not the world of tangible phenomena."[25] The denouement in Genesis 22:12 depends not on the revelation of new information from a new source, but on Abraham's newly complete understanding. Of course, this is possibly Maimonides' view even if Abraham did physically take Isaac to the mountaintop; it is necessary if not.

In sum, whether or not the story involved the physical body of Isaac, the story of the Akedah according to Maimonides is a narrative of Abraham's struggle to more deeply understand God's will. There is no contradiction within God, and no two powers in heaven; the initial revelation was an incomplete—but still authoritative—prophetic experience for Abraham, but this was supplemented and thereby overturned by the later prophetic revelation, in which Abraham fully understood the will of God.

In this sense, Maimonides' view is echoed by Levinas. Both Maimonides and Levinas argue that act 1 of the Akedah is surpassed, but not superseded, by act 2. For Maimonides, this is the difference between a seventh-level prophecy and an eleventh-level prophecy. For Levinas, "that Abraham obeyed the first voice is astonishing: that he had sufficient distance with respect to that obedience to hear the second voice—that is essential."[26] Both are necessary. But the second overwhelms the first. As Rabbi Norman Lamm puts it, "Binding Isaac on the altar was the act of *Akedat Yitzhak*, the sacrifice of Isaac; taking him off was the act of *Akedat Avraham*, the sacrifice of Abraham."[27]

Support for this understanding of Maimonides comes from Joseph ibn Kaspi, a prolific early fourteenth-century Provençal thinker.[28] Ibn Kaspi claimed to be merely articulating for the masses what Maimonides already wrote for the select few, so his understanding of the Akedah reflects, at least, the way he believed Maimonides understood it. Although Ibn Kaspi touches on the Akedah in numerous places in his dozens of books, the one most relevant to our discussion is found in the third chapter of his book *Gevia' Kesef* (*The Silver Goblet*).

The context is a theory of the difference between the two most common divine names. First is the name written with the consonants Y-H-W-H, but never pronounced that way in Jewish tradition, and written *yyy* by Ibn Kaspi (translated as "the Lord" in the passages below). Second is the generic word for God, *Elohim*, which is also used in the Bible as an epithet of the God of Israel (translated here as "God"). Ibn Kaspi's broad theory is that the use of the epithet "God" bespeaks an understanding of God that is distant and analytical and that is, in fact, the common understanding of God even among prophets. The use of the "personal" name "Lord" in a story, on the other hand, indicates that the character in the story has a deeper, personal understanding of God. With this, Ibn Kapi turns to Abraham.[29]

When he [= the biblical narrator] began the stories of Abraham, he began, "And the Lord said to Abram, 'Go for yourself,'" because Abraham was the first who developed the belief in the existence of the separate intellect. This opinion took him away from his land, and because of this he did all that he did. . . . And therefore, in the stories of Abraham, he is always very careful to say "the Lord," with the exception of some very few places.

In the Akedah, he did very well in using "God" when he commanded him to bring his son as a burnt offering, because this is in fact not desired by the Lord. Therefore in the preventing the act, he said "the angel of the Lord," and not "the angel of God," because the desisting is necessary for us by virtue of our apprehension of the existence of the separate intellect, and our clinging to it. And he did superbly because then when he mentioned the willingness to act, he said, "for you are a fearer of God, and you did not withhold your only son," because making his son into a burnt offering was a function of being a fearer of *God*, in other words, the heavenly spheres. This was also the result of his own imagination, because it was then the custom of all the nations to offer offerings and sacrifices. But when he got to the prevention, he said, "The Lord will see," instead of the earlier, "God will see."[30]

Ibn Kaspi introduces a striking theory here.[31] Within Genesis 22, there are two aspects of God with which Abraham interacts, so to speak. He is commanded to sacrifice his son by "God," but ordered to desist by (an angel of) "the Lord." And recall that these two names indicate different levels of apprehending God. The more distant, abstract understanding of God — indicated by the name "God" — commanded the sacrifice; the more intimate, personal understanding of God — indicated by the name "the Lord" — commanded the desistance. That within God there were mutually exclusive commandments does not bother Ibn Kaspi; he explains that the single and perfectly consistent God really does contain conflicting desires.[32] Again, the solution to this apparent riddle is that God is indeed complex, but that it was Abraham who changed, not God: when Abraham partially understood God, he thought he wanted child sacrifice, but when he understood God more intimately, he understood that God did not.[33]

The significance of this for our discussion lies in the structural parallels between Ibn Kaspi's interpretation of the Akedah and Maimonides' interpretation, as explicated earlier. Since Ibn Kaspi professes to be a disciple of Maimonides, this strengthens the possibility that we have properly understood Maimonides. Both thinkers solve the problem of the apparent contradiction within God by explaining that the change was not within God, but within Abraham's understanding of God. The climax of the story is thus the second "revelation" in Genesis 22:12, when Abraham arrives at a more complete and intimate understanding of God's will; he understands that, all things considered, God does not desire the sacrifice of Isaac after all.

What Maimonides and Ibn Kaspi offer, then, is a way of reading the Akedah that does not reject entirely either half of the chapter. Both the command to Abraham to sacrifice Isaac and the command to desist from doing so sincerely and perennially reflect the will of the biblical God. The second revelation is the one that has normative value, but this is not because the first was a mistake or a trick. God really does want the sacrifice of the "beloved son" but more wants that child to live.

It is certainly a psychological commonplace for a person to want something but to *not* want it even more. Consider a health-conscious person looking at a piece of cake. He may want the cake, although in the end he won't eat it. The rejection of the cake is a statement not of its despicability or fundamental abhorrence, but of a desire for health that is even more powerful than the desire for the confection. In the religious realm, this is a familiar sentiment as well, and it is worth considering three well-known examples.

The first is a claim recorded in the midrash that this type of internal conflict is religiously positive:

R. El'azar b. 'Azariah says: How do I know that a person should not say, "I don't want to wear *sha'atnez* [the forbidden mixture of wool and linen]" or "I don't want to eat pork" or "I don't want to have that illicit sexual relationship," but rather, "I do want to! But what can I do? My Father in heaven decreed against it." — This is what is taught, "I separated you from the nations, to be Mine." Thus one distances oneself from a sin, and therefore accepts the yoke of heaven.[34]

The ideal religious person, according to this midrash, has not altered her will to accord with the laws of the Torah, but stands in perennial conflict on the level of desire. She wants to taste the forbidden fruit but *more* wants to accept the yoke of heaven.

In two other texts, Jewish law operates with the knowledge that "what a person wants" is often complicated. If a person is coerced into selling a field, the sale is a valid sale.[35] The Talmud explains: many sellers would, on some level, prefer not to part with their property but are "coerced" by economic necessity. The human psyche is complex, and the legally necessary "will to sell" need not be the only sentiment; it only has to be the final one. Similarly, Maimonides himself rules that if a Jewish man refuses to issue the legal document of divorce (*get*) in a situation where he is required to, the court may physically coerce him to do so: "They strike him until he says, 'I want to!' Then he writes the *get*, and it is an acceptable *get*." Maimonides then explains that this is despite the rule that a *get* written under coercion is unacceptable:

> One who did not want to divorce, since he *does* want to be a member of the Jewish people, he *does* want to fulfill the commandments and distance himself from the sins; it is only his desires that got the best of him. Since he was beaten until his desire waned and then said, "I want to!," he actually divorced willingly.[36]

Again, there is a recognition that people are complex. Human desires do not follow the law of noncontradiction. We want and don't want at the same time, and sometimes with the same ferocity and passion. We hope for the wisdom to adjudicate between our desires, to know which "want" represents the best of us.

All that is left to say is that God, too, experiences the world in this way.[37] God wants child sacrifice, as an expression of love and commitment. But God *more* does not want it, as a reflection of a higher value (to be discussed in the next chapter). In the initial prophecy, Abraham accurately but incompletely understood God's will and set out to sacrifice Isaac. On the mountain, however, Abraham experienced a higher-level prophecy and attained a more complete understanding of God's will. Now he realized that although his previous understanding made some sense, it was incomplete and imperfect, and deeply flawed as a result. His new, better understanding led him to the conclusion that God did not want human sacrifice after all, although God may appreciate the sentiment behind it.

8

Rejecting Child Sacrifice

The interpretation of the Akedah that has been argued in the previous chapters opens crucial interpretive possibilities and raises crucial questions. This chapter will address the implications of the reading just offered, especially the question: if God does, to some extent, desire the sacrifice of children, why does God *more* not want it? What value is so transcendent that it disallows child sacrifice? Before turning to that, however, one other issue should be addressed: can God's prophets misunderstand God?

Do True Prophets Always Fully Understand God?

Biblical scholars and theologians have asked, "Does God lie to God's prophets?" A number of passages suggest that in fact God may do just that. One oft-cited passage is in 1 Kings 22. In this story, the prophet Micaiah tells the king of Israel that the four hundred prophets who have assured him of victory in battle are in fact prophesying truly — but were misled by God. This is a shrewd claim on Micaiah's part, because by the logic of his claim, the other prophets are in no position to defend themselves: they are sincere in their prophecy and in fact conveying what they were told by God. Only Micaiah claims to have insight into the backstory of their prophecy, which, he claims, was a lie planted by God in their mouths in order to lead the king to his death in battle.[1] "Put bluntly," explains Robert Goldenberg, "Micaiah's message is that God himself cannot be trusted."[2] But this is not because God is capricious, but because God may have many reasons for sharing messages — perhaps only partially true messages — with prophets. Even a true prophet, then, may be misleading—and even misled.

A similar notion may be implied in Isaiah 6:10, where Isaiah is given the following mandate: "Make the heart of this people fat, make their ears dull, and close their eyes / lest they see with their eyes, hear with their ears, and understand with their hearts—and return and be healed." The clear import of this mission is that the prophet is to mislead the people into thinking they are on the right track, so that they do not repent. If they repent, they will have to be forgiven, so God wants to ensure that they do not repent.[3]

The theological possibility of God feeding lies to prophets is explicitly mentioned in Ezekiel 14:9–10:

> And if the prophet is enticed to utter a prophecy, I the Lord have enticed that prophet, and I will stretch out My hand against him and destroy him from among My people Israel. They will bear their guilt—the prophet will be as guilty as the one who consults him.

The final line here seems unfair: God deceives a prophet in order to deceive the people and then punishes the people and the prophet. If the people earlier sinned in order to deserve this treatment, what did the prophet do? Perhaps the prophets also have pasts that lead to this point. Certainly, in the case of Micaiah, the impression one gets is that these prophets have long been in the false-prophecy business, telling the king what he wants to hear rather than the will of God. The Talmud asserts that the false prophets should have realized that their "prophecy" was a false one, because "no two prophets prophesy in the same style" (B. *Sanhedrin* 89b). This implies that a prophet constantly has to be checking her own experiences, interrogating whether this supposed prophetic experience was a real one or not.[4]

Obviously our case is different: God does not tell Abraham to sacrifice Isaac because of any deserved punishment. As a general principle, however, these cases are instructive. There is no guarantee that communication with God yields the correct answer. God may intentionally deceive. Or, in the case at hand, the prophet may simply incompletely comprehend. The prophecy is true but wrong.

Buber's approach to the Akedah is worth another brief discussion here. As we have already seen, Buber argues in "On the Suspension of the Ethical" that any reader of the story must raise the question of whether Abraham has *heard* correctly, before wondering what the appropriate *response* ought to be:[5] "Where, therefore, the 'suspension' of the ethical is concerned, the question of questions which takes precedence over every other is: Are you really addressed by the Absolute or by one of his apes?"[6] Buber is explicitly responding to what he (correctly) perceives as the dangers of Kierkegaard's reading of the narrative: "Ours is an age in which the suspension of the ethical fills the world in a caricaturized form.... False absolutes rule over the soul .... In the realm of Moloch honest men lie and compassionate men torture. And they really and truly believe that brother-murder will prepare the way for brotherhood!"[7]

Buber's question allows us to sharpen the point about prophecy that is true but wrong. For Maimonides, as we have seen, Abraham heard *correctly* but *incompletely*. By the end of the Akedah, however, he has heard *completely*. Abraham did not obey an ape rather than God: it was God both times. And yet God's will cannot be fully discerned from one revelation alone.[8] This thought brings us then to the final question: why did the angel stop Abraham from sacrificing Isaac?

Why Does God Not Want Child Sacrifice?

We return once more to the interplay of the two revelations to Abraham in the Akedah and the relationship between them. In the interpretation argued for here, the first revelation was true but an incomplete expression of the divine will, and the second, by completing it, overturned the conclusion of the first: God does not desire human sacrifice. The

REJECTING CHILD SACRIFICE

advantage of this interpretation is that the plain sense of the text, that God desired Abraham to sacrifice Isaac, does not have to be rejected, and yet by the end of the chapter, this has been eclipsed by an even stronger desire that Abraham *not* sacrifice Isaac. However, the biblical scholar Jon Levenson has argued against the latter half of this claim:

> [Many scholars] interpret the repeal of the demand as a repudiation of the underlying practice, without asking why the God who finally opposes child sacrifice initially commands it. Ezekiel in a similar situation has, as we have seen, an answer to this quandary: God gave Israel "laws that were not good . . . that [He] might render them desolate" (20:25–26). But nothing in Gen 22:1–19 suggests that the command to immolate Isaac in v 2 should be regarded as a law that is other than good. . . . In the Akedah, there is a commendation of the obedient father that is the reverse of the repudiation that so many scholars think they hear in this disquieting story.[9]

Indeed! The command to offer Isaac as a sacrifice was not "not good," and the obedient father certainly deserves commendation for his willingness to follow the command—and yet this story is in fact a repudiation of the underlying practice.

To complete the picture, one further point must be developed. Given the understandable desire on the part of people to offer their children as sacrifices and the understandable desire on the part of God to accept such sacrifices, we need to ask: so why are they rejected? Why does God *not* allow Abraham to carry through with the sacrifice of his son, so we would have not 'Akedat Yiṣḥaq, "the Binding of Isaac," but Sheḥiṭat Yiṣḥaq, "the Slaughtering of Isaac"?

To understand what the Torah is rejecting, closer attention must be paid to the logic of child sacrifice. It makes excellent religious sense that a person should want to sacrifice his most precious possessions to God and that God should be pleased with such an offering. The Bible takes for granted that this is a natural impulse: the first humans to acquire or produce anything, Cain and Abel, then offer some of their possessions on the altar.

Is a child a possession? This is not a simple question to answer. Children are literally the creation of their parents, and it is obvious that parents are entitled—in fact, obligated—to make many decisions for their children. No one could realistically claim that the autonomy a child deserves at birth or at a young age is tantamount to the autonomy deserved by adults. Children are dependent, and this affects their standing before the courts, before society, and before God.

The Laws of Hammurabi (§229–30) state:

> If a builder builds a house for a person, and does not construct it properly, and the house which he built falls and kills its owner, that builder shall be put to death.
> If it kills the son of the owner, the son of that builder shall be put to death.

The punishment, it could be argued, is perfectly just: one person killed another's son, so his own son must be put to death.[10] This is just *if the son is an adjunct of the father*. In the same way that a person who kills a neighbor's sheep is punished by the loss of his own sheep, a person who kills a neighbor's child is punished by the loss of his own child. On the assumption that the child is fundamentally defined as "his father's child," and not a person of his own, this law is elegant in its simplicity and its application of justice to the case at hand.

Does biblical thought share this assumption? The Bible apparently distinguishes between what God may do and what humans must do. God repeatedly claims to exact punishment from children for the sins of the parents.[11] Some prophets rejected this possibility, however.[12] The Rabbis comment on this discrepancy and provide a diachronic explanation for the difference: "R. Yose b. Ḥanina said: Moses our teacher instigated four decrees on Israel, which were later abolished by four prophets. . . . Moses said, 'He visits the sin of the father on the children,' but Ezekiel came along and abolished it: 'The soul that sins—it shall die.'"[13] Interestingly, modern scholars also think that there were diachronic changes in this regard and that various social changes led to changing standards of morality.[14] It is theologically coherent for God to act according to the best human norms of the day.

This is all in the divine realm, however. Consistently in biblical law, human courts are barred from doing so: "Fathers shall not be put to death because of their sons, and sons shall not be put to death because of the fathers; each person shall be put to death for his own sins" (Deut. 24:16).[15] More specifically, the very law stipulated in the Laws of Hammurabi is rejected in Exodus 21:28–31:

> If an ox gores a man or a woman, who dies, the ox shall surely be stoned, and its flesh may not be consumed, but the owner of the ox is not culpable. . . . If it gores a son or daughter, the same law shall be applied to him.

The final clause is best understood as a rejection of the practice elsewhere, which would have dictated that "if it gores a son or a daughter, the son or daughter of the ox's owner shall be put to death." Again, this is rejected by biblical law, which treats children as full people in this law. An ox that gores a person, child or adult, is to be put to death.

Why does the biblical law part ways with its Mesopotamian counterparts? The issue seems to be precisely the status of the child.[16] While in Mesopotamia children were legally seen as the property of their parents, and therefore appropriate vehicles for punishment of the parents, this was rejected in biblical thought. If this is rejected, other results follow. Primary for our purposes is the question of child sacrifice.

When the child is property of the parents, it makes eminently good sense that the child should be offered as a sacrifice by the parents. Recall the inscriptions from the tophets: "To my lady, Tanit, face of

Ba'al, and to the lord, to Ba'al Ḥammon, that which [the parents] vowed." The child has lost its life because of the vow of the parents. In fact, the child may have only been born in order to give the parents the opportunity to fulfill their vow. Child sacrifice depends on the assumption that the child is fully a possession of the parents.

If the Bible rejects this, it must reject child sacrifice as well. If the child is granted status as an autonomous individual, dependent for practical purposes on the parents but conceptually and legally independent, child sacrifice is simply murder. The murder of one person by another, against the victim's will, as an act of devotion, cannot be tolerated. Once children are seen as individuals, the same conclusion holds.

This, then, is the religious and philosophical dynamic of the Akedah. God commands Abraham to offer Isaac on the altar, reflecting God's sincere desire for human sacrifice. It is tempting to God, and tempting to God's servant, that the most precious possession be offered as a burnt offering, completely sacrificed to God. Abraham correctly understands this desire of God's and dutifully obeys. Abraham later—just in time—understands that although this is all correct, it is superseded by a more powerful lesson God has to teach: children, like all other human beings, cannot be mere adjuncts in someone else's religious experience. And so this is the ethical teaching of the Akedah: as much as it is enticing to do so, one person's religious fulfillment cannot come through harm to another. The trial of Abraham cannot involve the murder of Isaac.

Conclusion

The Demands of God and People

The notion that sincere individual faith can license the suspension of all ethical considerations is a deeply dangerous idea. If we are persuaded by Kierkegaard that when a person of faith claims to have a revelation, the rest of the world can only step back and observe, neither assenting nor condemning but only watching in admiration, we have ceded all rights to insist on societal values and norms. Thus, Kierkegaard's view, although offered as an interpretation of the story of the Akedah in Genesis 22, should not be taken as the meaning of that text.

The stakes here are not trivial. Many religious people do seek guidance in biblical stories, so how we read them makes all the difference. Reading Genesis 22 with Kierkegaard leads to an inability to explain why someone whose religion obligates them to marry more than one person, or to refuse contraceptive coverage, or to deny vaccinations to their children, or to shoot a mosque full of people, or to fly a plane into a building full of people is wrong. (And this is not, of course, to equate these acts morally.) According to Kierkegaard, all we could do would be to say that ethically speaking, these acts are wrong, but the person of faith may teleologically suspend the ethical.

We have seen over the course of the preceding pages that there is good reason to reject Kierkegaard's interpretation of the Akedah. Until the nineteenth century, the Jewish interpretive tradition did not see the "teleological suspension of the ethical" as the meaning or the import of the Akedah, and for good reason. The reading does not do

149

justice to the text, conflicts profoundly with fundamentals of Jewish thought and practice, and yields ethically unacceptable positions.

Having already articulated the crux of the alternative position, found in Maimonides, that is ethically preferable, I will close with Levinas again and a return to Caravaggio. Levinas, it will be recalled, emphasized that both halves of the narrative, and both revelations to Abraham, had to be appreciated: "That he obeyed the first voice is astonishing: that he had sufficient distance with respect to that obedience to obey the second voice—that is the essential."[1] This is the significant interpretive move found in Maimonides as well. For both the twelfth-century Spanish halakhist and rationalist and the twentieth-century Lithuanian-French religious phenomenologist, the key to the Akedah is in absorbing the lesson of the latter part of the narrative—the rejection of the sacrifice of Isaac—without abandoning the former part of the narrative—the command to offer Isaac as a sacrifice.

An intriguing question for the various interpreters is the identity of the "angel" in the story. The Hebrew mal'akh (like the Greek angelos) means simply "messenger," and of course God could use many different messengers. Fleshing out Levinas's approach, it has been suggested that the messenger is none other than Isaac himself: the Other, the face confronting Abraham.[2] It is when Abraham sees Isaac's face and perceives in him an Other, a full-fledged individual with an identity and personality of his own, that Abraham is commanded to not kill. As Levinas writes elsewhere, "To see a face is already to hear 'You shall not kill.'"[3] This is the most profound lesson: the need to appreciate that every other human being has the same autonomy and rights as I do.

Rabbinic texts are attuned to this basic principle: seeing the face of another is decentering. If I take note of another person in front of me, I can no longer think that I am most central: what makes her any less central than me? A midrash in Vayyiqra Rabbah,[4] for example, ponders the call of the beggar on the street, Zekhi bi, literally, "Give me charity." Rabbi Ḥaggai says, however, that it sounds like *Sekhi bi*, "Look at me!" He explains, "Look at me! Look at what I was, and look at what I am now." That act of looking—simply observing that this is a person before me—is central to the practice of charity, as it decenters our sense of the world. It is for just that reason that it is so natural to avert one's eyes from a beggar on the subway or the street. Looking at the beggar's face means grappling with his or her personhood, and this decentering is disconcerting.

This basic idea lies at the heart of the "Golden Rule," so ubiquitous that its radicality is sometimes missed. "Do not do to others as you would not want done to you," as Hillel expresses it in the Talmud,[5] or "Do to others as you want them to do to you," as Jesus formulates it (Matt. 7:12; Luke 6:31), the rule enjoins me to fundamentally realize that the next person has all the feelings, aspirations, pains, and self-centeredness that I do. Once that is fully absorbed, all else follows.

Within biblical law, this core teaching underlies the injunction "If you see your fellow's ass or ox fallen upon the road, do not ignore it! You must surely help him lift it" (Deut. 22:4). As biblical scholar Michael Fishbane perceived, this asks the person to overcome a state of "being within-oneself" and begin to see what is before oneself. It is so easy to see the world as centered around me. The law forces me to take account of the parallel experience of another.[6]

In chapter 5 we looked at Caravaggio's *The Sacrifice of Isaac*, where the artist drew our attention to the eye of Isaac, staring at us in terror from the canvas. To conclude, we turn to another painting of Caravaggio. The subject of this untitled work is debated. It is sometimes identified as a painting of Saint John the Baptist, but some have argued that this 1602 work, now in the Musei Capitolini in Rome, actually depicts "Isaac Laughing."[7]

Whether this identification reflects the original intention or not is difficult to say, but it does make good sense of the image. The boy rises from the altar, embracing the ram, who will take his place as a sacrifice and thus allow him to live. The laughter on his face,[8] his half-turned

Fig. 3. Caravaggio, untitled, Musei Capitolini, Rome, ca. 1602,
https://commons.wikimedia.org/wiki/File:Caravaggio_(Michelangelo
Merisi)-_Saint_John_the_Baptist_-_Google_Art_Project.jpg.

body, the embrace—this is the high point of a great drama, as Isaac is saved. The focus on Isaac has already been seen in Caravaggio. What this painting contributes is the end of the story. Removing Abraham from the picture altogether—an extraordinary omission in a painting of the Akedah[9]—allows the viewer's attention to focus exclusively on Isaac. And this is the crucial point: Isaac has finally been unbound.

If we may be so bold as to draw a lesson from the interpretation of the Akedah propounded here, it is that if confronted by a conflict between a divine imperative and our obligations toward other human beings, we should seek out the face of the Other. By doing so, we may be privileged to an even deeper understanding of the religious imperatives, and we may discover that these obligations and the obligations to the human Other are merely two sides of the same coin.

Life is messier than theology. There are times when we—even we—must kill another for a greater good. Examples are unfortunately too easy to think of, as they occur on a daily basis, even if the merits of many specific examples can be debated. But this sacrifice of another is necessitated not by faith, but by other Others. To protect some, one may be sacrificed; perhaps the performance or even planning of certain acts forfeits one's right to life. I do not deign to write the formulas for this moral calculus; as a society, we operate on the assumption that this is a legitimate calculus to employ. All this differs from theology. Here, the Akedah teaches, my faith cannot be proved and my merit cannot be secured through violence against another.

For Kierkegaard and the Malbim, the fact that Abraham was alone with God on the mountaintop is critical to understanding the religious point of the story: the fundamentally personal nature of faith, the incommunicability of religious devotion, the zealousness of the faithful that trumps even one's own moral compass. But in reality, Abraham was not alone on the mountain. Isaac was there as well, and despite the praise of Abraham as the knight of faith, it was Isaac whose life was actually on the line. Here is where these readings falter. It is all well and good to celebrate the personal and individual faith that animates some people's lives, but a society cannot afford to allow individuals' sense of religious devotion to take precedence over the welfare of others. As a society, we must allow knights of faith to ascend the mountain to be alone with God. But we must not allow them to bring Isaac along.

SOURCE ACKNOWLEDGMENTS

Excerpts from Uri Zvi Greenberg's "The Morning Sacrifice" are taken from *Uri Zvi Greenberg: The Collected Writings*, ed. Dan Miron (Jerusalem: Bialik, 1996), vol. 11, and appear by permission of David Greenberg. Text © the estate of the poet.

Excerpts from Uri Zvi Greenberg's "1923" are taken from *The Book of Indictment and Faith*, from Greenberg, *The Complete Writings*, ed. Dan Miron (Jerusalem: Bialik, 1991), vol. 3, and appear by permission of David Greenberg. Text © the estate of the poet.

Sebastian Brock's translation "Sarah and the Akedah" is taken from *Le Muséon* 87 (1974): 67–77 and appears by permission of Sebastian Brock.

Adam Baruch's "Akedah: Afterword" is taken from *Al Tishlaḥ Yadekha el ha-Naʾar*, ed. Arieh Ben-Gurion (Jerusalem: Keter, 2002), and appears by permission of Shira Aviad.

Excerpts from Hanoch Levin's *I Don't Understand You, Dad* are taken from *Mah Ikhpat la-Tzippor: Satires, Skits, Hymns* (Tel Aviv: ha-Kibbutz ha-Meʾuḥad, 1987) and appear by permission of Shimrit Ron, director of the Hanoch Levin Institute for Israeli Drama.

Bernard Septimus's translation "A Medieval Judeo-Spanish Poem on the Complementarity of Faith and Works and Its Intellectual Roots" is taken from *New Perspectives on Jewish-Christian Relations in Honor of David Berger*, ed. Elisheva Carlebach and Jacob J. Schacter (Leiden: Brill, 2012), and appears by permission of Bernard Septimus.

NOTES

Introduction

1. Bar-Asher, "Notes on Reading '*Aḥizat Moledet*,'" 71–72.
2. Auerbach, *Mimesis*, 3–23, and esp. 12. See also Redfield, "Behind Auerbach's 'Background,'" 121–50.
3. See the similar summary in Shinan, "Synagogues in the Land of Israel," 130–35.
4. Augustine, *Contra Faustum* 22.73.
5. See Greenstein, "Reading Pragmatically," 102–32.
6. Spiegel, "*Me-Aggadot ha-'Akedah*," translated as *The Last Trial*.
7. This text is found in the English translation on 148–49 and on 543–44 in the original Hebrew publication.
8. Kasher, "How Could God Command," 38–39.
9. Irshai, "The New Ascent of 'Akedah Theology,'" 273–304; Irshai, "Homosexuality and the 'Akedah Theology,'" 19–46; Irshai, "Religion and Morality," 1–17.

1. Jewish Experiences of the Akedah

1. On the antiquity of the merit of the Akedah conception, see Spiegel, *The Last Trial*, 86–120.
2. For the poem, see Septimus, "*Ḥananto le-Meah Peri*," 93; for comments, see Münz-Manor, "Narrating Salvation," 161–63.
3. Septimus makes this argument in "*Ḥananto le-Meah Peri*," 79–95.
4. For the question of languages in liturgical poems, see Kister, "*Shirat Bene Ma'arava*," 154.
5. *Tanḥuma* §18. For the use of the verse from Psalm 8:5 in connection with the Akedah, see already Tosefta *Soṭah* 6:5: "This passage [Psalm 8] was said about Isaac at the time of the Akedah."
6. Similar motifs are found, plausibly, at Qumran already, especially in 4Q225. For more on the motif of the jealous angels, and the relevance of

this motif to the Akedah, see M. Bernstein, "Angels at the Akedah," esp. 271–75. For an ambitious reconstruction of 4Q225, bringing it in line with later texts on the Akedah, see Kugel, "Exegetical Notes on 4Q225."

7. *Midrash Tanḥuma* (ed. Buber), Vayyera §46.

8. It seems likely, based on Jubilees and other texts, that there was a different, perhaps earlier, tradition of connecting the Akedah to Pesaḥ. The abandonment of this tradition is likely connected, at least in part, to the rise of the Christian tradition, which saw a triangle in the paschal sacrifice, the Akedah, and the crucifixion of Jesus.

9. B. *Rosh ha-Shanah* 16a.

10. The word for "mercy," *raḥamim*, means "love" in Aramaic. There may be a bilingual wordplay here, which leaves open the question of whether the primary emotion felt by Abraham toward Isaac on the altar was "love" or "mercy."

11. This is from the *Zikhronot* blessing in the *Musaf* prayer for Rosh Hashanah.

12. *Vayyiqra Rabbah*, Vayyiqra §2.

13. See G. Cohen, "The Story of Hannah and Her Seven Sons," and Joslyn-Siemiatkoski, "The Mother and Seven Sons."

14. Abraham is the heroic figure appealed to throughout the book.

15. B. *Gittin* 57b. See also the discussion in Spiegel, *The Last Trial*, 13–16. Oz and Oz-Salzberger, *Jews and Words*, 77, note that this woman is unusual within Jewish literature, "closer to Medea or Lady Macbeth than to most Jewish mothers, including the rough, primeval biblical brand." Note that the term *'akedah* in this passage means "offering," not "binding" (as the etymology would have it). This is true for many texts from the medieval and later periods.

16. Mintz, *Ḥurban*, 6, 90–92. In the realm of Jewish law, this same stance led to the privileging of communal custom of the "holy community" as authoritative. See Ta-Shma, "Law, Custom and Tradition."

17. The text is from the "Mainz Anonymous" chronicle, in Habermann, *Gezerot Ashkenaz ve-Tzarfat*, 96.

18. Yerushalmi, *Zakhor*, 38.

19. From most to least skeptical are the views of Ivan Marcus, Jeremy Cohen, and Robert Chazan. For representative publications, see I. Marcus, "From Politics to Martyrdom"; J. Cohen, *Sanctifying the Name of God*; Chazan, *God, Humanity, and History*.

20. For discussion, see Kanarek, "He Took the Knife," esp. 86.

21. No such verse exists; the chronicler has combined Isaiah 33:7 with something like Joel 2:10 or 4:15. Interestingly, in the Palestinian triennial cycle, Isaiah 33:7 was the haftarah for the reading of Genesis 22, suggesting an ancient association of that verse with this narrative.

22. Joel 2:10 and 4:15.

23. See Isaiah 5:30. Note that *ṣar* is taken to be part of the compound subject of *ḥašakh* by Rashi and other commentators *ad loc.*

24. Solomon b. Simson chronicle, in Habermann, *Gezerot Ashkenaz ve-Tzarfat*, 32. See the citations in Yerushalmi, *Zakhor*, 38; and Chazan, *European Jewry and the First Crusade*, 256. On the motif of the Akedah in the Crusade chronicles and other texts, see further Spiegel, *The Last Trial*, 17–28; Roos, *"God Wants It!"*, 87–105; Jeremy Cohen's analysis of the "Rachel of Mainz" story in *Sanctifying the Name of God*, 106–29; Yuval, *Two Nations in Your Womb*, 154–59.

25. See, for instance, the poem "The Lord Tests the Righteous" in Habermann, *Gezerot Ashkenaz ve-Tzarfat*, 111–12.

26. Translation from Spiegel, *The Last Trial*, 152; Spiegel, "Me-Aggadot ha-Akedah," 546.

27. Habermann, *Gezerot Ashkenaz ve-Tzarfat*, 43; see also Roos, *"God Wants It!"*, 91–92.

28. Theodor and Albeck, *Bereshit Rabbah*, 603, §56:12.

29. The attempts to deny that Christian martyrdoms were common (e.g., Moss, *The Myth of Persecution*) are not persuasive. Besides the hermeneutic of suspicion employed throughout the book—if any of the details in a story are implausible, the whole story is suspect—with regard to the Christian texts themselves, no attention is paid to other accounts, such as in Rabbinic literature, of Christian martyrdoms.

30. For the idea, if not the term, see also Boyarin, *Dying for God*.

31. The translated text is from the Palestinian *Targum* known as *Pseudo-Jonathan*, since it is often printed as *Targum Jonathan* but in fact has nothing to do with Jonathan ben 'Uzziel. A closely similar dialogue is reported in Theodor and Albeck, *Bereshit Rabbah*, 587–88, §56:4.

32. Saperstein, "A Sermon on the Akedah," 103, explains that sermons were usually offered on the beginning of the weekly Torah portion, not the end.

33. The text was published by Roth, "A Hebrew Elegy," 138. The original has an A-A-A-B rhyme scheme: *Ve-rav Yehuda teḥilla / asher haya ish tehilla / hiqriv ishto le-'olah / u-banav be-qerev yisra'el.*

34. On this choice, and the difference or lack thereof between German and Spanish Jews in the choices made under similar terrible circumstances, see Ben-Shalom, *"Kiddush Hashem."*

35. On the course of riots, based on fine-grained documentary evidence, see Gampel, *Anti-Jewish Riots,* 13–184.

36. For a succinct overview of Crescas's life and work, see Ben-Shalom, "Hasdai Crescas"; and Harvey, *Rabbi Ḥasdai Crescas.*

37. For the royal attempts to secure the safety of Crescas's family, see Gampel, *Anti-Jewish Riots,* 108–10.

38. Crescas's letter was included in the *Shevet Yehudah* of Solomon ibn Virga, a Spanish Jewish physician who lived a century later. In the Jerusalem 1991 edition, the letter appears on 248–50, and the quotation on 249.

39. Saperstein, "A Sermon on the Akedah," 111–13.

40. Gampel, *Anti-Jewish Riots,* 113n41, noting, "nothing of which is reflected in any of the documents."

41. Translation from Saperstein, "A Sermon on the Akedah," 111; Hebrew text on 121, lines 117–19.

42. Isaac Arama, a Spanish Jew of the fifteenth century, rejected this notion: "A person should not say, 'If God commands me to sacrifice this child of mine to Him, I would do it, like Abraham our father!' . . . The sacrifice of children, and their slaughter, is not pleasing to Him, may He be blessed, but only the submission and the subjugation." Arama, *Akedat Yiṣḥak: Bereshit,* 21; see Saperstein, "A Sermon on the Akedah," 115.

43. Barugel, *The* Sacrifice of Isaac *in Spanish and Sephardic Balladry.*

44. Barugel, *The* Sacrifice of Isaac *in Spanish and Sephardic Balladry,* 206.

45. Theodor and Albeck, *Bereshit Rabbah* 592–93, §55:8.

46. This may be suggested by the parallel drawn between Abraham's actions and those of Balaam. According to the midrash, the latter wakes up and saddles his own donkey out of hatred for the people he is going to curse. Thus, Abraham may be acting out of love for the person he is to sacrifice.

47. This poem is by R. Eliezer b. Nathan (Mainz, d. mid-twelfth century), published in Habermann, *Gezerot Ashkenaz ve-Tzarfat,* 86, discussed in this regard by Elitzur, *"Akedat Yitshak."*

48. U. Greenberg, "The Morning Sacrifice," 53.

49. Bahat, *Uri Zvi Greenberg,* 248. In this chapter, "The Akedah and the Jewish Tradition in His Poetry" (240–53), Bahat argues that Greenberg wants an Akedah, whereas the Jewish tradition resisted it and protested its immorality, concluding that Greenberg is more Christian than Jewish in this

regard. As the present chapter shows, this is not a fair depiction of pre-modern Jewish thought.

50. U. Greenberg, *The Book of Indictment and Faith*, 107.

51. This dynamic of real protests against God garbed in a style that is ostensibly pious is a major theme of Weiss, *Pious Irreverence*.

52. Although the word *raḥamin* properly means "love" in Aramaic, the phraseology here is clearly drawn from the Hebrew liturgical line "may your mercy overcome your anger" (*she-yikhbeshu raḥamekha et ka'askha*), found in B. *Berakhot* and in the liturgy in various places. Still there may well be bilingual wordplay at work, with Isaac goading his father to let his anger triumph over both his Aramaic "love" and his Hebrew "mercy." See also n. 10 above.

53. Text from Yahalom and Sokoloff, *Shirat Bene Ma'arava*, 126. See also M. Bernstein, "Angels at the Akedah," 286–87.

54. Van Bekkum, "Bound in Righteousness," esp. 154–55.

55. Münz-Manor, "Narrating Salvation," reads the dynamic somewhat differently here, also emphasizing "Abraham's hesitancy," but seeing Isaac as driven by "martyrological passion." The question is whether his passion is so extreme that it is meant to be somewhat parodic—as understood here—or sincere—as Münz-Manor reads it.

56. Münz-Manor, "Narrating Salvation," 163–64.

57. The text was published by Elitzur, *Rabbi El'azar be-Rabbi Qillir*, 185; see Elitzur's discussion of this motif in her introduction, 67–73, and in expanded form in an article, "Did Abraham Sin?," 221–23.

58. These passages are all cited in Elitzur, "Did Abraham Sin?," 221–23.

59. See Carmy, "Paradox, Paradigm, and the Birth of Inwardness," 466n14, noting that this understanding of the mishnah is reflected in the Yerushalmi, as well.

60. Theodor and Albeck, *Bereshit Rabbah*, 599, §56:4.

61. It is textually unclear who will consider Abraham a murderer. Some manuscripts have *hu omer*, "He [God] will say," and others have *'wmr*, which could be read as *'omar*, "I will say." See the apparatus in Theodor and Albeck, *Bereshit Rabbah*, 599.

62. Shagar, *Faith Shattered and Restored*, 8–9.

63. On this phenomenon in other biblical and Rabbinic texts, see Koller, "On Texts, Contexts, and Countertexts," 328–31.

64. The same is true in other Christian retellings. See, for instance, Pap. Bodmer 30, translated and discussed by van der Horst, "A New Early Christian

Poem." Here Abraham immediately tells Sarah of the delightful command he received from God, and Sarah responds with a speech to Isaac: "Keep courage, my dear child, for you have been happy in this life."

65. Brock, "Two Syriac Verse Homilies," text on 117–18, translation on 123 (with slight modifications here).

66. See discussion, with some examples, in Brock, "Sarah and the Akedah," 67–77.

67. For fuller discussion of the speeches given to Sarah in the Syriac poems, see Brock, "Two Syriac Verse Homilies," 70–76. On the role of Sarah in this poem, and the educational value of that role, see Eastman, "The Matriarch as Model," 241–59.

68. Text published in Brock, *Soghyatha Mgabbyatha*, 71.

69. *Va-yikra Rabbah* 29:9, and see the discussion of Weiss, *Pious Irreverence*, 62–63 and 209–10nn17–20.

70. For discussion, see J. Baumgarten, *Introduction to Old Yiddish Literature*, and especially Roman, "Early Ashkenazic Poems about the Binding of Isaac," who compares the Akedah *piyyuṭim* to the *Yudisher Shtam*.

71. For the text, see Frakes, *Early Yiddish Texts*, 316–28, and for the translation, see Frakes, *Early Yiddish Epic*, 149–55, here at 153. For a full study, see Matenko and Sloan, "The Aqedath Jiṣḥaq," 3–70.

72. Translation slightly modified from Frakes, *Early Yiddish Epic*, 154.

73. See B. *Qiddushin* 42b and elsewhere.

74. Frakes, *Early Yiddish Epic*, 155.

75. For a good survey, see Sagi, "The Meaning of the Akedah," 45–60.

76. Roskies, "The Holocaust According to the Literary Critics," 215.

77. See the analysis in Y. Feldman, *Glory and Agony*, 173–74.

78. Mintz, "Haim Gouri at 90," 36–39.

79. Elberg, *'Akedas Treblinke*.

80. See the discussion of G. Greenberg, "Ultra-Orthodox Reflections on the Holocaust," esp. 108, and further Akedah-oriented theological responses on 107–12.

81. Reiser, *Derashot mi-Shnot ha-Za'am*, 160–63, quotations from 162.

82. See Owen, *The Poems of Wilfred Owen*, 43.

83. Owen did not only blame the Akedah for the mentality of the soldiers prepared to die. He also looked askance at the ideology of patriotism, most famously in the poem "Dulce et Decorum est" (*Poems*, 60), which ends, "If you could hear, at every jolt, the blood / Come gargling from the froth-corrupted lungs, / Obscene as cancer, bitter as the cud / Of vile, incurable

sores on innocent tongues, / My friend, you would not tell with such high zest / To children ardent for some desperate glory, / The old Lie; Dulce et Decorum est / Pro patria mori." He also turned his attention to the passion of Jesus as a tragic model for people, especially in "At a Calvary near the Ancre" (*Poems*, 45).

84. L. Cohen, "The Story of Isaac." On Cohen's use of the Akedah in "The Story of Isaac" and his different take on it in "You Want It Darker" (2016), with the refrain, "*Hineni, hineni—*I'm ready, my Lord," see Diamond, "A Farewell 'Hineni' to Eliezer, the Cohen of Song."

85. On the Akedah in Israeli poetry, see Kartun-Blum, *A Story Like a Knife*; Kartun-Blum, *Profane Scriptures*; Forti, "The Topos of the 'Binding of Isaac.'" An anthology of Akedah-related poetry was edited by Arye Ben-Gurion, *Al Tishlaḥ Yadekha*. On the Akedah in Israeli narrative prose, see Y. Feldman, *Glory and Agony*. For the visual arts, see Ofrat, "The Binding of Isaac in Israeli Art," 124–53.

86. Y. Feldman, "From 'the Death of Holy Ones,' to 'the Joy of the Akedah,'" 107–51.

87. See the survey in Zerubavel, "*Qerav, Haqravah, Qorban*," esp. 67–69 and 75–81.

88. See Ohana, *The Origins of Israeli Mythology*, 117–22; Greenblum, "The Making of a Myth," esp. 141–42.

89. D. Knohl, *Siege in the Hills of Hebron*, 11. Note, too, that the third section in the book—in which the battles are actually narrated—is entitled "The Sacrifice."

90. See Y. Feldman, *Glory and Agony*, 42–128, for the surprisingly varied voices channeling the Akedah in Zionist culture in the years through World War II.

91. Baruch, "Akedah: Afterword," cited by Y. Feldman, *Glory and Agony*, 107 and discussed there on 108.

92. Levin, *Mah Ikhpat le-Tzippor*, 89–91. The text is also available at http://www .hanochlevin.com/sketches1-03/p89 (accessed February 2016).

93. The most famous example of the latter is the book *Siaḥ Loḥamim*, edited by Avraham Shapira. Note that this book was first published in October 1967, just *four months* after the June war.

94. This seems to be a mistake on Levin's part; according to the biblical narrative, Sarah was ninety at Isaac's birth, and Abraham was one hundred, and there is no obvious reason for a purposeful change.

2. Kierkegaard

1. See Patten, *Hegel's Idea of Freedom*, 25 and *passim*.
2. Kierkegaard's notes on Schelling's lectures are translated in Kierkegaard, *The Concept of Irony/Schelling Lecture Notes*. The editors' introduction to the volume is very helpful on this period in Kierkegaard's life.
3. Letter to Emil Boesen, February 27, 1842, in Kierkegaard, *Letters and Documents*, 139–40, and see also the very similar next letter, #70, addressed to his brother on 141–42.
4. He was profoundly affected by Hegel, even as he tried to see a way through him or around him; see especially Stewart, *Kierkegaard's Relations to Hegel Reconsidered*. In Copenhagen, too, there was no escape from Hegel: the Danish philosopher Hans Lassen Martensen, a lecturer (and later a professor) at the University of Copenhagen and a devoted preacher of Hegel, particularly provoked Kierkegaard.
5. Aroosi, "The Causes of Bourgeois Culture," 71–92.
6. See Kierkegaard, "A First and Last Declaration," 527–31, esp. 529, and the comments of Evans, *Kierkegaard's Ethic of Love*, 38. (Climacus is another pseudonym of Kierkegaard's, but the "first and last declaration" is signed by Kierkegaard himself.) For an overview of approaches to the question of pseudonymy, see Poole, "The Unknown Kierkegaard," 48–75.
7. See especially Evans, *Kierkegaard's Ethic of Love*, 63–66, and contra, e.g., Kemp, "In Defense of a Straightforward Reading," 49–70.
8. In fact, Evans, *Kierkegaard's Ethics of Love*, 61–84, argues that "ethics" means something different in *Fear and Trembling* than in Kierkegaard's other books.
9. Westphal, *Kierkegaard's Critique of Reason and Society*, 78–81, notes that whereas Hegel found the state to be the locus of divinity in the world, Kierkegaard points to Jesus and Abraham. Further on Hegel as the target of Kierkegaard's criticisms, see Westphal, 76; Evans, *Kierkegaard's Ethic of Love*, 66–71; and Simmons, "What About Isaac?," esp. 323–24.
10. Kierkegaard, *Fear and Trembling*, 22.
11. Kierkegaard, *Fear and Trembling*, 23–24.
12. Kierkegaard, *Fear and Trembling*, 29.
13. Kierkegaard, *Fear and Trembling*, 30.
14. Crocker, "Sacrifice in Kierkegaard's *Fear and Trembling*," 125–39, esp. 128.
15. Kierkegaard, *Fear and Trembling*, 39.
16. Kierkegaard, *Fear and Trembling*, 51.

17. Kierkegaard, *Fear and Trembling*, 66.

18. Kierkegaard, *Fear and Trembling*: "The tragic hero is soon finished and at peace; he makes the infinite movement and is now secure in the universal. The knight of faith, on the contrary, is kept sleepless, for he is constantly being tried" (68). "Abraham is therefore at no moment a tragic hero but something entirely different, either a murderer or a believer. Abraham lacks the middle term that saves the tragic hero. That is why I can understand a tragic hero but cannot understand Abraham, even though in a certain demented sense I admire him more than all others" (52).

19. Kierkegaard, *Fear and Trembling*, 20.

20. Kierkegaard, *Fear and Trembling*, 52.

21. Kierkegaard, *Fear and Trembling*, 100.

22. This is emphasized by Tilley, "Rereading the Teleological Suspension," 145–70.

23. Blanshard, *Reason and Belief*, 235.

24. See also the comments of Outka, "God as the Subject of Unique Veneration," 214–15.

25. Kierkegaard, *Fear and Trembling*, 49.

26. Kierkegaard, *Fear and Trembling*, 49.

27. Kierkegaard, *Fear and Trembling*, 106.

28. For this idea, Kierkegaard did not need Hegel in particular. All of his contemporary Protestant liberal thinkers were working to equate religion with ethics, casting Jesus as primarily a teacher of ethics; see Evans, *Kierkegaard's Ethic of Love*, 83.

29. Kierkegaard, *Fear and Trembling*, 47; see also 60–61.

30. Climacus (Kierkegaard), *Concluding Unscientific Postscript*, 44–45.

31. According to Rae, "Kierkegaard, the Self, Authenticity," 75–97, *Fear and Trembling* is primarily about authenticity to the self, which is not wrong, but ignores the religious nature of the authenticity envisioned, and "to the self" may not fully capture what Johannes says about Abraham's motivation, which is both "for God" and "for himself" simultaneously.

32. Kierkegaard, *On Authority and Revelation*, 178–89.

33. Kierkegaard, *On Authority and Revelation*, 182.

34. He was a direct student of Martensen (see n. 4 above).

35. On Adler himself, see Koch, "Adolph Peter Adler," 1–22.

36. Sagi, *Kierkegaard, Religion, and Existence*, 115–35.

37. Sontag, "Introduction to the Torchbook Edition," vii-xl, esp. xxxiii.

38. Kierkegaard, *On Authority and Revelation*, 27–28.

39. Kierkegaard, *On Authority and Revelation*, 46.
40. Kierkegaard, *On Authority and Revelation*, 15.
41. See his commentary on Genesis 22:4, for example.
42. Kierkegaard, *On Authority and Revelation*, 69–142.
43. This aspect of the book is particularly emphasized by Cavell, "Kierkegaard's *On Authority and Revelation*," 165–79, who argues that the book is relevant for the later question of the authenticity of the artist. See also Jones, "Some Remarks on Authority and Revelation in Kierkegaard," 232–51.
44. Westphal, *Kierkegaard's Critique of Reason and Society*, 36–40.
45. Jones, "Some Remarks," 240.
46. Cooper, "Søren Kierkegaard," esp. 48 and 58–59. Cooper writes that, philosophically speaking, this last point is the weakest element in Kierkegaard's thought.
47. Kierkegaard, *Fear and Trembling*, 49.
48. Kierkegaard, *Fear and Trembling*, 63.
49. Kierkegaard, *Fear and Trembling*, 65.
50. Kierkegaard, *Fear and Trembling*, 100.
51. See Simmons, "What About Isaac?," 336.
52. On the Pauline style of Hebrews, see Rothschild, *Hebrews as Pseudepigraphon*.
53. Augustine, *The City of God*, 545.
54. Again, this is likely already found in Paul's letters, in particular Romans 8:32, where Paul speaks of God as "He who did not withhold [*epheisato*] his own son, but gave him up for all of us." This is an echo of Genesis 22:16, where God says to Abraham, "Because you have not withheld [*epheisō*] your only son. . . ." For more on this, see Good, "Isaac Typology in the New Testament"; Paczkowski, "The Sacrifice of Isaac in Early Patristic Exegesis"; Kessler, *Bound by the Bible*, 57–64. Fascinating examples from the Syriac writers Ephraem the Syrian and Jacob of Serūg are discussed by Griffith, "Disclosing the Mystery."
55. Wilken, "Melito, the Jewish Community at Sardis, and the Sacrifice of Isaac," 53–69; see also Clements, "The Parallel Lives of Early Jewish and Christian Texts and Art," 207–40.
56. For the text, see Melito of Sardis, *On Pascha and Fragments*, 74 (Greek) and 75 (English), and see the next fragment on 76–77. See also the discussion in Cohick, *The Peri Pascha Attributed to Melito of Sardis*, 42–44.

57. This insight, in different terms, is Gellman's: see *Abraham! Abraham!*, 43–55.
58. *Mishnah Makkot* 3:16. The translation of the passage from Isaiah is in light of the use made of it by the Mishnah. For further discussion, see Steinmetz, *Punishment and Freedom*, esp. 94–95 with the notes.
59. The poem is found in a fifteenth-century manuscript in the Municipal Library of Porto, Portugal. It was discussed in a paper by Michelle Hamilton in 2006, and the manuscript was described and the poem was published by John Zemke, "In Memorial Charles Cook," 333–47. The poem was further discussed by Septimus, "A Medieval Judeo-Spanish Poem," 227–39, and Hamilton, *Beyond Faith*, 58–87. Much of the analysis here derives from the learned treatments of Septimus and Hamilton.
60. Naḥmanides, commentary on Genesis 22:1. Naḥmanides relies conceptually and linguistically on *Mishnah Makkot* 3:16 here; see Septimus, "A Medieval Judeo-Spanish Poem," 227–39, and further the analysis of Steinmetz, *Punishment and Freedom*, 69–105.
61. See Nissim b. Reuben Gerondi, *Commentary*, 280–81.
62. Kierkegaard, *Fear and Trembling*, 8.
63. According to Zerubavel, "*Qerav, Haqravah, Qorban*," 61–99, the ambiguity of the word "sacrifice" in other languages, particularly Russian, has had profound ideological effects.
64. This is the summary of Crocker, "Sacrifice in Kierkegaard's *Fear and Trembling*," 125.
65. On these parallels, see especially J. Levenson, *The Death and Resurrection of the Beloved Son*, 104–10, with further insights on the significance of these parallels; and Simon, "The Banishment of Ishmael," 377–80.
66. J. Levenson, *Death and Resurrection*, 104–5.
67. See, however, chapter 1, at n. 59, for a tradition that Abraham was in fact praying.
68. For example, Theodor and Albeck, *Bereshit Rabbah*, 611, §56:19. See, e.g., Ibn Ezra's commentary: "It did not mention Isaac, for he is subservient to [Abraham]. One who says that he slaughtered him and left him, and only later did he come back to life, has contradicted the biblical text." An additional comment appears in some manuscripts of Ibn Ezra (Paris 177 and Lutzki 827; see the edition at mg.alhatorah.org): "One who says that he went to study Torah with Shem, the son of Noah, his ancestor, is better. But the truth is that he brought him down with him." The first rejected

view is found in *Pirqe de-Rabbi Eliezer* §31; the second is found in *Bereshit Rabbah* 56:11.

69. Abarbanel, *Commentary*, 1.277.

3. Jewish Parallels

1. This is a theme begun in Taylor, *Sources of the Self*, and then developed at great length in *A Secular Age*.

2. This paragraph is a summary of Taylor, *Sources of the Self*, 285–302.

3. Within the history of ideas, Friedrich Schleiermacher is a crucially important figure for this story, but pursuit of this would take us too far afield. See the comments of Batnitzky, *How Judaism Became a Religion*, 25–27, 126–27.

4. For a good explication of these issues in Persian-period Jewry, see Beal, *The Book of Hiding*.

5. See also Lichtenstein, "Religion and State," 776.

6. Gellman, *Abraham! Abraham!*, 1.

7. T. Hartman and Buckholtz, *Are You Not a Man of God?*, 35. See also Batnitzky, *How Judaism Became a Religion*, 111–15.

8. See Stern, *The Genius*, 135–42, esp. 140.

9. Batnitzky, *How Judaism Became a Religion*, 16–25.

10. Clive, "'The Teleological Suspension of the Ethical' in Nineteenth-Century Literature," 78, 84.

11. Gellman, *The Fear, the Trembling, and the Fire*, and Gellman, *Abraham! Abraham!* The latter, later book makes less-sweeping claims about the existentialism latent in Hasidic (especially Izbicer) thought. See also Magid, "Hasidism and Existentialism?," 279–94.

12. See Gellman, *Abraham! Abraham!*, 4–6.

13. Leiner, *Mei ha-Shiloaḥ*, 2.19; see also 1.29.

14. Despite this, it must be noted the Hebrew is not ambiguous in the normal sense, since the phrase *le-ha'alot le-* means "offer as a sacrifice," as is seen even later in the same chapter. No one has ever read the phrase *va-ya'alehu le-'olah* in Genesis 22:13 as meaning that Abraham "lifted up" the ram (and then possibly took it down). The ambiguity, if it exists, is whether this is the normal idiomatic use of *le-ha'alot le-* or a homonymous phrase with the same verb in a non-idiomatic sense.

15. Theodor and Albeck, *Bereshit Rabbah*, 604, §56:12.

16. Zucker, *Commentaries of Rav Sa'adia Gaon to Genesis*, 114 (Arabic) and 401 (Hebrew). For further discussion, see Schlossberg, "The Place of the Binding

of Isaac in R. Sa'adia's Gaon's Polemic against Islam," 115–29. Other philosophically minded exegetes rejected this, however. Maimonides, for example, argues that the will of God was entirely clear to Abraham, as we will see.

17. R. Levi b. Gershon, "Interpretation of the Words," on Genesis 22:1.

18. Leiner, *Mei ha-Shiloah*, 2.19.

19. Gellman's argument is actually far more complicated, because, building on something Rabbi Leiner writes about a different biblical narrative, he suggests that Abraham may have successfully rid himself of all parental feelings and yet still loved Isaac—and that this love is the "angel" of Genesis 22:12.

20. This is the aspect of the Izbicer's thought that has attracted the most contemporary attention. For a striking list of examples from the *Mei ha-Shiloah* where the Izbicer justifies "sinful" behavior as justified by a personal religious impulse motivating it, see Gellman, *Abraham! Abraham!*, 69–70.

21. Leiner, *Mei ha-Shiloah*, 1.29.

22. This point is well argued in Daniel Rynhold's review of Gellman, *Abraham! Abraham!* Meir, "The Interpretation of the Binding of Isaac in the Dialogical Thought of Martin Buber," especially 287–91, also rejects Gellman's claim of a similarity between the Izbicer and Kierkegaard, seeing the Izbicer as closer to Buber. (This, too, is uncompelling: for the Izbicer, the test was for Abraham to rid himself of all "attachment" for Isaac—a far cry from Buber.)

23. For an overview of the Hatam Sofer's life and thought, see Katz, "Towards a Biography of the Hatam Sofer," 403–43.

24. For a discussion of Chajes's relationship with Schreiber, including to what extent Schreiber really respected Chajes and to what extent he was simply being kind in an effort to keep Chajes from becoming a reformer, see Hutner David, *The Dual Role of Rabbi Zvi Hirsch Chajes*, 443–56. The letter discussed here is mentioned on 456.

25. It is published as §208 in *The Responsa of the Hatam Sofer*, vol. 1 (*Orah Hayyim*).

26. As Rabbi Sofer indicates, Maimonides (*Guide*, 3.29–31) and Nahmanides (commentary to Leviticus 1:9) debated whether there is a "significance" to sacrifices. Maimonides argued that sacrifices were instituted only as a concession to the psychological and spiritual states of the Israelites after the Exodus, but that God has no desire for them. Rabbi Sofer suggests that even Maimonides only denied the transcendent value of sacrifices to quiet the cynics; really he agreed with Nahmanides that they have inherent worth.

27. Interestingly, Rabbi Leiner (*Mei ha-Shiloah*, 1.29) argues the precise opposite: Abraham was profoundly unsure of what God wanted, but he resolved the ambiguity somehow and then conveyed his understanding to Isaac. For Isaac, then, there was no uncertainty and no hesitation, whereas for Abraham the act was fraught with doubt. This is why the episode is a trial for Abraham (Gen. 22:1) and not Isaac.

28. A structurally similar interpretation is found in the work of R. Yehudah Aryeh Leib Alter (1847–1905), *Sefat Emet*, 1.67b. Alter argues that Abraham so thoroughly identified with the divine will that he had no trouble fulfilling any aspect of God's will and therefore never had to actually *obey* God. In Alter's terminology, following God through profound identification is called "service out of love," and obedience for its own sake is "service out of fear." In order to test whether Abraham could in fact serve God out of fear, God had to command him to do something that was *not* in accordance with the divine will. For Rabbi Alter, as for the Malbim and Kierkegaard, Abraham had to decide whether to follow the direct command of God or what he knew to be the will of God—which in this case did not agree. For further discussion, and the suggestion that Rabbi Alter is specifically trying to undercut the possibility of "sinning for the sake of heaven" (above, n. 19), see Gellman, *The Fear, the Trembling, and the Fire*, 86–92.

29. The Malbim mentions works of Kant by name and grapples with Kant's epistemological thought explicitly. Furthermore, other passages within Malbim's commentaries seem to be informed by modern philosophical thought. He appears to have read Leibniz in German translation, and he apparently read the periodicals *Kokhvei Yitzhaq, Otzar Nehmad, Kerem Hemed, Bikkure ha-'Ittim, Me'assefim,* and *Bikkurim,* through which modern critical thinking was distilled to Jewish intellectuals. Malbim also was interested in scholarship regarding the Bible, although of course he found there much with which he could not agree. For intellectual profiles and these details, see Berger, "Malbim's Secular Knowledge," 24–46, and Rosenbloom, *Ha-Malbim*.

30. See Malik, *Receiving Søren Kierkegaard*, esp. 283–392.

4. Jewish Followers

1. Jacobs, "The Problem of the Akedah," 8. It must be said, however, that the sources cited by Jacobs as evidence of a Jewish Kierkegaardian reading (which include Maimonides) fail to reveal anything of the sort, with the possible exception of Philo.

2. Fox, "Kierkegaard and Rabbinic Judaism," 115–24, argues that "the Rabbis'
understanding of the akedah differs from Kierkegaard's" and that "a properly Jewish theology must follow the rabbinic tradition and reject the views
of Kierkegaard." Halevi, "Kierkegaard and the Midrash," 13–28, suggests
that Kierkegaard "re-created . . . the essential features of the Rabbinic interpretation of Abraham," but this is rightly disputed by Green, "Abraham,
Isaac, and the Jewish Tradition," 1–21, who emphasizes just how foreign
Kierkegaard's line of thought was to Jewish philosophy before 1800. Green
does, however, strike a different note in a later essay, arguing that there
may be some substantive parallels in Jewish thought to Kierkegaard: Green,
"*Fear and Trembling*: A Jewish Appreciation," 139–42. Most pointedly, Ze'ev
Levy concludes his discussion with the assertion that "what Kierkegaard
extols and glorifies, Judaism condemns as sacrilege." See Ze'ev Levy, "On
the *Aquedah* [*sic passim*] in Modern Philosophy," 106.

3. Buber, *Between Man and Man*, 40–81.

4. Steinberg, *Anatomy of Faith*, 147.

5. For an overview of his thought, with bibliography and brief biographical
summary, see Rynhold, "Yeshayahu Leibowitz."

6. Ben-Yeruḥam and Ḳolits, *Negation for Negation's Sake*, a collection of essays
criticizing Leibowitz's thought, sometimes trenchant and sometimes vir-
ulent (and sometimes both), was published in Hebrew in 1983. In English,
reviews of Leibowitz's thought were written in the wake of the publication of *Judaism, Human Values, and the Jewish State*. See, for example, the
generally appreciative piece by Halbertal, "The Scourge of Reason," 35–38,
which notes, "His interpretation is sometimes too simple or too shrill. An
examination of the halakha itself reveals an extensive interest in human
needs and values." And see Mirsky, "Judaism, Human Values and the Jewish State," 18–20, who describes the way in which Leibowitz constructs
Judaism, and then notes, "There are, of course, a number of empirical
holes to be punched through this construct."

7. See, for example, Benbassat, "Yeshayahu Leibowitz," 151: "Leibowitz's concept of Judaism, I claim, is therefore neither deontological nor teleological
(or maybe both). It is a paradoxical position that posits duty and an end-
determination as mutually conditioned."

8. Ben Pazi, "The Religious Thought of Yeshayahu Leibowitz," 193–202.

9. Leibowitz, "Maimonides—the Abrahamic Man," 20–22. The publication
of the English translation in *Judaism* included reactions by Agus, Halevi,
and Schultz and a response by Leibowitz. The passages here have been re-

translated here from the Hebrew original, as the published English version
has a number of infelicitous renderings, one of which was pointed out by
Leibowitz in his later response.

10. The observation that this essay was written in response to Strauss's presence in Jerusalem in 1955 was made by Harvey, "Leibowitz on Abrahamic
Man," 347 with n. 2.

11. For an appreciation of the essay in this vein, see Harvey, "Leibowitz on
Abrahamic Man," 352. Generally, Leibowitz's writings of the 1950s contained all of his distinctive thought, at least in incipient form. Mirsky
noted, echoing an observation made about someone else, that Leibowitz hit on one idea early in his life, and clung to it "with all the tenacity of
genius" ("Judaism, Human Values and the Jewish State," 18).

12. The interpretation of Maimonides offered by Leibowitz is more reflective
of Leibowitz's thought than Maimonides'; see Harvey, "On Yeshayahu Leibowitz," 141–49.

13. Leibowitz, "Abraham and Job," 391–94.

14. See especially Sagi, "The Trial of the Akedah," 121–34. For a farther-
ranging comparison of Leibowitz with Kierkegaard, see Benbassat,
"Yeshayahu Leibowitz," 141–63.

15. Sagi, "The Trial of the Akedah," 124–25.

16. See also Harvey, "Leibowitz on Abrahamic Man," 347–52, noting a key
difference between the two readings: "Kierkegaard's Abraham can go
sacrifice his son because he believes that in the end he will not have to
sacrifice him, while Leibowitz's Abraham can go sacrifice his son because
in his eyes, 'all human thoughts, human emotions, and human values are
cancelled and nullified by the fear of God and the love of God.'"

17. Sagi, "The Trial of the Akedah," 121–34; see also Fagenblat, "Lacking All
Interest," 1–2.

18. See Benbassat, "Yeshayahu Leibowitz," 154.

19. Leibowitz, "Religious Praxis," 14–15. The Hebrew original appeared in 1953.
As Elie Jesner pointed out (p.c.), Leibowitz conflates "man's natural incli-
nations or drives" with an ethical system. Certainly they are not the same,
but Leibowitz does not seem to realize the difference between the two and
paints ethics with the same self-service idolatry brush.

20. Sagi, "The Meaning of the Akedah," 54: "In the whole history of Jewish
thought, until Soloveitchik and Leibowitz, there is no evidence of any
attempt to make the *Akedah* a life-shaping ideal."

21. See the comments of Waltke, *The Book of Proverbs: Chapters 1–15*, 100–101, discussing the expression in biblical narratives and wisdom literature. See also Forti, "The Polarity of Wisdom and Fear of God," 45–57.

22. For a more extended critique of Leibowitz along these lines, see D. Hartman, *A Living Covenant*, 98, who writes, "I allow that the Torah may challenge some accepted current patterns of behavior, but I cannot imagine that it requires us to sacrifice our ability to judge what is just and fair."

23. See D. Hartman, *A Living Covenant*, 309n5, for this example of a counter-text as well.

24. Naḥmanides, commentary on Genesis 6:2; see also 6:13.

25. See also the related comment on Leviticus 19:2, on the meaning of "be holy."

26. For trenchant criticism of his approach to scriptural texts, see Sagi, "Contending with Modernity," 439–40.

27. Sagi, "Contending with Modernity," 422; Harvey, "Comments on Rabbi Soloveitchik," 106n16; and Saks, "Letters on Religion without Theology," 93–94n6.

28. Sagi, "Contending with Modernity," 421–41. See also Sagi, "Rabbi Soloveitchik and Professor Leibowitz," 131–48. Much of the portrait of Soloveitchik presented here is based on two works, *Halakhic Man* and *Mah Dodekh mi-Dod*, both of which are explicitly descriptive of *others* and do not necessarily reflect Soloveitchik's own thought. This problem in interpreting Soloveitchik has been a central one; see the discussion in Possen, "J. B. Soloveitchik," 189–210. Sagi is probably mistaken in taking these texts as Soloveitchik's own thought, however. This is comparable to the problem of pseudepigrapha in Kierkegaard's writings: clearly, these themes are central to Soloveitchik's thought, but they may not reflect his own thinking on these themes. This problem leads Sagi to paint a portrait of Soloveitchik that is far less nuanced, and far more like Leibowitz, than is seen elsewhere in his writings.

29. D. Hartman, *A Living Covenant*, 109.

30. Not surprisingly, the philosophers most cited in the dissertation are—besides Cohen himself—Soloveitchik's advisor Maeir, Cassirer, and Natorp, the latter two being the most prominent neo-Kantians of the Marburg school.

31. Solowiejczyk, *Das reine Denken*, 110.

32. This astute point was made by Possen, "J. B. Soloveitchik," 194–95.

33. Solowiejczyk, *Das reine Denken*, 110.

34. This essay was published in *Tradition* 7.2 (1965), 5–67, and has been reprinted a number of times, including as a stand-alone book: *The Lonely Man of Faith*. Citations below will cite page numbers in the book.

35. As will be discussed below, for Kierkegaard the anachronistic label of "existentialist," while technically inexact, is conceptually appropriate.

36. Soloveitchik, *Lonely Man of Faith*, 39.

37. Soloveitchik, *Lonely Man of Faith*, 47–48. Possen, "J. B. Soloveitchik," 198–99, writes that this passage "echoes *Fear and Trembling* directly, modulating its language in a Jewish key."

38. Possen, "J. B. Soloveitchik," 198, writes that Soloveitchik in "Lonely Man of Faith" defines his loneliness "in another, still more Kierkegaardian way." See also Sztuden, "Adam the First," 8–19, esp. 17–18 on Kierkegaard's influence in "The Lonely Man of Faith." Singer and Sokol, "Joseph Soloveitchik: Lonely Man of Faith," 247–48, argue that although "Soloveitchik borrows a broad array of concepts and terms from thinkers such as Kierkegaard and Martin Buber in giving expression to his existentialism, . . . what he has to say is based on his personal religious experience. Existential thought, then, plays the same role in 'The Lonely Man of Faith' that neo-Kantian philosophy does in 'Halakhic Man'—it is a packaging device." The same view is echoed by Wolfson, "Eternal Duration and Temporal Compression," 195–96. This seems wrong. The whole idea that one would write a book "based on his personal religious experience" betrays the influence of existentialism! It is true, as Wolfson says, that Soloveitchik did not accept existentialism uncritically (on this see below), but this does not mean that he was not deeply influenced by that body of thought, and especially the early varieties that circulated in interwar Germany. Along similar lines, Wurzburger, "The Maimonidean Matrix," 176–78, notes that Soloveitchik understands that the creativity mandated in emulation of God finds its highest fulfillment in the scientific realm, which is a far cry from the understanding of earlier rabbinic writers, including his direct forebears. But Wurzburger denies that this reflects the influence of Cohen, preferring instead to see this as Maimonidean influence. But of course R. Ḥayyim of Volozhin also read Maimonides and came to a very different view. The novel elements in Soloveitchik's thought must be sought in his novel influences. It is eminently plausible that the encounter with Cohen led him to privilege a view he knew anyway to be that of Maimonides. See another example in Munk, *The Rationale of Halakhic Man*, 107–10, noting that Soloveitchik's interpretation of *ehyeh asher ehyeh* is in line with both

Maimonides and Hermann Cohen. Which is the primary influence? Contrast Munk's view, summarized also on 127–28.

39. Soloveitchik, *Lonely Man of Faith*, 4–5.
40. Kierkegaard, *Fear and Trembling*, 66–67.
41. Kierkegaard, *Fear and Trembling*, 63–65.
42. The diachronic point was made by Kaplan, "From Cooperation to Conflict," esp. 55 and 63–64n21. Dr. Joshua Feigelson (p.c.) plausibly suggests that the shift is to be connected to the personal crises Soloveitchik suffered then. See also Ziegler, *Majesty and Humility*, 31–33.
43. Soloveitchik, "Catharsis," 45–46.
44. For discussion of the masculine imagery of conquest, as opposed to the feminine imagery of retreat, in Soloveitchik's thought elsewhere, see Kolbrener, *The Last Rabbi*, 67–74.
45. Soloveitchik, "Majesty and Humility," 38–39. See also Soloveitchik, *Abraham's Journey*, 69–70.
46. Soloveitchik, "Majesty and Humility," 39.
47. Soloveitchik, "Majesty and Humility," 39–40.
48. Soloveitchik, "Majesty and Humility," 40n22. On this passage, see D. Hartman, *A Living Covenant*, 82–84.
49. Soloveitchik, "Majesty and Humility," 25.
50. Jacobs, "The Problem of the Akedah in Jewish Thought," 7. As will be discussed, this appears to be a vast oversimplification of Soloveitchik's thought in general and of his interpretations of the Akedah in particular.
51. Turner, "Sacrifice and Repentance," 302–3: "Soloveitchik, then, clearly follows Cohen and Rosenzweig in seeing sacrifice as a breakage of human will. The goal of repentance, for him too, is to recast the role of human will in human civilization."
52. Soloveitchik, *Abraham's Journey*, 11–12.
53. Soloveitchik, "Thoughts on Prayer," 94–95, 254–55.
54. See D. Hartman, *A Living Covenant*, 131–49; D. Hartman, *Love and Terror in the God Encounter*, 167–212; D. Hartman, "Prayer and Religious Consciousness," 105–25.
55. D. Hartman, "Prayer and Religious Consciousness," 123.
56. Prayer occupies an important place in Soloveitchik's thought. See Lichtenstein, "Prayer," 287–301, and D. Schwartz, *Philosophical Thought of Rabbi Soloveitchik*.
57. Soloveitchik, *The Lonely Man of Faith*, 51–66.

58. Soloveitchik, "Majesty and Humility," 33. In the original, *"kivyakhol,"* which indicates a statement that could be considered theologically problematic were it to be taken too literally or seriously, is written in Hebrew script. On the term, see Fishbane, *Biblical Myth & Rabbinic Mythmaking,* 325–404.

59. For yet another theme of prayer emphasized by Soloveitchik, the profound need for petition, see Held, *Abraham Joshua Heschel,* 300–301n96.

60. Sagi, "The Meaning of the Akedah," 54.

61. T. Hartman and Buckholtz, *Are You Not a Man of God?,* 43.

62. Soloveitchik, "Confrontation," 98. This essay received attention in the press; see Irving Spiegel, "Rabbi Says Faiths Are Not Related: Urges Each to Recognize the 'Individuality' of Others," *New York Times,* August 16, 1964, A7.

63. Soloveitchik, "The Community," 7–24. Note that this was presented at a meeting of the Conference of Jewish Communal Service.

64. Soloveitchik, "The Community," 3.

65. Solovetichik, "The Community," 10.

66. Soloveitchik, "The Community," 9–10.

67. Soloveitchik, "The Community," 11–12.

68. Soloveitchik, "Confrontation," 102.

69. Soloveitchik, "Confrontation," 109.

70. Soloveitchik, *Community, Covenant, and Commitment,* 134–35.

71. There is also a feminist critique of this reasoning to be offered: it is all well and good to desire "aloneness," but *someone* has to be with the kids. And if the man must be alone, does that undercut the woman's chance for a meaningful prayer experience?

72. For comments on this aspect of Soloveitchik's thought, see Stern, "Other Theologies," 27–30.

73. D. Hartman, *A Living Covenant,* 101–8, argues that Soloveitchik's claims that Jewish people of faith are "lonely" is intelligible only "if one identifies loneliness with uniqueness." Hartman rejects this move, though, on grounds that will soon be directly relevant to our topic: "People who believe that authentic faith requires that they follow the model of the Akedah may sacrifice thousands of innocent human beings in the name of their 'insane' love for God" (103).

74. Soloveitchik, *The Emergence of Ethical Man.*

75. Soloveitchik, *The Emergence of Ethical Man,* 153–54.

76. Soloveitchik, *The Emergence of Ethical Man,* 154.

77. Soloveitchik, *The Emergence of Ethical Man,* 154.

78. Soloveitchik, *The Emergence of Ethical Man,* 150.

79. See, e.g., Kaufman, "An Emphatic Plea for Please," 195–98.
80. Soloveitchik, *The Emergence of Ethical Man*, 155–56.
81. Soloveitchik, *The Emergence of Ethical Man*, 156–57n2.
82. Ozar, "Yeridah le-Zorekh Aliyyah," 170–71.
83. For full and relevant surveys, see Malik, *Receiving Søren Kierkegaard*, and the articles in *Kierkegaard's International Reception — Northern and Western Europe*, esp. Schulz, "Germany and Austria," 307–419.
84. Gordon, *Continental Divide*, 67.
85. Arendt, "Soren Kierkegaard," 293–303, quoted in Moyn, "Transcendence, Morality, and History," 24–25. Moyn writes, "It is really only thanks to the German interwar discovery of his philosophy that he became the canonical figure he remains today. It is possible, almost, to say that Kierkegaard is a twentieth-century rather than a nineteenth-century philosopher."
86. The fullest discussion of Heidegger's influence on Soloveitchik is a four-page footnote in Wolfson, "Eternal Duration and Temporal Compresence," 208–12n37, which begins, "Worthy of a separate investigation is the intriguing resemblance between Soloveitchik's affirmation of the compresence of the three temporal modes in the eternality of the moment and the three ecstasies of time in the thought of Heidegger." Relatedly, Herskowitz, "The Moment and the Future," 87–99, shows that Soloveitchik and Kierkegaard share a conception of "the moment" that appears to be another indication of Kierkegaard's influence on Soloveitchik. Herskowitz also notes, however, that the same view of time is found in Heidegger. Herskowitz suggests (97–99) that both Soloveitchik and Heidegger were influenced by Kierkegaard, which seems eminently reasonable, but we should also recall that Soloveitchik was likely influenced by Heidegger as well, and so he may have received this view both directly from the Dane as well as mediated by the sage of Freiburg. See also Herskowitz, "Rabbi Joseph B. Soloveitchik's Endorsement and Critique," 373–90, on Soloveitchik's thinking about the Volk of Israel, especially as it relates to his critique of Heidegger.
87. Some reports place Soloveitchik at the Davos conference in 1929 where Heidegger and Cassirer debated the proper interpretation of Kant and the point of philosophy; see Gordon, "Continental Divide," 227n14. He does not appear in the rosters of those actually present, however, and therefore Gordon does not mention him in *Continental Divide*; see Wolfson, "Eternal Duration and Temporal Compresence," 212n37. Wolfson also cites Soloveitchik's own testimony (offered in at least two different contexts) that he attended Heidegger's lectures, although it is not clear where or when.

88. On this event, from both philosophical and historical perspectives, see Gordon, *Continental Divide*.

89. If everyone was struggling with Scheler (Gordon, *Continental Divide*, 70–76 and *passim*), so, too, was Soloveitchik (see Soloveitchik, *Halakhic Mind*, 120n52, and Ozar, "The Emergence of Max Scheler," 178–206). If Buber was struggling with Cohen and Heidegger, so, too, was Soloveitchik.

90. Again, see Sagi, "The Meaning of the Akedah," 54, cited in n. 29.

91. As we have seen, Soloveitchik does speak sometimes about the religious person discovering ethics on her own and only later discovering that her views agree with the divine will, but this line of thought has been far less influential among Jewish thinkers trying to understand Soloveitchik in the past half-century.

5. Criticizing Kierkegaard

1. Habermas, "Reply to My Critics," 368–70.

2. To some extent, the fact that *The Halakhic Mind* was not published until 1986 can explain the view of Singer and Sokol discussed and rejected in the previous chapter, n. 38.

3. On this essay, see Sacks, "Rabbi J. B. Soloveitchik's Early Epistemology," 75–87; A. Levenson, "Joseph Soloveitchik's *The Halachic Mind*," 55–63; Kolbrener, "Towards a Genuine Jewish Philosophy," 21–43. The aspect that has garnered the most attention is Soloveitchik's critique of Maimonides' approach to the commandments in the *Guide*; see Rynhold, *Two Models of Jewish Philosophy*, 89–100; Stambovsky, "R. Soloveitchik's Causal Critique of Maimonides," 307–30.

4. Cassirer, *Einstein's Theory of Relativity*, and Natorp, *Die logischen Grundlagen der exakten Wissenschaften*; for discussion, see Luft, *The Space of Culture*, 79–80. The path from Cassirer to Kuhn is not far; see Friedman, "Ernst Cassirer and Thomas Kuhn," 239–52.

5. Soloveitchik, *Halakhic Mind*, 3–36.

6. Soloveitchik, *Halakhic Mind*, 54.

7. Soloveitchik, *Halakhic Mind*, 55. For an analysis of Eckhart, see McGinn, *The Mystical Thought of Meister Eckhart*.

8. Soloveitchik, *Halakhic Mind*, 55.

9. Soloveitchik, *Halakhic Mind*, 77.

10. Soloveitchik, *Halakhic Mind*, 80.

11. Soloveitchik, *Halakhic Man*, 59. See Possen, "J. B. Soloveitchik," 198.

12. This has been examined from numerous angles. For angles relevant to our inquiry, see Moyn, "Judaism against Paganism," 22–58; Habermas, "Work and Weltanschauung," 431–56; Gordon, *Continental Divide*, 341–57.

13. Arendt, "Heidegger at Eighty," 302.

14. Novak, "Buber's Critique of Heidegger," 134–36.

15. Tillich, "Heidegger and Jaspers," 24, cited in Gordon, *Continental Divide*, 342.

16. Even in *The Lonely Man of Faith*, Soloveitchik includes a long note on the dangers of Kierkegaard's thought unchecked; see 101–2n1. On this passage see Possen, "J. B. Soloveitchik," 199–201.

17. This is the thrust of the final, brief chapter of *The Halakhic Mind*.

18. For a different criticism of this claim, see Brafman, "Universalism and Particularism in Contemporary Philosophy of Halakha," 63–78.

19. Kierkegaard, *Fear and Trembling*, 70.

20. T. Hartman and Buckholtz, *Are You Not a Man of God?*, 43.

21. Soloveitchik, "Thoughts on Prayer," 254–55.

22. Gellman, "And Sarah Died," 62.

23. Biala, "The End of Sacrificial Religiosity."

24. Irshai, "Religion and Morality," 1–17; Irshai and Waldoks, "Modern Orthodox Feminism in Israel," 1–94.

25. Irshai and Waldoks, "Modern Orthodox Feminism in Israel," 24n48.

26. As noted by Munk, *The Rationale of Halakhic Man*, 40.

27. This is well articulated by Irshai, "Religion and Morality," 2.

28. Irshai and Waldoks, "Modern Orthodox Feminism in Israel," 24–25.

29. Halbertal, *On Sacrifice*, 73.

30. Halbertal, *On Sacrifice*, 73–74.

31. Caravaggio painted the theme a few years later, as well; the ca. 1605 painting hangs in Princeton University and can be seen at https://www.caravaggio-foundation.org/The-Sacrifice-Of-Isaac-C.-1605.html. The renderings of each character and the scene as a whole are entirely different from the 1601 painting.

32. J. Bernstein, "Forgetting Isaac," 170–75. Bernstein's interpretation of Caravaggio as a critique of Kierkegaard relies on Marin, *To Destroy Painting*, 141.

33. Theodor and Albeck, *Bereshit Rabbah*, 599, §56:4. Besides its theological motivation, the midrash plays on a word in the verse, reading Greek *se*, "you," instead of Hebrew *śeh*, "sheep."

34. Theodor and Albeck, *Bereshit Rabbah*, 599, §56:4. See also on Genesis 22:6, Theodor and Albeck, *Bereshit Rabbah*, 598, §56:3.

35. Diez-Macho, *Targum Neofiti*, 1.125.

36. Qur'ān 37:102–3. For philological discussion, especially of the word *'aslamā* here and of its Jewish background (compare *hishlim libbo*), see Kister, *"Islām,"* 397–401. For discussion of the difficult words at the end of that line, see Calder, "The *Sa'y* and the *Jabīn*."

37. Fackenheim, *Encounters between Judaism and Modern Philosophy*, 35.

38. Fackenheim, *Encounters between Judaism and Modern Philosophy*, 69–70.

39. Noted by (among others) Zierler, "In Search of a Feminist Reading of the Akedah," 20.

40. Buber, *Between Man and Man*, 52.

41. This was a major critique of Heidegger voiced by Buber in his inaugural Jerusalem lectures, as discussed by Novak, "Buber's Critique of Heidegger," 130–31—and note the connection to Kierkegaard noted on 131. See Buber, *Between Man and Man*, 140–44.

42. Elsewhere, Buber voices a different critique of Kierkegaard, questioning whether the content of the divine command should be taken as self-evidently clear, as will be discussed.

43. Fackenheim, *Encounters between Judaism and Modern Philosophy*, 48–49. Prosser, "Conscientious Subjectivity in Kierkegaard and Levinas," 406–7, argues that while both Kierkegaard and Levinas assume the need for conscientious subjectivity, Kierkegaard believes this is only possible in a relationship with God, whereas Levinas believes that meeting the human Other produces the same result, rendering the divine superfluous.

44. Jewish mysticism did introduce an ideal of *hitbodedut*, and this was picked up and developed in Hasidism—which, as already discussed, grew up in the same environment that gave rise to Kierkegaard's thought; note in this regard T. Hartman and Buckholtz, *Are You Not a Man of God?*, 35: "The Hassidic turn to inwardness, like Kierkegaard's, emerged in protest of what was perceived as the lifeless stagnancy of formalistic institutionalized religion." Even there, however, one does not approach the loneliness of Kierkegaard's knight of faith. For discussion of earlier strands of such thought in Judaism, in medieval and early modern times, see Idel, "*Hitbodedut* as Concentration," 405–38, who notes that "rabbinic Judaism . . . took shape as the religion of Jewish communities" and that Jewish mysticism was revolutionary in this regard.

45. See Anderson, "Celibacy or Consummation in the Garden?," 121–48.

46. See, e.g., Haran, "From Early to Classical Prophecy," 385–97.

47. Herskowitz, "The Moment and the Future," 96–97.

48. Levinas, *Proper Names*, 68. This is from a chapter entitled "Kierkegaard: Existence and Ethics," 66–74; originally in German in *Schweizer Monatshefte* 43 (1963).

49. See Steinberg, *Anatomy of Faith*, 147 (cited above in chapter 4, n. 4), and the other sources cited there, n. 2. Similarly, Gumbiner, "Existentialism and Our Father Abraham," 143–48, wrote that the Kierkegaardian view is "ethically and religiously impossible from the Jewish standpoint"; see also the comments of Gordis, "The Faith of Abraham," 417n14.

50. Jacobs, "The Problem of the *Akedah* in Jewish Thought," 3–4, goes on to state that "the opposite view, the 'pro-Kierkegaardian' interpretation of the Akedah, is, however, also found in Jewish thought." The sources mustered to buttress this claim do not stand up to scrutiny, however. He relies on Maimonides, in large part, but as will be discussed, Maimonides is irrelevant to the Kierkegaardian question.

51. This critique has come especially from neuroscience and neuroscientifically informed philosophy. In the context of the Akedah, see the comments of Zierler, "In Search of a Feminist Reading of the Akedah," 10–26; T. Hartman and Buckholtz, *Are You Not a Man of God?*, 38.

52. Levinas, *Proper Names*, 76–77. This chapter ("A Propos of 'Kierkegaard vivant,'" 75–79) was originally two interventions in *Kierkegaard vivant* (Paris: Gallimard, Collection 'Idées' no. 106, 1966), prepared for publication in *Noms propres* by Levinas.

53. See Graetz, "Trauma and Recovery," 42.

54. D. Hartman, *A Heart of Many Rooms*, 12–14 (quotation from 14); see also D. Hartman, *A Living Covenant*, 43–44.

55. D. Hartman, *A Heart of Many Rooms*, 13.

56. D. Hartman, *A Living Covenant*, 43–44.

57. See the discussion of Hartman in Tucker, "Redeeming the Akeidah, Halakhah and Ourselves," 11–15.

58. On the dynamics of the Divine in this story, see Rashbam's commentary to Genesis 18:1, 16, and 22, and Sommer, *The Bodies of God*, 40–41.

59. God is consistently depicted as needing to "go down" to investigate human actions. Compare, e.g., Genesis 11:5: "The Lord came down to see the city and the tower, which mortals had built."

60. Carmy and Shatz, "The Bible as a Source for Philosophical Reflection," 13.

61. Wettstein, "The Faith of Abraham," 11n19. Similarly, see Zierler, "In Search of a Feminist Reading of the Akedah," 20; see also Korn, "Windows on the World," 5. Gordis, "The Faith of Abraham," 116, on that last appended page,

too, notes that "Abraham is being commanded to give up all that is most precious to him in the world, but he is not being asked to surrender his loyalty to the moral law."

62. For Jewish ways of approaching this problem, modern and ancient, see Sagi, "The Punishment of Amalek," 323–46; L. Feldman, *Remember Amalek!*

63. Relatedly—but differently—Sagi and Statman, "Divine Command Morality and Jewish Tradition," 39–67, argue that there is very little in the annals of Jewish thought that suggests a DCM approach. In part, they explain, this is because the traditional image of God is one of a just and merciful God, and therefore it seemed obvious that people should act the same way as well.

64. Levinas, "Kierkegaard: Existence and Ethics," 68.

65. Fackenheim, *Encounters between Judaism and Modern Philosophy*, 63.

66. Ellenson, "Emil Fackenheim and the Revealed Morality of Judaism," 402–13, argues that in a covenant the individual must retain moral authority and be able to demur or reject God's command. God may not like it (cf. Saul), but it is incumbent upon people to subject commands to their sense of morality.

6. On Child Sacrifice

1. J. Levenson, *Death and Resurrection of the Beloved Son*, 13, argues that since the denouement states clearly that the reward is for being willing to sacrifice, a proper reading must focus on the trial, rendering the ending anticlimactic. This seems to overstate the proper methodological conclusion.

2. Levinas, "A Propos of 'Kierkegaard vivant,'" 76–77.

3. For thoughts in this direction, see Halbertal, *On Sacrifice*, 24–25.

4. For reviews of the evidence, see Brown, *Late Carthaginian Child Sacrifice*; Stavrakopoulou, *King Manasseh and Child Sacrifice*; Vainstub, "Human Sacrifices in Canaan and Israel," 117–204; and the full discussion by Xella, "'Tophet,'" 259–81. (The entire double issue of *Studi Epigrafici e Linguistici*, edited by Xella, was devoted to the theme of "The Tophet in the Phoenician Mediterranean," and contains many valuable papers.) See also Tigay, *Deuteronomy*, 464–65 with the notes (Excursus 15); Martin, *The Art of Contact*, 97–98.

5. Tertullian, *The Apology*, 9.2–4, translated by Thelwall in *The Ante-Nicene Fathers*, 3.25. As for whether the Romans opposed this practice and how, note Rives, "Tertullian on Child Sacrifice," 54–63.

6. Cleitarchus, *Scholia to Plato's Republic*, 1.337A, cited and translated in Mosca, "Child Sacrifice in Canaanite and Israelite Religion," 22.

7. For a full collection, see Xella, "Sacrifici di Bambini," 59–100.

8. This is the paraphrase offered by Stager, *Rites of Spring*, 7, of the reasons other scholars resist the idea that child sacrifice was practiced by the Phoenicians, at least at Carthage. Stager's monograph is a thorough review of the evidence that it was practiced.

9. Xella et al., "Phoenician Bones of Contention," 1200. Quinn, *In Search of the Phoenicians*, 92–112, calls this "the circle of the Tophet."

10. Stager, "The Rite of Child Sacrifice," 1–11; Stager and Wolff, "Child Sacrifice at Carthage," 31–51.

11. P. Smith et al., "Aging Cremated Infants," 859–74; P. Smith et al., "Age Estimations," 1191–99; against the challenge of J. Schwartz et al., "Skeletal Remains from Punic Carthage," e9177; J. Schwartz et al., "Carthaginian Infant Sacrifice Revisited," 738–45; J. Schwartz, "The Mythology of Carthaginian Child Sacrifice," 103–25; and J. Schwartz et al., "Two Tales of One City," 442–54.

12. For a suggested etymology of this deity's name, and a connection to the tophet, see Xella, "Sull' etimologia de (Baal) Hammon," 27–31.

13. A very clear photograph of the stele on which this inscription appears is in Vainstub, "Human Sacrifices in Canaan and Israel," 141.

14. Xella et al., "Phoenician Bones of Contention," 1204.

15. See Vainstub, "Human Sacrifices in Canaan and Israel," 153–56 with references. The stele from Pozo Moro, sometimes said to visually represent a child sacrifice, is best left aside, as its imagery is both unique and complex. For the stele, see Almagro-Gorbea, "Les Reliefs Orientalisant de Pozo Moro," 123–36 and plate 1; Brown, *Late Carthaginian Child Sacrifice*, 70–72. For discussions, see M. Smith, *The Early History of God*, 174–75, and especially Rundin, "Pozo Moro," 425–47.

16. For the reading and extensive historical discussion, see Pitard, "The Identity of the Bir-Hadad," 3–21.

17. For further discussion, see Ginsberg, "Psalms and Inscriptions," 159–71. Ginsberg suggests that the text of Isaiah 38:9–20 (*mikhtav* or *mikhtam*) was on an inscription erected by Hezekiah in Jerusalem to repay the vow made when he was sick.

18. Logan, "Rehabilitating Jephthah," 665–85; compare Monroe, "Disembodied Women," 35–52. See also D. Marcus, *Jephthah and His Vow*, and M.

Smith, "Child Sacrifice as the Extreme Case and Calculation," 3–17, with further references.

19. This is emphasized by J. Levenson, *The Death and Resurrection of the Beloved Son*, 13–14.

20. Excerpts from Philo's *Phoenician History* are preserved through citation by Eusebius, quoted here from A. Baumgarten, *The Phoenician History of Philo of Byblos*, 244–45. Philo also reports that the model for all this was Kronos himself, who offered up his only son, "who was therefore called Ieoud (for an only son is thus called even now by the Phoenicians)," on account of a war. Ieoud seems to reflect the Hebrew/Phoenician word *yaḥid*, "only one," the same epithet used in the story of the Akedah to refer to Isaac. See discussion in A. Baumgarten, *The Phoenician History*, 251.

21. Moshe Weinfeld argued that "passing through the fire" did not entail death: "The Worship of Molech," 133–54. This was adequately rebutted on philological grounds by M. Smith, "A Note on Burning Babies," 477–79.

22. Note that Hezekiah, Ahaz's son and Manasseh's father, did have ample opportunity to offer a child sacrifice, when Sennacherib campaigned against Judah in 701 BCE, but is not said to have done so. This silence may be part of the reason for the biblical valorization of Hezekiah.

23. See the discussion of Aubet, *The Phoenicians and the West*, 212–56 (esp. 245–56). Aubet argues that child sacrifice was an elite phenomenon not only in the Levant, but in the central Mediterranean as well, but this cannot make sense of the vast numbers in the tophet of Carthage. It is possible that Carthage was exceptional even within the central Mediterranean, but this requires more data from the other sites.

24. For an approach to the tophet along these lines, see Bonnet, "On Gods and Earth," 373–87. Quinn, *In Search of the Phoenicians*, 98–101, less plausibly suggests that the practice may have been more common earlier in the Levant but then declined or perhaps was banned (as in Judah), leading some Phoenicians who particularly treasured the practice of child sacrifice to leave the Phoenician homeland and found colonies in the central Mediterranean.

25. For discussions and opposing conclusions, see J. Levenson, *The Death and Resurrection of the Beloved Son*, 3–17, and Milgrom, "Were the Firstborn Sacrificed," 49–55. See also Stavrakopoulou, *King Manasseh and Child Sacrifice*, 179–91, and Lange, "'They Burn Their Sons and Daughters,'" 109–32.

26. See M. Greenberg, *Ezekiel 1–20*, 368–70. See also Patton, "'I Myself Gave Them Laws,'" 73–90; Mein, *Ezekiel and the Ethics of Exile*, 117–19; and the

somewhat different approach of Hahn and Bergsma, "What Laws Were 'Not Good'?," 201–18.

27. See chapter 1, at n. 31. This version is from the *Targum Pseudo-Jonathan*. See also Theodor and Albeck, *Bereshit Rabbah*, 587–88, §55:4 and the parallels noted in the notes there. Schoenfeld, *Isaac on Jewish and Christian Altars*, esp. 95–100, argues that for both Rashi and the Gloss—but not many other Northern French interpreters—Genesis 22 was fundamentally a story of chosenness, relying in large part on Rashi's paraphrase of this midrash.

28. Halbertal, *On Sacrifice*, 24–25.

7. Maimonides and the Divine Will

1. For a thorough discussion of Maimonides' approach to biblical interpretation, see M. Cohen, *Opening the Gates of Interpretation*, and the voluminous literature cited there.

2. This point is made by Even-Chen, *'Aḳedat Yiṣḥaḳ*, 52.

3. Kant, *The Conflict of the Faculties*, 115. As Boehm, *The Binding of Isaac*, 114–15, has charted, Kant turned to this criticism of Abraham repeatedly, as it was a key example of some of the central issues he was grappling with in his thought about reason and faith. In *Religion within the Boundaries of Mere Reason*, written in 1793, Kant argued that God could never command something unethical, and adds in parentheses: "e.g., if a father were ordered to kill his son who, so far as he knows, is totally innocent" (Kant, *Religion within the Boundaries of Mere Reason*, 100). This was written when the then king of Prussia, Frederick William II, was already unhappy with Kant's ideas on religious matters; in fact, he had made Kant promise not to comment publicly on religion; see Derrida, "Vacant Chair," esp. 44. Despite the clear import of this comment, Kant kept the reference implicit to avoid provoking the king. It was only after Frederick William II's death in 1797 that Kant wrote *The Conflict of the Faculties*, and there he includes a more explicit discussion, arguing again that Abraham should have disobeyed, since God was not the one who issued the command.

4. Buber, "On the Suspension of the Ethical," esp. 103. Many interpreters understand the interplay between the version in Samuel and the version in Chronicles differently; see, for example, the hypotheses of Japhet, *I & II Chronicles*, 373–75, and Stokes, "The Devil Made David Do It," 91–106.

5. Buber's essay is poignant but rests on little of substance. Leora Batnitzky notes some of the weakness in her introduction to the 2016 edition of *Eclipse of God*, xx. For more on the "problem of hearing" in Buber's

thought, see Sagi, "The Akedah—The Problem of Obedience or the Problem of Hearing," 248–62.

6. See Carmy, "An Individualist Religious Thinker," 200. See also the discussion in chapter 3, n. 14 and the accompanying text.

7. Evans, *Kierkegaard's Ethic of Love*, 306–15.

8. Evans, *Kierkegaard's Ethic of Love*, 308–9.

9. That Maimonides "answers" Kant here was noted by Fackenheim, *Encounters between Judaism and Modern Philosophy*, 40, and Boehm, *The Binding of Isaac*, 116–17.

10. Saadia Gaon, *Book of Beliefs and Doctrines*, 140 (chapter 3, §9). Abraham ibn Ezra, in his commentary to Genesis 22:1, at the end of s.v. *ve-ha-Elohim nissah*, alludes to Saadia's question, but brushes it aside: "Since Scripture says at the outset 'tested,' all questions have been removed." As will soon be explained, however, that does not solve the actual problem Saadia and Maimonides had in mind.

11. The topic of prophecy in medieval religious philosophy has attracted a lot of attention. For Maimonides, see Kreisel, *Prophecy*, 148–311, and see the entire work for a wider-ranging discussion.

12. Maimonides, *Guide*, 2.36. This being so, it is incoherent to simply say, as Ibn Ezra does, that God was simply "testing" Abraham in Genesis 22:2, and there is therefore no problem.

13. See the discussion in Kellner, "Maimonides and Gersonides on Mosaic Prophecy," 62–79.

14. The high levels of prophecy ascribed to Abraham by Maimonides had a profound effect on how subsequent philosophers dealt with Abraham. For the Karaite evidence, see Lasker, *From Judah Hadassi to Elijah Bashyatchi*, 217–28.

15. This is well developed by Even-Chen, *'Akedat Yiṣḥak*, 42–47, and Boehm, *The Binding of Isaac*, 73–85.

16. In fact, in the *Guide*, 3.24, Maimonides mentioned in passing that this was a dream: "as he was commanded, even though this command was in a dream or a vision." The notion that the vision came at night is found earlier in *Pirqe de-Rabbi Eliezer* §31 ("On the same night, the Holy One, blessed be He, revealed Himself to Abraham") and the Qur'ān; see Kister, "Islām," 398.

17. A parallel interpretation was offered in modern times by Israeli biblical scholar Israel Knohl. For Knohl, the name *Elohim* indicates the "numinous, irrational, and amoral dimension of God," while the Tetragrammaton signifies the rational and moral aspect. Thus, when Abraham obeys the

command, he shows that he "obeys *Elohim*," but the actual sacrifice is prevented by an angel of the Lord. See Knohl, *Divine Symphony*, 106–8; "In the Face of Death," 88.

18. There is a fascinating parallel approach in the work of Maimonides' Spanish Sufi contemporary, Ibn 'Arabi (1165–1240). Interpreting the Qur'ānic version of the story, Ibn 'Arabi writes that Abraham was commended for acting on his dream, in which he saw that he was killing Isaac as a sacrifice, but that in fact this was an incomplete understanding: "God says to Abraham, calling him, 'O Abraham, you believed what you saw,' and He does not say, 'You were right concerning what you saw,' namely your son, because he did not interpret what he saw, but took it at face value, although visions require interpretation." In fact, according to Ibn 'Arabi, "it was a ram that appeared in the form of Abraham's son in the dream, while Abraham believed what he saw." See Ibn al-'Arabi, *The Bezels of Wisdom*, 99.

19. Boehm, *The Binding of Isaac*, 73–85, argues that Maimonides actually meant to say that Abraham doubted God's original command, as this is the only reason he would have obeyed the angel at the later stage, but this seems unnecessary as *each* prophecy is entirely true in the eyes of the prophet.

20. Profiat Duran (on *Guide* 2.46) and other interpreters have understood Maimonides to believe that the Akedah never actually occurred. The evidence for this reading is reviewed by Nuriel, *Revealed and Hidden*, 154–57.

21. See Maimonides, *Mishneh Torah*, Laws of the Temple (*Bet ha-Beḥira*) 2:2, in addition to the passages in the *Guide* discussed here (especially 3:24). See further the sources and discussion in Shapiro, *Changing the Immutable*, 67–73.

22. On the Akedah as a trial in the thought of Maimonides, see S. Feldman, "The Binding of Isaac," 105–33, and J. Cohen, "Philosophical Exegesis in Historical Perspective," esp. 136, as well as Even-Chen, *'Aḳedat Yiṣḥak*, 47–52.

23. Diamond, "'Trial' as Esoteric Preface," 1–30. See also Diamond, "Abarbanel's Exegetical Subversion," 75–100.

24. Diamond, "'Trial' as Esoteric Preface," 19–26.

25. Diamond, "'Trial' as Esoteric Preface," 26.

26. Levinas, *Proper Names*, 77.

27. Lamm, "The Greatest Trial," 5. The view that the latter part of the Akedah is the more important part is also that of Geiger; for references and discussion, see Koltun-Fromm, "Historical Memory in Abraham Geiger's

Account," 119–21. This is vehemently opposed by Samson Raphael Hirsch in his commentary on Genesis 22:11.

28. For a bio-bibliography of Ibn Kapi, see Mesch, *Studies in Joseph Ibn Caspi*, 43–58, and for a synthesis and analysis of his philosophical views, see Kasher and Kahan, "Joseph Kaspi."

29. For analysis, see Boehm, *The Binding of Isaac*, 63–70.

30. The text is from Herring, *Joseph ibn Kaspi's Gevia' Kesef*, 8 (in Hebrew) and 140–44 in English; the translation is somewhat modified from that offered by Herring.

31. He returns to this theory in chapter 14 of *Gevia' Kesef* as well (see Herring, 33, for the Hebrew text, and Herring, 230–31, for the English translation). A somewhat different analysis of Ibn Kaspi's interpretation of the Akedah is provided by Kasher, "How Could God Command," 27–37.

32. See Mesch, *Studies in Joseph Ibn Caspi*, 87, for discussion of this point.

33. As Mesch, *Studies in Joseph ibn Caspi*, 93, points out, Ibn Kaspi says that even Moses "did not arrive at his full perfection immediately," and this is certainly true for Abraham as well.

34. *Sifra*, Qedoshim 4.9.12.

35. B. *Bava Meṣia'* 47b.

36. Maimonides, *Mishneh Torah*, Laws of Divorce 2:20.

37. Maimonides himself, of course would reject this talk of God as conflicted and person-like.

8. Rejecting Child Sacrifice

1. See discussion in Roberts, "Does God Lie?," 211–20. Contrast Moberly, "Does God Lie to His Prophets?," 1–23, who argues that Micaiah's claims are merely rhetorical and not meant to be taken seriously as theology, as well as Yael Shemesh, "Lies by Prophets," 81–95, who argues that prophets do not say things that are outright false, but they do deceive. Neither of these does justice to the texts discussed here.

2. Goldenberg, "The Problem of False Prophecy," 94.

3. See the discussion in I. Knohl, "Does God Deceive?," 275–91. The only point to be emphasized against Knohl is that "lest they repent" presupposes sin. The condemnation is not without any background whatsoever, although it may well be—as Knohl argues—that Isaiah himself has not been involved in any previous attempts at repentance.

4. Last Stone, "Between Truth and Trust," 337–66.

5. Buber, "On the Suspension of the Ethical," 100–105. See also the discussion and criticism of Buber above in chapter 7, n. 5.

6. Buber, "On the Suspension of the Ethical," 104.

7. Buber, "On the Suspension of the Ethical," 104–5.

8. Elsewhere, Buber (*On the Bible*, 166–71) suggests a somewhat different key to Abraham's evolving understating of the divine will. False prophets, according to Buber, think that the divine will is static, while true prophets know that the right answer varies. Abraham need not have been wrong the first time to have been right the second time. This is a theme echoed by Fackenheim, *Encounters between Judaism and Modern Philosophy*, 70, as well. He contrasts Kantian thought, which "rules out all surprise when it affirms the intrinsic value of humanity to be simply absolute," to Abraham and thereafter all who "receive the Torah," who go through multiple stages of revelation, culminating in the experience "to receive, in surprise as well as gratitude, the value of humanity as a gift that Divinity might have withheld and that is yet given forever."

9. J. Levenson, *Death and Resurrection of the Beloved Son*, 113.

10. See also, e.g., Laws of Hammurabi §209–10: "209. If a man strikes a freeborn woman so that she loses her unborn child, he shall pay ten shekels for her loss. If the woman dies, his daughter shall be put to death." In the Middle Assyrian Laws, the same principle is applied to a man's wife: if the man rapes an unmarried girl, his wife is to be raped as punishment (A 55); if he strikes a woman and causes a miscarriage, punishment is again to be exacted from his wife (A 50). For discussion, see Yaron, "The Middle Assyrian Laws and the Bible," 555–56.

11. See Exodus 20:4–5, 34:7; Deuteronomy 5:9; and many narratives.

12. See Ezekiel 14 and 18, among others.

13. B. *Makkot* 24a. In another version, in *Ba-midbar Rabbah* §19, God proposes the principle of "visiting the sin of the parents on the children," and Moses convinces God to change to individualized justice. A synchronic explanation for the discrepancy is provided on B. *Berakhot* 7a, and another one in *Pesikta de-Rav Kahana* 25:7. In that latter text, there is a debate between "Torah" and "prophecy"; other views are attributed to "wisdom" and, finally, God—who has a view that differs from all of the rest.

14. See the sophisticated discussion in Halpern, "Jerusalem and the Lineages," 11–107.

15. M. Greenberg, "Some Postulates of Biblical Criminal Law," 21–22; Tigay, *Deuteronomy*, 227.

16. M. Greenberg, "Some Postulates of Biblical Criminal Law," 20–27, crediting Umberto Cassuto with this insight; Frymer-Kensky, "Tit for Tat," 230–34; and Wright, *Inventing God's Law*, 212 and notes on 450. As Wright notes (tentatively), "The statement of this principle in Deut 24:16 makes explicit what is implicit in [Exodus]."

Conclusion

1. Levinas, "A Propos of 'Kierkegaard vivant,'" 75–79.
2. Stolle, "Levinas and the Akedah," 137–39, and Shankman, *Other Others*, 9, 15–16.
3. Levinas, *Difficult Freedom*, cited by Stolle, "Levinas and the Akedah," 139.
4. Margaliot, *Midrash Wayyiqra Rabbah*, 783–84 (§34:10).
5. B. *Shabbat* 31a. The same formulation is found in a Late Egyptian Wisdom text: "That which you hate to be done to you, do not do it to another" (a literal equivalent of Hillel's Aramaic *mai de-seni lakh*), and in Tobit 4:15. See Jasnow, *A Late Period Hieratic Wisdom Text*, 95.
6. Fishbane, *Sacred Attunement*, 190.
7. Rudolph and Ostrow, "Isaac Laughing," 646–81. See also Varriano, *Caravaggio*, 98. This is rejected by Graham-Nixon, *Caravaggio*, 225–26.
8. Stroumsa, "Christ's Laughter," 267–88, argued that docetism (an ancient heresy whose fundamental claim was that Jesus was not actually sacrificed) may have been based on a tight analogy between Jesus and Isaac. The evidence is the docetic texts mention that Jesus laughed when another was killed in his place; Isaac, whose name means "laughter," was also saved at the last minute by substitution. See also Goldstein and Stroumsa, "The Greek and Jewish Origins of Docetism," 423–41, who emphasize the Greek notion of substitution—including in the story of Iphigenia—by an *eidolon*.
9. Rudolph and Ostrow, "Isaac Laughing," 671–72.

BIBLIOGRAPHY

Abarbanel, Isaac. *Commentary on the Torah.* 5 vols. Jerusalem: Bene Arba'el, 1964.

Agus, Jacob. "Kierkegaard and Pascal to the Rescue!" *Judaism* 6 (1957): 273.

Almagro-Gorbea, Martín. "Les Reliefs Orientalisant de Pozo Moro (Albacete, Espagne)." In *Mythe et personification: Actes du colloque du Grand Palais (Paris), 7–8 mai 1977,* edited by Jacqueline Duchemin, 123–36 and plate 1. Centre de recherches mythologiques de l'Université de Paris 10. Paris: Belles Lettres, 1980.

Alter, Yehudah Aryeh Leib. *Sefat Emet.* 2 vols. Jerusalem: n.p., 1971.

Anderson, Gary. "Celibacy or Consummation in the Garden? Reflections on Early Jewish and Christian Interpretations of the Garden of Eden." *Harvard Theological Review* 82 (1989): 121–48.

Arendt, Hannah. "Heidegger at Eighty." In *Heidegger and Modern Philosophy: Critical Essays,* edited by Michael Murray, 293–303. New Haven: Yale University Press, 1978 [originally in German in *Merkur* 10 (1969): 893–902]).

Aroosi, Jamie. "The Causes of Bourgeois Culture: Kierkegaard's Relation to Marx Considered." *Philosophy and Social Criticism* 42 (2015): 71–92.

Aubet, Maria Eugenia. *The Phoenicians and the West: Politics, Colonies, and Trade.* 2nd ed. Translated by Mary Turton. Cambridge: Cambridge University Press, 2001.

Auerbach, Erich. *Mimesis: The Representation of Reality in Western Literature.* Translated by Willard R. Trask. Princeton: Princeton University Press, 1953.

Augustine. *The City of God.* Translated by Gerald G. Walsh and Grace Monahan. Fathers of the Church 14. Washington DC: Catholic University of America Press, 1952.

Bahat, Yaakov. *Uri Zvi Greenberg: Criticism and Analysis of His Poetry and Thought.* Jerusalem and Tel Aviv: Yaḥdav and Dvir, 1983.

Bar-Asher, Moshe. "Notes on Reading 'Aḥizat Moledet' by A. B. Yehoshua." *Kivvunim Ḥadashim* 19 (2009): 64–72.

Baruch, Adam. "Akedah: Afterword." In *Al Tishlaḥ Yadekha el ha-Na'ar,* edited by Arieh Ben-Gurion, 129. Jerusalem: Keter, 2002.

Barugel, Alberto. *The* Sacrifice of Isaac *in Spanish and Sephardic Balladry*. American University Studies. Series II, Romance Languages and Literatures 116. New York: Peter Lang, 1990.

Batnitzky, Leora. *How Judaism Became a Religion: An Introduction to Modern Jewish Thought*. Princeton: Princeton University Press, 2011.

Baumgarten, Albert I. *The Phoenician History of Philo of Byblos: A Commentary*. Études préliminaires aux religions orientales dans l'Empire romain 89. Leiden: Brill, 1981.

Baumgarten, Jean. *Introduction to Old Yiddish Literature*. Edited and translated by Jerold C. Frakes. Oxford: Oxford University Press, 2005.

Beal, Timothy. *The Book of Hiding: Gender, Ethnicity, Annihilation, and Esther*. Biblical Limits. London: Routledge, 1997.

Benbassat, Roi. "Yeshayahu Leibowitz: Jewish Existentialism." *Religious Studies* 51 (2015): 141–63.

Ben-Gurion, Arye, ed. *Al Tishlaḥ Yadekha el ha-Na'ar—Songs and Thought on the Akedah*. Jerusalem: Keter, 2002 [Hebrew].

Ben Pazi, Hanokh. "The Religious Thought of Yeshayahu Leibowitz as 'Radical Theology' after the Shoah." *'Iyyun* 57 (2008): 193–202.

Ben-Shalom, Ram. "Hasdai Crescas: Portrait of a Leader at a Time of Crisis." In *The Jew in Medieval Iberia, 1100–1500*. Edited by Jonathan Ray, 309–51. Jews in Space and Time. Boston: Academic Studies Press, 2012.

———. "*Kiddush Hashem* (Martyrdom) and Jewish Martyrology in Aragon and Castille in the Year 1391: Between Sepharad and Ashkenaz." *Tarbiz* 70 (2001): 227–82 [Hebrew].

Ben-Yeruḥam, Ḥ., and Ḥ. 'E. Ḳolits, eds. *Negation for Negation's Sake: Against Yeshayahu Leibowitz—A Collection of Studies and Notes*. Jerusalem: El ha-Shorashim, 1983.

Berger, David. "Malbim's Secular Knowledge and His Relationship to the Spirit of the Haskalah." *Yavneh Review* 5 (1966): 24–46.

Bernstein, J. M. "Forgetting Isaac: Faith and the Philosophical Impossibility of a Postsecular Society." In *Habermas and Religion*, edited by Craig Calhoun, Eduardo Mendieta, and Jonathan VanAntwerpen, 154–75. Cambridge: Polity, 2013.

Bernstein, Moshe J. "Angels at the Akedah: A Study in the Development of a Midrashic Motif." *Dead Sea Discoveries* 7 (2000): 263–91.

Biala, Tamar. "The End of Sacrificial Religiosity." *De'ot* 40 (2008) [Hebrew].

Blanshard, Brand. *Reason and Belief*. London: Allen & Unwin, 1974.

Boehm, Omri. *The Binding of Isaac: A Religious Model of Disobedience*. Library of Hebrew Bible / Old Testament Studies 468. New York and London: T & T Clark, 2007.

Bonnet, Corinne. "On Gods and Earth: The Tophet and the Construction of a New Identity in Punic Carthage." In *Cultural Identity in the Ancient Mediterranean*, edited by Erich S. Gruen, 373–87. Getty Research Institutes Issues & Debates. Los Angeles: Getty, 2017.

Boyarin, Daniel. *Dying for God: Martyrdom and the Making of Christianity and Judaism*. Stanford: Stanford University Press, 1999.

Brafman, Yonatan. "Universalism and Particularism in Contemporary Philosophy of Halakha: Soloveitchik, Novak, Habermas." In *Das Prinzip Aufklärung zwischen Universalismus und partikularem Anspruch*, edited by Kristina-Monika Hinneburg and Grazyna Jurewicz, 63–78. Munich: Fink, 2014.

Brock, Sebastian. "Sarah and the Akedah." *Le Muséon* 87 (1974): 67–77.

———. *Soghyatha Mgabbyatha*. Monastery of St. Ephrem, 1982.

———. "Two Poems, Jewish and Christian, on Genesis 22: Common and Distinctive Elements in Exegesis." In *Oriental Studies and Interfaith Dialogue: Essays in Honour of József Szécsi*, edited by Máté Hidvégi, 43–55. Budapest: L'Harmatta, 2018.

———. "Two Syriac Verse Homilies on the Binding of Isaac." *Le Muséon* 99 (1986): 61–129.

Brown, Shelby. *Late Carthaginian Child Sacrifice and Sacrificial Monuments in Their Mediterranean Context*. JSOT/ASOR Monograph Series 3. Sheffield: JSOT Press, 1991.

Buber, Martin. *Between Man and Man*. New York: Macmillan, 1965 (originally 1945).

———. *On the Bible: Eighteen Studies*. Edited by Nahum M. Glatzer. New York: Schocken, 1968.

———. "On the Suspension of the Ethical." *Eclipse of God: Studies in the Relation Between Religion and Philosophy*, 100–105. Princeton: Princeton University Press, 2016 (originally 1952).

Calder, N. "The *Sa'y* and the *Jabīn*: Some Notes on the Qur'ān 37: 102-103." *Journal of Semitic Studies* 31 (1986): 17–26.

Carmy, Shalom. "An Individualist Religious Thinker, without Grand Narrative." In Rabbi Shagar (Shimshon Gershon Rosenberg), *Faith Shattered and Restored: Judaism in the Postmodern Age*, edited by Zohar Maor, translated by Elie Leshem, 193–207. Jerusalem: Maggid, 2017.

———. "Paradox, Paradigm, and the Birth of Inwardness: On R. Kook and the Akeda." In *Hazon Nahum: Studies in Jewish Law, Thought, and History Pre-*

sented to Dr. Norman Lamm, edited by Yaakov Elman and Jeffrey S. Gurock, 459–78. New York: Michael Scharf Publication Trust of the Yeshiva University Press; Hoboken NJ: Ktav, 1997.

Carmy, Shalom, and David Shatz. "The Bible as a Source for Philosophical Reflection." In *History of Jewish Philosophy*, edited by Daniel H. Frank and Oliver Leaman, 10–29. New York: Routledge, 1997.

Cassirer, Ernst. *Einstein's Theory of Relativity*. Chicago: Open Court, 1923. Originally published as *Zur Einsteinschen Relativitätstheorie: Erkenntnistheoretische Betrachtungen*. Berlin: Bruno Cassirer, 1921.

Cavell, Stanley. "Kierkegaard's *On Authority and Revelation*." In *Must We Mean What We Say? A Book of Essays*, 165–79. Cambridge: Cambridge University Press, 1969.

Chazan, Robert. *European Jewry and the First Crusade*. Berkeley: University of California Press, 1987.

———. *God, Humanity, and History: The Hebrew First Crusade Chronicles*. Berkeley: University of California Press, 2000.

Clements, Ruth. "The Parallel Lives of Early Jewish and Christian Texts and Art: The Case of Isaac the Martyr." In *New Approaches to the Study of Biblical Interpretation in Judaism of the Second Temple Period and in Early Christianity: Proceedings of the Eleventh International Symposium of the Orion Center for the Study of the Dead Sea Scrolls and Associated Literature, Jointly Sponsored by the Hebrew University Center for the Study of Christianity, 9–11 January, 2007*, edited by Gary A. Anderson, Ruth A. Clements, and David Satran, 207–40. STDJ 106. Leiden: Brill, 2013.

Clive, Geoffrey. "'The Teleological Suspension of the Ethical' in Nineteenth-Century Literature." *Journal of Religion* 34 (1954): 75–87.

Cohen, Gerson. "The Story of Hannah and Her Seven Sons in Hebrew Literature." In *Mordecai M. Kaplan Jubilee Volume*, edited by M. Davis, 109–22. New York: Jewish Theological Seminary, 1953. Reprinted in Cohen, *Studies in the Variety of Rabbinic Culture*, 39–60. JPS Scholars of Distinction Series. Philadelphia: Jewish Publication Society, 1991.

Cohen, Jeremy. "Philosophical Exegesis in Historical Perspective: The Case of the Binding of Isaac." In *Divine Omniscience and Omnipotence in Medieval Philosophy: Islamic, Jewish and Christian Perspectives*, edited by Tamar Rudavsky, 135–42. Synthese Historical Library—Texts and Studies in the History of Logic and Philosophy 25. Dordrecht: Reidel, 1985.

———. *Sanctifying the Name of God: Jewish Martyrs and Jewish Memories of the First Crusade*. Philadelphia: University of Pennsylvania Press, 2006.

Cohen, Leonard. "The Story of Isaac." From *Songs from a Room*. New York: Columbia, 1969.

———. "You Want It Darker." From *You Want It Darker*. New York: Columbia, 2016.

Cohen, Mordechai Z. *Opening the Gates of Interpretation: Maimonides' Biblical Hermeneutics in Light of His Geonic-Andalusian Heritage and Muslim Milieu.* Études sur le judaïsme medieval 48. Leiden: Brill, 2011.

Cohick, Lynn H. *The* Peri Pascha *Attributed to Melito of Sardis: Setting, Purpose, and Sources.* Brown Judaic Studies 327. Providence RI: Brown Judaic Studies, 2000.

Cooper, David E. "Søren Kierkegaard." In *The Blackwell Guide to Continental Philosophy*, edited by Robert C. Solomon and David Sherman, 43–61. Malden MA: Blackwell, 2003.

Crocker, Sylvia Fleming. "Sacrifice in Kierkegaard's *Fear and Trembling*." *Harvard Theological Review* 68 (1975): 125–39.

Derrida, Jacques. "Vacant Chair: Censorship, Mastery, Magisteriality." In *Eyes of the University, Right to Philosophy 2*, 43–63. Stanford: Stanford University Press, 2004.

Diamond, James A. "Abarbanel's Exegetical Subversion of Maimonides' 'Akedah: Transforming a Knight of Intellectual Virtue into a Knight of Existential Faith." In *The Hebrew Bible in Fifteenth-Century Spain: Exegesis, Literature, Philosophy, and the Arts*, edited by Jonathan Decter and Arturo Prats, 75–100. Études sur le judaïsme médiéval 54. Leiden: Brill, 2012.

———. "A Farewell 'Hineni' to Eliezer, the Cohen of Song." *Jerusalem Post*, November 15, 2016. http://www.jpost.com/Opinion/A-farewell-hineni-to-Eliezer-the-Cohen-of-song-472723.

———. "'Trial' as Esoteric Preface in Maimonides' *Guide of the Perplexed*: A Case Study in the Interplay of Text and Prooftext." *Journal of Jewish Thought & Philosophy* 7 (1997): 1–30.

Eastman, David L. "The Matriarch as Model: Sarah, the Cult of the Saints, and Social Control in a Syriac Homily of Pseudo-Ephrem." *Journal of Early Christian Studies* 21 (2013): 241–59.

Elberg, Simcha. *'Akedas Treblinke: Gedanken un Refleksen*. Shanghai: North China Press, 1946 [Yiddish].

Elitzur, Shulamit. "*'Akedat Yiṣḥak*: With Tears or Joy? The Influence of the Crusades on the Biblical Story in Piyyuṭim." *'Eṭ la-Da'at* 1 (1997): 15–35 [Hebrew].

———. "Did Abraham Sin by Binding Isaac?" In *'Aḳedat Yiṣḥaḳ le-Zar'o: Mabbat be-'Ayin Yisra'elit le-zikhro shel Yiṣḥaḳ Hirschberg hy"d*, edited by Israel Rozenson and Binyamin Lau, 215–24. Jerusalem: ha-Ḳeren le-hanṣaḥat Yiṣḥaḳ Hirshberg, 2003.

———. *Rabbi El'azar be-Rabbi Qillir, Qedushta'ot le-Yom Mattan Torah.* Jerusalem: Meḳiṣe Nirdamim, 2000) [Hebrew].

Ellenson, David. "Emil Fackenheim and the Revealed Morality of Judaism." *Judaism* 25 (1976): 402–13.

Evans, C. Stephen. *Kierkegaard's Ethic of Love: Divine Commands and Moral Obligations.* Oxford: Oxford University Press, 2004.

Even-Chen, Alexander. *'Aḳedat Yiṣḥaḳ: In Mystical and Philosophical Interpretation of the Bible.* Tel Aviv: Yedi'ot Aharonot—Sifre Hemed, 2006 [Hebrew].

Fackenheim, Emil L. *Encounters between Judaism and Modern Philosophy: A Preface to Future Jewish Thought.* New York: Basic Books, 1973.

Fagenblat, Michael. "Lacking All Interest: Levinas, Leibowitz, and the Pure Practice of Religion." *Harvard Theological Review* 97 (2004): 1–32.

Feldman, Louis H. *Remember Amalek! Vengeance, Zealotry, and Group Destruction in the Bible According to Philo, Pseudo-Philo, and Josephus.* Monographs of the Hebrew Union College 31. Cincinnati: HUC Press, 2004.

Feldman, Seymour. "The Binding of Isaac: A Test-Case of Divine Foreknowledge." In *Divine Omniscience and Omnipotence in Medieval Philosophy: Islamic, Jewish and Christian Perspectives*, edited by Tamar Rudavsky, 105–33. Synthese Historical Library—Texts and Studies in the History of Logic and Philosophy 25. Dordrecht: Reidel, 1985.

Feldman, Yael. "From 'the Death of Holy Ones' to 'the Joy of the Akedah,' or the 'Invention' of the Akedah as a Heroic Figure in the Zionist Discourse." *Yisrael* 12 (2007): 107–51.

———. *Glory and Agony: Isaac's Sacrifice and National Narrative.* Stanford: Stanford University Press, 2010.

Fishbane, Michael. *Biblical Myth & Rabbinic Mythmaking.* Oxford: Oxford University Press, 2003.

———. *Sacred Attunement: A Jewish Theology.* Chicago: University of Chicago Press, 2008.

Forti, Tova. "The Polarity of Wisdom and Fear of God in the Eden Narrative and in the Book of Proverbs." *Biblische Notizen* 149 (2011): 45–57.

———. "The Topos of the 'Binding of Isaac' (the Akedah) in Modern Hebrew Poetry." In *Unbinding the Binding of Isaac*, edited by Mishael M. Caspi and John T. Greene, 193–210. Lanham MD: University Press of America, 2007.

Fox, Marvin. "Kierkegaard and Rabbinic Judaism." *Judaism* 2 (1953): 115–24.

Frakes, Jerold C. *Early Yiddish Epic*. Syracuse: Syracuse University Press, 2014.

———. *Early Yiddish Texts, 1100-1750*. Oxford: Oxford University Press, 2004.

Friedman, Michael. "Ernst Cassirer and Thomas Kuhn: The Neo-Kantian Tradition in History and Philosophy of Science." *Philosophical Forum* 39 (2008): 239–52.

Frymer-Kensky, Tikva. "Tit for Tat: The Principle of Equal Retribution in Near Eastern and Biblical Law." *Biblical Archaeologist* 43 (1980): 230–34.

Gampel, Benjamin R. *Anti-Jewish Riots in the Crown of Aragon and the Royal Response, 1391-1392*. Cambridge: Cambridge University Press, 2016.

Gellman, Jerome. *Abraham! Abraham! Kierkegaard and the Hasidim on the Binding of Isaac*. Aldershot, England: Ashgate, 2003.

———. "And Sarah Died." *Tradition* 32, no. 1 (1997): 62.

———. *The Fear, the Trembling, and the Fire: Kierkegaard and Hasidic Masters on the Binding of Isaac*. Lanham MD: University Press of America, 1994.

Ginsberg, H. L. "Psalms and Inscriptions of Petition and Acknowledgment." In *Louis Ginzberg Jubilee Volume*, 159–71. New York: American Academy for Jewish Research, 1945.

Goldenberg, Robert. "The Problem of False Prophecy: Talmudic Interpretations of Jeremiah 28 and 1 Kings 22." In *The Biblical Mosaic: Changing Perspectives*, edited by Robert Polzin and Eugene Rothman, 87–103. Philadelphia and Chico CA: Fortress and Scholars, 1982.

Goldstein, Ronnie, and Guy G. Stroumsa. "The Greek and Jewish Origins of Docetism: A New Proposal." *Zeitschrift für Antikes Christentum* 10 (2006): 423–41.

Good, J. Edwin "Isaac Typology in the New Testament." *New Testament Studies* 14 (1968): 583–89.

Gordis, Robert. "The Faith of Abraham: A Note on Kierkegaard's 'Teleological Suspension of the Ethical.'" *Judaism* 25 (1976): 414–19; 26 (1977): 116.

Gordon, Peter E. "Continental Divide: Ernst Cassirer and Martin Heidegger at Davos, 1929—An Allegory of Intellectual History." *Modern Intellectual History* 1 (2004): 219–48.

———. *Continental Divide: Heidegger, Cassirer, Davos*. Cambridge MA: Harvard University Press, 2010.

Graetz, Naomi. "Trauma and Recovery: Abraham's Journey to the *Akeidah*." *CCAR Journal* 58, no. 4 (2012): 29–50.

Graham-Nixon, Andrew. *Caravaggio: A Life Sacred and Profane*. New York: W. W. Norton, 2010.

Green, Ronald M. "Abraham, Isaac, and the Jewish Tradition: An Ethical Reappraisal." *Journal of Religious Ethics* 10 (1982): 1–21.

———. "*Fear and Trembling*: A Jewish Appreciation." *Kierkegaard Studies Yearbook 2002*, 137–49.

Greenberg, Gershon. "Ultra-Orthodox Reflections on the Holocaust: 1945 to the Present." In *Contemporary Responses to the Holocaust*, edited by Konrad Kwiet and Jürgen Matthäus, 87–121. Praeger Series on Jewish and Israeli Studies. Westport CT: Praeger, 2004.

Greenberg, Moshe. *Ezekiel 1-20*. Anchor Bible 22. Garden City NY: Doubleday, 1983.

———. "Some Postulates of Biblical Criminal Law." In *Yehezkel Kaufmann Jubilee Volume*, edited by Menahem Haran, 5–28. Jerusalem: Magnes, 1960.

Greenberg, Uri Zvi. *The Book of Indictment and Faith*. Jerusalem and Tel Aviv: Sedan, 1937 [Hebrew]. Reprinted and cited from *Uri Zvi Greenberg: The Complete Writings*, vol. 3 edited by Dan Miron. Jerusalem: Bialik, 1991.

———. "The Morning Sacrifice." *Sulam* 13 (1963) [Hebrew]. Reprinted in *Uri Zvi Greenberg: The Collected Writings*, vol. 11, edited by Dan Miron, 53. Jerusalem: Bialik, 1996.

Greenblum, Dror. "The Making of a Myth: The Story of Kfar Etzion in Religious Zionism, 1948–1967." *Israel Studies* 21 (2016): 132–56.

Greenstein, Edward L. "Reading Pragmatically: Interpreting the Binding of Isaac." In *Words, Ideas, Worlds: Biblical Essays in Honour of Yairah Amit*, edited by Athalya Brenner and Frank H. Polak, 102–32. Hebrew Bible Monographs 40. Amsterdam Studies in the Bible and Religion 5. Sheffield: Sheffield Academic, 2012.

Griffith, Sidney H. "Disclosing the Mystery: The Hermeneutics of Typology in Syriac Exegesis." In *Interpreting Scriptures in Judaism, Christianity, and Islam*, edited by Mordechai Z. Cohen and Adele Berlin, 46–64. Cambridge: Cambridge University Press, 2016.

Gumbiner, J. H. "Existentialism and Our Father Abraham." *Commentary* 5, no. 2 (February 1948): 143–48.

Habermann, A. M. *Gezerot Ashkenaz ve-Tzarfat*. Jerusalem: Tarshish, 1946.

Habermas, Jürgen. "Reply to My Critics." In *Habermas and Religion*, edited by Craig Calhoun, Eduardo Mendieta, and Jonathan VanAntwerpen, 347–90. Cambridge: Polity, 2013.

———. "Work and Weltanschauung: The Heidegger Controversy from a German Perspective." *Critical Inquiry* 15 (1989): 431–56.

Hahn, Scott Walker, and John Sietze Bergsma. "What Laws Were 'Not Good'? A Canonical Approach to the Theological Problem of Ezekiel 20:25–26." *Journal of Biblical Literature* 123 (2004): 201–18.

Halbertal, Moshe. *On Sacrifice*. Princeton: Princeton University Press, 2012.

———. "The Scourge of Reason." *New Republic* 208, no. 111 (March 15, 1993): 35–38.

Halevi, Jacob. "Kierkegaard and the Midrash." *Judaism* 4 (1955): 13–28.

Halpern, Baruch. "Jerusalem and the Lineages in the Seventh Century BCE: Kinship and the Rise of Individual Moral Liability." In *Law and Ideology in Monarchic Israel*, edited by Baruch Halpern and Deborah W. Hobson, 11–107. JSOT Supplement 124. Sheffield: Sheffield Academic, 1991.

Hamilton, Michelle M. *Beyond Faith: Belief, Morality and Memory in a Fifteenth-Century Judeo-Iberian Manuscript*. The Medieval and Early Modern Iberian World 57. Leiden: Brill, 2014.

Haran, Menahem. "From Early to Classical Prophecy: Continuity and Change." *Vetus Testamentum* 27 (1977): 385–97.

Hartman, David. *A Heart of Many Rooms: Celebrating the Many Voices within Judaism*. Woodstock VT: Jewish Lights, 2001.

———. *A Living Covenant: The Innovative Spirit in Traditional Judaism*. New York: Free Press, 1985. Reprint, Woodstock VT: Jewish Lights, 1997.

———. *Love and Terror in the God Encounter: The Theological Legacy of Rabbi Joseph B. Soloveitchik*. Woodstock VT: Jewish Lights, 2001.

———. "Prayer and Religious Consciousness: An Analysis of Jewish Prayer in the Works of Joseph B. Soloveitchik, Yeshayahu Leibowitz, and Abraham Joshua Heschel." *Modern Judaism* 23 (2003): 105–25.

Hartman, Tova, and Charlie Buckholtz. *Are You Not a Man of God? Devotion, Betrayal, and Social Criticism in Jewish Tradition*. Oxford: Oxford University Press, 2014.

Harvey, Warren Ze'ev. "Comments on Rabbi Soloveitchik and Maimonidean Philosophy." In *Faith in Changing Times*, edited by Avi Sagi, 100–101. Jerusalem: World Zionist Organization, 1996 [Hebrew].

———. "Leibowitz on Abrahamic Man, Belief, and Nihilism." In *Abraham, Father of Believers: His Images in Light of the History of Philosophy*, edited by Moshe Hallamish, Hannah Kasher, and Yohanan Silman, 347–52. Ramat Gan: Bar Ilan University Press, 2002 [Hebrew].

———. "On Yeshayahu Leibowitz: 'The Faith of Maimonides.'" *'Iyyun* 30 (1981): 141–49 [Hebrew].

———. *Rabbi Ḥasdai Crescas*. Jerusalem: Merkaz Zalman Shazar, 2010 [Hebrew].

Held, Shai. *Abraham Joshua Heschel: The Call of Transcendence*. Bloomington: Indiana University Press, 2013.

Herring, Basil. *Joseph ibn Kaspi's Gevia' Kesef: A Study in Medieval Jewish Philosophic Bible Commentary*. New York: Ktav, 1982.

Herskowitz, Daniel. "The Moment and the Future: Kierkegaard's *Øieblikket* and Soloveitchik's View of Repentance." *AJS Review* 40 (2016): 87–99.

———. "Rabbi Joseph B. Soloveitchik's Endorsement and Critique of Volkish Thought." *Journal of Modern Jewish Studies* 14 (2015): 373–90.

Hutner David, Bruria. *The Dual Role of Rabbi Zvi Hirsch Chajes: Traditionalist and Maskil*. PhD diss., Columbia University, 1971.

Ibn al-'Arabi. *The Bezels of Wisdom*. Translated and introduction by R. W. J. Austin. New York: Paulist Press, 1980.

Ibn Virga, Solomon. *Shevet Yehudah*. Jerusalem: Sepharadic Library, 1991.

Idel, Moshe. "*Hitbodedut* as Concentration in Ecstatic Kabbalah." In *Jewish Spirituality*. Vol. 1, *From the Bible through the Middle Ages*, edited by Arthur Green, 405–38. New York: Crossroad, 1986.

Irshai, Ronit. "Homosexuality and the 'Akedah Theology': A Comparison of Modern Orthodoxy and the Conservative Movement." *Journal of Jewish Ethics* 4 (2018): 19–46.

———. "The New Ascent of 'Akedah Theology' and Its Moral, Halakhic, and Gender Implications." *Jerusalem Studies in Jewish Thought* 25 (2017): 273–304 [Hebrew].

———. "Religion and Morality: *Akedah* Theology and Cumulative Revelation as Contradictory Theologies in Jewish Modern-Orthodox Feminism." *Journal of Modern Jewish Studies* 15 (2016): 1–17.

Irshai, Ronit, and Tanya Zion Waldoks. "Modern Orthodox Feminism in Israel between Nomos and Narrative." *Mishpat u-Mimshal* 15 (2013): 1–94 [Hebrew].

Jacobs, Louis. "The Problem of the Akedah in Jewish Thought." In *Kierkegaard's* Fear and Trembling: *Critical Appraisals*, edited by Robert L. Perkins, 1–9. University: University of Alabama Press, 1981.

Japhet, Sara. *I & II Chronicles: A Commentary*. OTL. Louisville: Westminster John Knox, 1993.

Jasnow, Richard. *A Late Period Hieratic Wisdom Text (P. Brooklyn 47.218.135)*. Studies in Ancient Oriental Civilizations 52. Chicago: Oriental Institute of the University of Chicago, 1992.

Jones, Joe R. "Some Remarks on Authority and Revelation in Kierkegaard." *Journal of Religion* 57 (1977): 232–51.

Joslyn-Siemiatkoski, Dan. "The Mother and Seven Sons in Late Antique and Medieval Ashkenazi Judaism: Narrative Transformations and Communal Identity." In *Dying for the Faith, Killing for the Faith: Old-Testament Faith-Warriors (1 and 2 Maccabees) in Historical Perspective*, edited by Gabriela Signori, 125–46. Brill's Studies in Intellectual History 206. Leiden: Brill, 2012.

Kanarek, Jane. "He Took the Knife: Biblical Narrative and the Formation of Rabbinic Law." *AJS Review* 34 (2010): 65–90.

Kant, Immanuel. *The Conflict of the Faculties*. Translated and introduction by Mary J. Gregor. Lincoln: University of Nebraska Press, 1992.

———. *Religion within the Boundaries of Mere Reason*. Edited and translated by Allen W. Wood and George di Giovanni. Introduction by Robert Merrihew Adams. Cambridge: Cambridge University Press, 1998.

Kaplan, Lawrence. "From Cooperation to Conflict: Rabbi Professor Emanuel Rackman, Rav Joseph B. Soloveitchik, and the Evolution of American Orthodoxy." *Modern Judaism* 30 (2010): 46–68.

Kartun-Blum, Ruth. *Profane Scriptures: Reflections on the Dialogue with the Bible in Modern Hebrew Poetry*. Cincinnati: HUC Press, 1999.

———. *A Story Like a Knife: 'Akedah and Song*. Tel Aviv: Hakibbutz Hameuchad, 2013 [Hebrew].

Kasher, Hannah. "How Could God Command Us to Perform Such an Abomination?! Critique of the Akedah According to R. Joseph Ibn Kaspi." *'Eṭ la-Da'at* 1 (1997): 37–47 [Hebrew].

Kasher, Hannah, and Moshe Kahan. "Joseph Kaspi." Stanford Encyclopedia of Philosophy. Updated January 15, 2019. http://plato.stanford.edu/entries/kaspi-joseph/.

Katz, Jacob. "Towards a Biography of the Hatam Sofer." In *Divine Law in Human Hands: Case Studies in Halakhic Flexibility*, 403–43. Jerusalem: Magnes Press, 1998.

Kaufman, Stephen A. "An Emphatic Plea for Please." *Maarav* 7 (1991): 195–98.

Kellner, Menachem Marc. "Maimonides and Gersonides on Mosaic Prophecy." *Speculum* 52 (1977): 62–79.

Kemp, Ryan. "In Defense of a Straightforward Reading of *Fear and Trembling*." *Kierkegaard Studies Yearbook* 2013, no. 1 (2013): 49–70.

Kessler, Edward. *Bound by the Bible: Jews, Christians and the Sacrifice of Isaac*. Cambridge: Cambridge University Press, 2004.

Kierkegaard, Søren. *The Concept of Irony/Schelling Lecture Notes*. Edited and translated by Howard V. Hong and Edna H. Hong. Kierkegaard's Writings 2. Princeton: Princeton University Press, 1989.

———. *Fear and Trembling*. Translated by Sylvia Walsh. Edited and introduction by C. Stephen Evans. Cambridge Texts in the History of Philosophy. Cambridge: Cambridge University Press, 2006.

———. *Fear and Trembling/Repetition*. Translated with notes by Howard V. Hong and Edna H. Hong. Kierkegaard's Writings 6. Princeton: Princeton University Press, 1983.

———. "A First and Last Declaration." In *Concluding Unscientific Postscript to the Philosophical Crumbs*, edited and translated by Alastair Hannay, 527–31. Cambridge Texts in the History of Philosophy. Cambridge: Cambridge University Press, 2009.

———. *Letters and Documents*. Edited and translated by Henrik Rosenmeier. Kierkegaard's Writings 25. Princeton: Princeton University Press, 1978.

———. *On Authority and Revelation: The Book on Adler, or a Cycle of Ethico-Religious Essays*. Translated with an introduction and notes by Walter Lowrie. New York: Harper & Row, 1966. Originally published 1955 by Princeton University Press.

Kister, Menahem. "*Islām*: Midrashic Perspectives on a Quranic Term." *Journal of Semitic Studies* 63 (2018): 381–406.

———. "*Shirat Bene Ma'arava*: Aspects of the World of Anonymous Poetry." *Tarbiz* 76 (2007): 105–84 [Hebrew].

Knohl, Dov. *Siege in the Hills of Hebron*. Introduction by Abba Eban. New York and London: Thomas Yoseloff, 1958.

Knohl, Israel. *The Divine Symphony: The Bible's Many Voices*. Philadelphia: Jewish Publication Society, 2003.

———. "Does God Deceive? An Examination of the Dark Side of Isaiah's Prophecy." In *Mishneh Todah: Studies in Deuteronomy and Its Cultural Environment in Honor of Jeffrey H. Tigay*, edited by Nili Sacher Fox, David A. Glatt-Gilad, and Michael J. Williams, 275–91. Winona Lake IN: Eisenbrauns, 2008.

———. "In the Face of Death: Mortality and Religious Life in the Bible, in Rabbinic Literature and in the Pauline Letters." In *Self, Soul and Body in Religious Experience*, edited by Albert I. Baumgarten, Jan Assmann, and Guy G. Stroumsa, 87–95. Studies in the History of Religions 78. Leiden: Brill, 1998.

Koch, Carl Henrik. "Adolph Peter Adler: A Stumbling Block and an Inspiration for Kierkegaard." In *Kierkegaard and His Danish Contemporaries*, tome 2, *Theology*, edited by Jon Stewart, 1–22. Kierkegaard Research: Sources, Reception, and Resources 7. Surrey: Ashgate, 2009.

Kolbrener, William. *The Last Rabbi: Joseph Soloveitchik and Talmudic Tradition*. Bloomington: Indiana University Press, 2016.

———. "Towards a Genuine Jewish Philosophy: *Halakhic Mind*'s New Philosophy of Religion." *Tradition* 30, no. 3 (Spring 1996): 21–43.

Koller, Aaron. "On Texts, Contexts, and Countertexts." *Prooftexts* 35 (2015): 328–44.

Koltun-Fromm, Ken. "Historical Memory in Abraham Geiger's Account of Modern Jewish Identity." *Jewish Social Studies* 7 (2000): 109–26.

Korn, Eugene. "Windows on the World—Judaism Beyond Ethnicity: A Review of *Abraham's Journey* by Joseph B. Soloveitchik, edited by David Shatz, Joel B. Wolowelsky and Reuven Ziegler, and *Future Tense* by Rabbi Jonathan Sacks." *Meorot* 8 (2010): 1–9.

Kreisel, Howard. *Prophecy: The History of an Idea in Medieval Jewish Philosophy*. Dordrecht: Kluwer, 2001.

Kugel, James. "Exegetical Notes on 4Q225 'Pseudo-Jubilees.'" *Dead Sea Discoveries* 13 (2006): 73–98.

Lamm, Norman. "The Greatest Trial." *Derasha* for the Second Day of Rosh Hashanah, September 14, 1969, Jewish Center, New York City. https://archives.yu .edu/gsdl/collect/lammserm/index/assoc/HASHc7ed.dir/doc.pdf.

Lange, Armin. "'They Burn Their Sons and Daughters—That Was No Command of Mine' (Jer 7:31): Child Sacrifice in the Hebrew Bible and in the Deuteronomistic Jeremiah Redaction." In *Human Sacrifice in Jewish and Christian Tradition*, edited by Karin Finsterbusch, Armin Lange, and K. F. Diethard Römheld, 109–32. Leiden: Brill, 2007.

Lasker, Daniel J. *From Judah Hadassi to Elijah Bashyatchi: Studies in Late Medieval Karaite Philosophy*. Supplements to the Journal of Jewish Thought and Philosophy 4. Leiden: Brill, 2008.

Last Stone, Suzanne. "Between Truth and Trust: The False Prophet as Self-Deceiver?" *Hebraic Political Studies* 4 (2009): 337–66.

Leibowitz, Yeshayahu. "Abraham and Job." In *Judaism, the Jewish People, and the State of Israel*, 391–94. Jerusalem and Tel Aviv: Schocken, 1975 [Hebrew].

———. *Judaism, Human Values, and the Jewish State*. Edited by Eliezer Goldman. Cambridge MA: Harvard University Press, 1992.

———. "Maimonides—Abrahamic Man." *Be-Terem* 211 (1955): 20–22 [Hebrew]. English translation: "Maimonides—the Abrahamic Man." *Judaism* 6 (1957): 148–54.

———. "Religious Praxis." In *Judaism, Human Values, and the Jewish State*, edited by Eliezer Goldman, 1–29. Cambridge MA: Harvard University Press, 1992.

———. "[Response]." *Judaism* 7 (1958): 74–75.

Leiner, Mordechai Joseph. *Mei ha-Shiloaḥ.* Edited by Gershon Henoch of Radzin. 2 vols. Jerusalem: Institute for the Publication of the Rebbe from Izbica-Radzin, 1995. Originally published posthumously, 1858.

Levenson, Alan T. "Joseph Soloveitchik's *The Halachic Mind*: A Liberal Critique and Appreciation." *CCAR Journal* 41 (1994): 55–63.

Levenson, Jon D. *The Death and Resurrection of the Beloved Son: The Transformation of Child Sacrifice in Judaism and Christianity.* New Haven: Yale University Press, 1993.

Levin, Hanoch. *Mah Ikhpat la-Tzippor: Satires, Skits, Hymns.* Tel Aviv: ha-Kibbutz ha-Me'uḥad, 1987 [Hebrew].

Levinas, Emmanuel. *Difficult Freedom.* Translated by Séan Hand. Baltimore: Johns Hopkins University Press, 1990.

———. "Kierkegaard: Existence and Ethics." In *Proper Names*, translated by Michael B. Smith, 66–74. London: Athlone, 1996.

———. *Proper Names.* Translated by Michael B. Smith. London: Athlone, 1996.

Levy, Ze'ev. "On the *Aquedah* in Modern Philosophy." *Journal of Jewish Thought and Philosophy* 15 (2007): 85–108.

Lichtenstein, Aharon. "Prayer in the Thought of Rabbi Joseph B. Soloveitchik zt"l." *Shanah be-Shanah* (1999): 287–301 [Hebrew].

———. "Religion and State." In *Contemporary Jewish Religious Thought: Original Essays on Critical Concepts, Movements, and Beliefs*, edited by Arthur A. Cohen and Paul Mendes-Flohr, 773–78. New York and London: Free Press and Macmillan, 1987.

Logan, Alice. "Rehabilitating Jephthah." *Journal of Biblical Literature* 128 (2009): 665–85.

Luft, Sebastian. *The Space of Culture: Towards a Neo-Kantian Philosophy of Culture (Cohen, Natorp, and Cassirer).* Oxford: Oxford University Press, 2015.

Magid, Shaul. "Hasidism and Existentialism? A Review Essay." *Modern Judaism* 15 (1995): 279–94.

Malik, Habib C. *Receiving Søren Kierkegaard: The Early Impact and Transmission of His Thought.* Washington DC: Catholic University of America Press, 1997.

Marcus, David. *Jephthah and His Vow*. Lubbock: Texas Tech University Press, 1986.

Marcus, Ivan G. "From Politics to Martyrdom: Shifting Paradigms in the Hebrew Narratives of the 1096 Riots." *Prooftexts* 2 (1982): 40–52.

Margaliot, Mordechai. *Midrash Wayyiqra Rabbah: Based on Manuscripts and Genizah Fragments*. New York: Jewish Theological Seminary of American, 1993. Reprint of 1953–60 ed. [Hebrew].

Marin, Louis. *To Destroy Painting*. Chicago: University of Chicago Press, 1994. Reprint of French 1977 ed.

Martin, S. Rebecca. *The Art of Contact: Comparative Approaches to Greek and Phoenician Art*. Philadelphia: University of Pennsylvania Press, 2017.

Matenko, Percy, and Samuel Sloan, "The Akedath Jiṣḥaq: A Sixteenth Century Yiddish Epic." In *Two Studies in Yiddish Culture*, 3–70. Leiden: Brill, 1962.

McGinn, Bernard. *The Mystical Thought of Meister Eckhart: The Man from Whom God Hid Nothing*. New York: Herder and Herder, 2001.

Mein, Andrew. *Ezekiel and the Ethics of Exile*. Oxford: Oxford University Press, 2001.

Meir, Ephraim. "The Interpretation of the Binding of Isaac in the Dialogical Thought of Martin Buber: Between Kierkegaard and Hasidut." In *Abraham, Father of Believers: His Images in Light of the History of Philosophy*, edited by Moshe Hallamish, Hannah Kasher, and Yohanan Silman, 281–93. Ramat Gan: Bar Ilan University Press, 2002) [Hebrew].

Melito of Sardis. *On Pascha and Fragments*. Edited and translated by Stuart George Hall. Oxford: Clarendon, 1979.

Mesch, Barry. *Studies in Joseph Ibn Caspi: Fourteenth-Century Philosopher and Exegete*. Études sur le judaïsme médiéval 8. Leiden: Brill, 1975.

Milgrom, Jacob. "Were the Firstborn Sacrificed to YHWH? To Molek? Popular Practice or Divine Demand?" In *Sacrifice in Religious Experience*, edited by Albert I. Baumgarten, 49–55. Leiden: Brill, 2002.

Mintz, Alan. "Haim Gouri at 90." *Jewish Review of Books*, Summer 2014, 36–39.

———. *Ḥurban: Responses to Catastrophe in Hebrew Literature*. Syracuse: Syracuse University Press, 1996.

Mirsky, Yehudah. "Judaism, Human Values and the Jewish State." *New Leader* 75, no. 11 (September 7, 1992): 18–20.

Moberly, R. W. L. "Does God Lie to His Prophets? The Story of Michaiah ben Imlah as a Test Case." *Harvard Theological Review* 96 (2003): 1–23.

Monroe, Lauren S. "Disembodied Women: Sacrificial Language and the Deaths of Bat-Jephthah, Cozbi, and the Bethlehemite Concubine." *Catholic Biblical Quarterly* 75 (2003): 35–52.

Mosca, Paul G. "Child Sacrifice in Canaanite and Israelite Religion." PhD thesis, Harvard University, 1975.

Moss, Candida. *The Myth of Persecution: How Early Christians Invented a Story of Martyrdom*. New York: HarperOne, 2013.

Moyn, Samuel. "Judaism against Paganism: Emmanuel Levinas's Response to Heidegger and Nazism in the 1930s." *History & Memory* 10 (1998): 25–58.

———. "Transcendence, Morality, and History: Emmanuel Levinas and the Discovery of Søren Kierkegaard in France." *Yale French Studies* 104 (2004): 22–54.

Munk, Reinier. *The Rationale of Halakhic Man: Joseph B. Soloveitchik's Conception of Jewish Thought*. Amsterdam Studies in Jewish Thought 3. Amsterdam: J. C. Gieben, 1996.

Münz-Manor, Ophir. "Narrating Salvation: Verbal Sacrifices in Late Antique Liturgical Poetry." In *Jews, Christians, and the Roman Empire: The Poetics of Power in Late Antiquity*, edited by Natalie B. Dohrmann and Annette Yoshiko Reed, 154–66, 315–19. Jewish Culture and Contexts. Philadelphia: University of Pennsylvania Press, 2013.

Natorp, Paul. *Die logischen Grundlagen der exakten Wissenschaften*. 2nd ed. Leipzig: Teubner, 1921.

Nissim b. Reuben Gerondi. *Commentary on the Torah*. Edited by Leon Feldman. Jerusalem: Makhon Shalom, 1968 [Hebrew].

Novak, David. "Buber's Critique of Heidegger." *Modern Judaism* 5 (1985): 125–40.

Nuriel, Avraham. "Parables Which Are Not Said to Be Parables in the *Guide for the Perplexed*." *Da'at* 25 (1990): 85–91 [Hebrew].

———. *Revealed and Hidden in Medieval Jewish Philosophy*. Jerusalem: Magnes, 2000 [Hebrew].

Ofrat, Gideon. "The Binding of Isaac in Israeli Art." In *Within a Local Context*, 124–53. Tel Aviv: Hakibbutz Hameuchad, 2004 [Hebrew].

Ohana, David. *The Origins of Israeli Mythology: Neither Canaanites Nor Crusaders*. Cambridge: Cambridge University Press, 2012.

Outka, Gene. "God as the Subject of Unique Veneration: A Response to Ronald M. Green." *Journal of Religious Ethics* 21 (1993): 211–15.

Owen, Wilfred. *The Poems of Wilfred Owen*. Introduction and notes by Owen Knowles. Ware: Wordsworth, 1994.

Oz, Amos, and Fania Oz-Salzberger. *Jews and Words*. New Haven: Yale University Press, 2012.

Ozar, Alex S. "The Emergence of Max Scheler: Understanding Rabbi Joseph Soloveitchik's Philosophical Anthropology." *Harvard Theological Review* 109 (2016): 178–206.

———. "Yeridah le-Ẓorekh Aliyyah: Rabbi Joseph B. Soloveitchik on Autonomy and Submission." *Torah u-Madda Journal* 17 (2017): 150–73.

Paczkowski, Mieczyslaw. "The Sacrifice of Isaac in Early Patristic Exegesis." In *The Sacrifice of Isaac in the Three Monotheistic Religions*, edited by Frederic Manns, 101–21. Jerusalem: Franciscan Printing Press, 1995.

Patten, Alan. *Hegel's Idea of Freedom*. Oxford Philosophical Monographs. Oxford: Oxford University Press, 1999.

Patton, Caroline. "'I Myself Gave Them Laws That Were Not Good': Ezekiel 20 and the Exodus Traditions." *Journal for the Study of the Old Testament* 69 (1996): 73–90.

Pitard, Wayne T. "The Identity of the Bir-Hadad of the Melqart Stela." *Bulletin of the American Schools for Oriental Research* 272 (1988): 3–21.

Poole, Roger. "The Unknown Kierkegaard: Twentieth-Century Receptions." In *The Cambridge Companion to Kierkegaard*, edited by Alastair Hannay and Gordon D. Marino, 48–75. Cambridge: Cambridge University Press, 1998.

Possen, David D. "J. B. Soloveitchik: Between Neo-Kantianism and Kierkegaardian Existentialism." In *Kierkegaard's Influence on Theology*, tome 3, *Catholic and Jewish Theology*, edited by Jon Stewart, 189–210. Kierkegaard Research: Sources, Reception and Resources 10. New York: Routledge, 2012.

Prosser, Brian T. "Conscientious Subjectivity in Kierkegaard and Levinas." *Continental Philosophy Review* 35 (2002): 397–422.

Quinn, Josephine. *In Search of the Phoenicians*. Princeton: Princeton University Press, 2017.

Rae, Gavin. "Kierkegaard, the Self, Authenticity and the Teleological Suspension of the Ethical." *Critical Horizons* 11 (2010): 75–97.

Redfield, James Adam. "Behind Auerbach's 'Background': Five Ways to Read What Biblical Narratives Don't Say." *AJS Review* 39 (2015): 121–50.

Reiser, Daniel. *Derashot mi-Shnot ha-Za'am: Derashot ha-Admo"r mi-Piaseczna be-Ghetto Warsaw, 1940–1942: Critical Edition Based on the Author's Autograph, with an Introduction, Notes, and Sources*. Jerusalem: Herzog Academic College, Yad Vashem, World Union of Jewish Studies, 2017.

Rives, James B. "Tertullian on Child Sacrifice." *Museum Helveticum* 51 (1994): 54–63.

Roberts, J. J. M. "Does God Lie? Divine Deceit as a Theological Problem in Israelite Prophetic Literature." In *Congress Volume 1986*, edited by John A. Emerton, 211–20. VT Supplement 40. Leiden: Brill, 1988.

Roman, Oren. "Early Ashkenazic Poems about the Binding of Isaac." *Naharaim* 10 (2016): 175–94.

Roos, Lena. *"God Wants It!": The Ideology of Martyrdom in the Hebrew Crusade Chronicles and Its Jewish and Christian Background*. Medieval Church Studies 6. Turnhout, Belgium: Brepols, 2006.

Rosenbloom, Noah H. *Ha-Malbim: Exegesis, Philosophy, Knowledge, and Mystery in the Writings of Rabbi Meir Leibush Malbim*. Jerusalem: Mossad ha-Rav Kook, 1988 [Hebrew].

Roskies, David G. "The Holocaust According to the Literary Critics." *Prooftexts* 1 (1981): 209–16.

Roth, Cecil. "A Hebrew Elegy on the Martyrs of Toledo, 1391." *Jewish Quarterly Review* 39 (1948): 123–50.

Rothschild, Clare K. *Hebrews as Pseudepigraphon: The History and Significance of the Pauline Attribution of Hebrews*. WUNT 235. Tübingen: Mohr Siebeck, 2009.

Rudolph, Conrad, and Steven Ostrow. "Isaac Laughing: Caravaggio, Non-traditional Imagery and Traditional Identification." *Art History* 24 (2001): 646–81.

Rundin, John S. "Pozo Moro, Child Sacrifice, and the Greek Legendary Tradition." *Journal of Biblical Literature* 123 (2004): 425–47.

———. "[Review of Gellman, *Abraham! Abraham!*]." In *Religious Studies* 41 (2005): 116–20.

Rynhold, Daniel. *Two Models of Jewish Philosophy: Justifying One's Practices*. Oxford: Oxford University Press, 2005.

———. "Yeshayahu Leibowitz." Stanford Encyclopedia of Philosophy. Summer 2011 ed., edited by Edward N. Zalta. http://plato.stanford.edu /archives/sum2011/entries/leibowitz-yeshayau/.

Saadia Gaon. *The Book of Beliefs and Doctrines*. Edited and translated by Joseph Qafih. New York: Sura Institute of Yeshiva University, 1970 [Arabic and Hebrew].

Sacks, Jonathan. "Rabbi J. B. Soloveitchik's Early Epistemology: A Review of *The Halakhic Mind*." *Tradition* 23, no. 3 (Spring 1988): 75–87.

Sagi, Avi. "The Aḳedah: The Problem of Obedience or the Problem of Hearing—Between Kierkegaard and Buber." *'Iyyun* 37 (1988): 248–62 [Hebrew].

———. "Contending with Modernity: Scripture in the Thought of Yeshayahu Leibowitz and Joseph Soloveitchik." *Journal of Religion* 77 (1997): 421–41.

———. *Kierkegaard, Religion, and Existence: The Voyage of the Self*. Translated by Batya Stein. Amsterdam: Rodopi, 2000.

———. "The Meaning of the Akedah in Israeli Culture and Jewish Tradition." *Israel Studies* 3 (1998): 45–60.

———. "The Punishment of Amalek in Jewish Tradition: Coping with the Moral Problem." *Harvard Theological Review* 87 (1994): 323–46.

———. "Rabbi Soloveitchik and Professor Liebowitz as Theoreticians of Halakhah." *Da'at* 29 (1992): 131–48.

———. "The Trial of the Akedah: A Comparative Study in the Thought of Kierkegaard and Leibowitz." *Da'at* 23 (1989): 121–34.

Sagi, Avi, and Daniel Statman. "Divine Command Morality and Jewish Tradition." *Journal of Religious Ethics* 23 (1995): 39–67.

Saks, Jeffrey. "Letters on Religion without Theology." *Tradition* 34, no. 3 (2000): 88–94.

Saperstein, Marc. "A Sermon on the Akedah from the Generation of the Expulsion and Its Implications for 1391." In *Exile and Diaspora: Studies in the History of the Jewish People Presented to Professor Haim Beinart*, edited by Aharon Mirsky, Avraham Grossman, and Yosef Kaplan, 103–24. Jerusalem and Madrid: Ben Zvi Institute and the Hebrew University, and Consejo Superior de Investigaciones Científicas, 1991.

Schlossberg, Eliezer. "The Place of the Binding of Isaac in R. Sa'adia Gaon's Polemic against Islam." In *Abraham, Father of Believers: His Images in Light of the History of Philosophy*, edited by Moshe Hallamish, Hannah Kasher, and Yohanan Silman, 115–29. Ramat Gan: Bar Ilan University Press, 2002 [Hebrew].

Schoenfeld, Devorah. *Isaac on Jewish and Christian Altars: Polemic and Exegesis in Rashi and the Glossa Ordinaria*. Fordham Series in Medieval Studies. New York: Fordham University Press, 2013.

Schulz, Heiko. "Germany and Austria: A Modest Head Start: The German Reception of Kierkegaard." In *Kierkegaard's International Reception—Northern and Western Europe*, edited by Jon Stewart, 307–419. Kierkegaard Research: Sources, Reception and Resources 8/I. London: Routledge, 2009.

Schwartz, Dov. *The Philosophical Thought of Rabbi Soloveitchik*. Vol. 3, *Prayer as Experience*. Ramat Gan: Bar Ilan University Press, 2015 [Hebrew].

Schwartz, Jeffrey H. "The Mythology of Carthaginian Child Sacrifice." In *Diversity of Sacrifice: Form and Function of Sacrificial Practices in the Ancient World and Beyond*, edited by Carrie Ann Murray, 103–25. IEMA Proceedings 5. Albany: State University of New York Press, 2016.

Schwartz, Jeffrey H., Frank Houghton, Luca Bondioli, and Roberto Macchiarelli. "Carthaginian Infant Sacrifice Revisited." *Antiquity* 86 (2012): 738–45.

Schwartz, Jeffrey H., Frank Houghton, Luca Bondioli, and Roberto Macchiarelli. "Two Tales of One City: Data, Inference and Carthaginian Infant Sacrifice." *Antiquity* 91 (2017): 442–54.

Schwartz, Jeffrey H., Frank Houghton, Roberto Macchiarelli, and Luca Bondioli. "Skeletal Remains from Punic Carthage Do Not Support Systematic Sacrifice of Infants." *PLOS ONE* 5, no. 2 (2010): e9177.

Septimus, Bernard. "Ḥananto le-Meah Peri: From Early *Piyyuṭ* to the Babylonian Talmud." *Lešonenu* 71 (2009): 79–95 [Hebrew].

———. "A Medieval Judeo-Spanish Poem on the Complementarity of Faith and Works and Its Intellectual Roots." In *New Perspectives on Jewish-Christian Relations in Honor of David Berger*, edited by Elisheva Carlebach and Jacob J. Schacter, 227–39. Brill Reference Library of Judaism. Leiden: Brill, 2012.

Shagar (Shimshon Gershon Rosenberg), Rabbi. *Faith Shattered and Restored: Judaism in the Postmodern Age*. Translated by Elie Leshem. Edited by Zohar Maor. Jerusalem: Maggid, 2017.

Shankman, Steven. *Other Others: Levinas, Literature, Transcultural Studies*. SUNY Series in Contemporary Jewish Thought. Albany: State University of New York Press, 2010.

Shapira, Avraham, ed. *Siaḥ Loḥamim: Chapters of Listening and Contemplation*. Tel-Aviv: Qevutsat ḥaverim tse'irim me-ha-tenu'ah ha-qibutsit, 1967.

Shapiro, Marc B. *Changing the Immutable: How Orthodox Judaism Rewrites Its History*. Oxford: Littman Library of Jewish Civilization, 2015.

Shemesh, Yael. "Lies by Prophets and Other Lies in the Hebrew Bible." *Journal of the Ancient Near Eastern Society* 29 (2002): 81–95.

Shinan, Avigdor. "Synagogues in the Land of Israel: The Literature of the Ancient Synagogue and Synagogue Archaeology." In *Sacred Realm: The Emergence of the Synagogue in the Ancient World*, edited by Steven Fine, 130–52. New York: Oxford University Press and the Yeshiva University Museum, 1996.

Simmons, J. Aaron. "What About Isaac? Rereading *Fear and Trembling* and Rethinking Kierkegaardian Ethics." *Journal of Religious Ethics* 35 (2007): 319–45.

Simon, Uriel. "The Banishment of Ishmael: The Akedah Preceding the Akedah of Isaac." In *'Aḳedat Yiṣḥaḳ le-Zar'o: Mabbat be-'Ayin Yisra'elit le-*

zikhro shel Yiṣḥaḳ Hirschberg hy"d, edited by Israel Rozenson and Binyamin Lau, 377–80. Jerusalem: Ha-Ḳeren le-hanṣaḥat Yiṣḥaḳ Hirshberg, 2003.

Singer, David, and Moshe Sokol. "Joseph Soloveitchik: Lonely Man of Faith." *Modern Judaism* 2 (1982): 227–72.

Smith, Mark S. "Child Sacrifice as the Extreme Case and Calculation." In *Not Sparing the Child: Human Sacrifice in the Ancient World and Beyond,* edited by V. Daphna Arbel, Paul C. Burns, J. R. C. Cousland, Richard Menkis, and Dietmar Neufeld, 3–17. London and New York: Bloomsbury, 2015.

———. *The Early History of God: Yahweh and the Other Deities in Ancient Israel.* 2nd ed. Grand Rapids: Eerdmans, 2002.

Smith, Morton. "A Note on Burning Babies." *Journal of the American Oriental Society* 95 (1975): 477–79.

Smith, Patricia, Gal Avishai, Joseph A. Greene, and Lawrence E. Stager. "Aging Cremated Infants: The Problem of Sacrifice at the Tophet of Carthage." *Antiquity* 85 (2011): 859–74.

Smith, Patricia, Lawrence E. Stager, Joseph A. Greene, and Gal Avishai. "Age Estimations Attest to Infant Sacrifice at the Carthage Tophet." *Antiquity* 87 (2013): 1191–99.

Soloveitchik, Joseph B. *Abraham's Journey: Reflections on the Life of the Founding Patriarch.* Edited by David Shatz, Joel B. Wolowelsky, and Reuven Ziegler. Hoboken NJ: Ktav for the Toras HoRav Foundation, 2008.

———. "Catharsis." *Tradition* 17, no. 2 (Spring 1978): 38–54. Reprinted in *Confrontation and Other Essays,* 41–61. Jerusalem: Maggid, 2015.

———. *Community, Covenant, and Commitment: Selected Letters and Communications of Rabbi Joseph B. Soloveitchik.* Edited by Nathaniel Helfgot. MeOtzar HoRav 4. Hoboken NJ: Ktav for the Toras HoRav Foundation, 2005.

———. "The Community." *Tradition* 17, no. 2 (Spring 1978): 7–24. Reprinted in *Confrontation and Other Essays,* 1–23. Jerusalem: Maggid, 2015.

———. "Confrontation." *Tradition* 6, no. 2 (Spring 1964): 5–29. Reprinted in *Confrontation and Other Essays,* 85–115. Jerusalem: Maggid, 2015.

———. *The Emergence of Ethical Man.* Edited by Michael S. Berger. Hoboken NJ: Ktav for the Torah HoRav Foundation, 2005.

———. *Halakhic Man.* Translated by Lawrence Kaplan. Philadelphia: Jewish Publication Society, 1983. Originally published as *"Ish ha-Halakhah." Talpiot* 1 (1944): 651–735 [Hebrew].

———. *The Halakhic Mind: An Essay on Jewish Tradition and Modern Thought.* New York: Macmillan, 1986.

————. "The Lonely Man of Faith." *Tradition* 7, no. 2 (1965): 5–67. Reprinted as *The Lonely Man of Faith*. Introduction by David Shatz. New York: Double-day Three Leaves, 2006.

————. "Majesty and Humility." *Tradition* 17, no. 2 (Spring 1978): 25–37. Reprinted in *Confrontation and Other Essays*, 25–40. Jerusalem: Maggid, 2015.

————. "Thoughts on Prayer." *Ha-Darom* 47 (1978): 84–106 [Hebrew]. Reprinted in *Ish ha-Halakha: Galui ve-Nistar*, 239–71. Jerusalem: World Zionist Organization, 1979.

Solowiejczyk, Josef. *Das reine Denken und das Seinskonstituierung bei Hermann Cohen*. PhD diss., Friedrich-Wilhelms-Universität zu Berlin, 1932.

Sommer, Benjamin D. *The Bodies of God and the World of Ancient Israel*. Cambridge: Cambridge University Press, 2008.

Sontag, Frederick. "Introduction to the Torchbook Edition." In Kierkegaard, *On Authority and Revelation*, vii–xl.

Spiegel, Shalom. *The Last Trial: On the Legends and Lore of the Command to Abraham to Offer Isaac as a Sacrifice: The Akedah*. Philadelphia: Jewish Publication Society, 1967.

————. "Me-Aggadot ha-'Aḳedah: A Liturgical Poem on the Slaughter of Isaac and His Resurrection by R. Ephraim of Bonn." In *Sefer ha-Yovel li-khvod Alexander Marx on his Seventieth Birthday*, Hebrew section, 471–547. New York: Jewish Theological Seminary, 1950 [Hebrew]. Translated as Spiegel, *The Last Trial*.

Stager, Lawrence E. "The Rite of Child Sacrifice at Carthage." In *New Light on Ancient Carthage*. Edited by J. G. Pedley, 1–11. Ann Arbor: University of Michigan Press, 1980.

————. *Rites of Spring in the Carthaginian Tophet*. Eighth BABESCH Byvanck Lecture. Leiden: BABESCH Foundation, 2014.

Stager, Lawrence E., and Samuel R. Wolff. "Child Sacrifice at Carthage — Religious Rite or Population Control? Archaeological Evidence Provides Basis for a New Analysis." *Biblical Archaeology Review* 10, no. 1 (1984): 31–51.

Stambovsky, Phillip. "R. Soloveitchik's Causal Critique of Maimonides as a Religious Philosopher." *Journal of Jewish Studies* 63 (2012): 307–30.

Stavrakopoulou, Francesca. *King Manasseh and Child Sacrifice: Biblical Distortions of Historical Realities*. BZAW 338. Berlin and New York: De Gruyter, 2004.

Steinberg, Milton. *Anatomy of Faith*. Edited with an introduction by Arthur A. Cohen. New York: Harcourt Brace, 1960.

Steinmetz, Devora. *Punishment and Freedom: The Rabbinic Construction of Criminal Law*. Divinations. Philadelphia: University of Pennsylvania Press, 2008.

Stern, Eliyahu. *The Genius: Elijah of Vilna and the Making of Modern Judaism.* New Haven: Yale University Press, 2103.

———. "Other Theologies: The Social Thought of Rabbi J. B. Soloveitchik and Emmanuel Levinas." BA honors thesis, Yeshiva University, 2002.

Stewart, Jon. *Kierkegaard's Relations to Hegel Reconsidered.* Cambridge: Cambridge University Press, 2003.

Stokes, Ryan E. "The Devil Made David Do It . . . Or Did He? The Nature, Identity, and Literary Origins of the *Satan* in 1 Chronicles 21:1." *Journal of Biblical Literature* 128 (2009): 91–106.

Stolle, Jeffrey. "Levinas and the Akedah: An Alternative to Kierkegaard." *Philosophy Today* 45 (2001): 132–43.

Stroumsa, Guy G. "Christ's Laughter: Docetic Origins Reconsidered." *Journal of Early Christian Studies* 12 (2004): 267–88.

Sztuden, Alex. "Adam the First." *Tradition* 49 (2016): 8–19.

Ta-Shma, Israel M. "Law, Custom and Tradition in Early Jewish Germany— Tentative Reflections." *Sidra* 3 (1987): 85–161.

Taylor, Charles. *A Secular Age.* Cambridge MA: Harvard University Press, 2007.

———. *Sources of the Self: The Making of the Modern Identity.* Cambridge MA: Harvard University Press, 1989.

Thelwall, S. *The Ante-Nicene Fathers: Translations of the Writings of the Fathers Down to A.D. 325.* Vol. 3. Grand Rapids MI: Eerdmanns, 1989. American reprint of the Edinburgh edition / revised and chronologically arranged, with brief prefaces and occasional notes, by A. Cleveland Coxe.

Tigay, Jeffrey H. *Deuteronomy.* JPS Torah Commentary. Philadelphia: Jewish Publication Society, 1996.

Tilley, J. Michael. "Rereading the Teleological Suspension: Resignation, Faith, and Teleology." Verstrynge, 145–70. Berlin: De Gruyter, 2012.

Tucker, Ethan. "Redeeming the Akeidah, Halakhah and Ourselves." Hadar. https://www.hadar.org/torah-resource/redeeming-akeidah-halakhah-and -ourselves.

Turner, Yossi. "Sacrifice and Repentance: The Religious Thought of Hermann Cohen, Franz Rosenzweig, and Joseph B. Soloveitchik." *The Actuality of Sacrifice: Past and Present,* edited by Alberdina Houtman, Marcel Poorthuis, Joshua J. Schwartz, and Joseph Turner, 287–304. Jewish and Christian Perspectives 28. Leiden: Brill, 2015.

Vainstub, Daniel. "Human Sacrifices in Canaan and Israel." In *Israel and Its Land, Texts and History: Proceedings of a Conference in Honor of Shmuel Aḥituv at His Retirement*, edited by Zipporah Talshir, 117–204. Be'er Sheva 19. Be'er Sheva: Ben Gurion University Press, 2010 [Hebrew].

van Bekkum, Wout. "Bound in Righteousness: Variances and Versions of the *Aqedah* Story in Jewish Hymnography (Piyyut)." In *Religious Stories in Transformation: Conflict, Revision and Reception*, edited by Alberdina Houtman, Tamar Kadari, Marcel Poorthuis, and Vered Tohar, 144–64. Jewish and Christian Perspectives Series 31. Leiden: Brill, 2016.

van der Horst, Pieter W. "A New Early Christian Poem on the Sacrifice of Isaac (Pap. Bodmer 30)." In *Le Codex des Visions*, 155–72. Recherches et rencontres 18. Geneva: Librairie Droz, 2002. Reprinted in van der Horst, *Jews and Christina in Their Graeco-Roman Context: Selected Essays on Early Judaism, Samaritanism, Hellenism, and Christianity*, 190–205. WUNT 196. Tübingen: Mohr Siebeck, 2006.

Varriano, John. *Caravaggio: The Art of Realism*. University Park PA: Penn State University Press, 2010.

Waltke, Bruce K. *The Book of Proverbs: Chapters 1–15*. NICOT. Grand Rapids MI: Eerdmans, 2004.

Weinfeld, Moshe. "The Worship of Molech and of the Queen of Heaven and Its Background." *Ugarit Forschungen* 4 (1972): 133–54.

Weiss, Dov. *Pious Irreverence: Confronting God in Rabbinic Judaism*. Philadelphia: University of Pennsylvania Press, 2017.

Westphal, Merold. *Kierkegaard's Critique of Reason and Society*. University Park PA: Penn State University Press, 1991 [first published 1987].

Wettstein, Howard. "The Faith of Abraham." http://philosophy.ucr.edu/wp-content/uploads/2015/09/akedah2.pdf.

Wilken, Robert M. "Melito, the Jewish Community at Sardis, and the Sacrifice of Isaac." *Theological Studies* 37 (1976): 53–69.

Wolfson, Elliot R. "Eternal Duration and Temporal Compresence: The Influence of Ḥabad on Joseph B. Soloveitchik." In *The Value of the Particular: Lessons from Judaism and the Modern Jewish Experience — Festschrift for Steven T. Katz on the Occasion of His Seventieth Birthday*, edited by Michael Zank and Ingrid Anderson, with the assistance of Sarah Leventer, 195–238. Leiden: Brill, 2015.

Wright, David P. *Inventing God's Law: How the Covenant Code of the Bible Used and Revised the Laws of Hammurabi*. Oxford: Oxford University Press, 2009.

Wurzburger, Walter. "The Maimonidean Matrix of Rabbi Joseph B. Soloveitchik's Two-Tiered Ethics." In *Through the Sound of Many Voices: Writings*

Contributed on the Occasion of the 70th Birthday of W. Gunther Plaut, 172–83, edited by Jonathan V. Plaut. Toronto: Lester & Orpen Dennys, 1982.

Xella, Paolo. "Sacrifici di Bambini nel Mondo Fenicio e Punico nelle Testimonianze in Lingua Greca e Latina—I." *Studi Epigrafici e Linguistici* 26 (2009): 59–100.

———. "Sull' etimologia de (Baal) Hammon." *Studi Epigrafici e Linguistici* 27 (2010): 27–31.

———. "'Tophet': An Overall Interpretation." *Studi Epigrafici e Linguistici* 29–30 (2012–13): 259–81.

Xella, Paolo, Josephine Quinn, Valentina Melchiorri, and Peter van Dommelen. "Phoenician Bones of Contention." *Antiquity* 87 (2013): 1199–207.

Yahalom, Joseph, and Michael Sokoloff. *Shirat Bene Ma'arava: Aramaic Poems of the Jews of the Land of Israel in the Byzantine Period*. Jerusalem: Israel Academy of Sciences, 1999 [Hebrew].

Yaron, Reuven. "The Middle Assyrian Laws and the Bible." *Biblica* 51 (1970): 549–57.

Yerushalmi, Yosef Hayim. *Zakhor: Jewish History and Jewish Memory*. Seattle: University of Washington Press, 1989 [first edition 1982].

Yuval, Israel. *Two Nations in Your Womb: Perceptions of Jews and Christians in Late Antiquity and the Middle Ages*. Translated by Barbara Harshav and Jonathan Chipman. S. Mark Taper Foundation Book in Jewish Studies. Berkeley: University of California Press, 2006.

Zemke, John. "In Memorial Charles Cook, Mentor of Samuel G. Armistead." In *Spain's Multicultural Legacies—Studies in Honor of Samuel G. Armistead*, edited by Adrienne L. Martín and Cristina Martínez-Carazo, 333–47. Newark DE: Juan de la Cuesta, 2008.

Zerubavel, Yael. "*Qerav, Haqravah, Qorban*: Developments within the Ideology of Patriotic Sacrifice in Israel." In *Patriotism: We Love You, Homeland*, edited by Avner Ben-Amos and Daniel Bar-Tal, 61–99. Tel Aviv: Deyonun, Tel-Aviv University, 2004 [Hebrew].

Ziegler, Reuven. *Majesty and Humility: The Thought of Rabbi Joseph B. Soloveitchik*. The Rabbi Soloveitchik Library 3. Brookline and Jerusalem: Maimonides School and Urim, 2012.

Zierler, Wendy. "In Search of a Feminist Reading of the Akedah." *Nashim* 9 (2005): 10–26.

Zucker, Moshe. *Commentaries of Rav Sa'adia Gaon to Genesis*. New York: Jewish Theological Seminary of America, 1984.

GENERAL INDEX

INDEX OF TEXTS

CPSIA information can be obtained
at www.ICGtesting.com
Printed in the USA
LVHW111747300820
664584LV00013B/417